THE
BURNING

Black Wall Street and the
Tulsa Race Massacre of 1921

THE
BURNING

Black Wall Street and the
Tulsa Race Massacre of 1921

Tim Madigan
adapted for young people by
Hilary Beard

HENRY HOLT AND COMPANY
NEW YORK

Henry Holt and Company, *Publishers since 1866*

Henry Holt® is a registered trademark of Macmillan Publishing Group, LLC

120 Broadway, New York, NY 10271 • mackids.com

Library of Congress Cataloging-in-Publication Data is available.

ISBN 978-1-250-78769-9

Our books may be purchased in bulk for promotional, educational, or business use. Please contact your local bookseller or the Macmillan Corporate and Premium Sales Department at (800) 221-7945 ext. 5442 or by email at MacmillanSpecialMarkets@macmillan.com.

First edition, 2021 / Designed by Mallory Grigg

Printed in the United States of America

10 9 8 7 6 5 4 3 2 1

CONTENTS

Introduction

When I first received the invitation to adapt *The Burning* for young readers, I was intrigued by the opportunity to help share an account of the Tulsa Race Massacre—a story that simultaneously encompasses one of the great horrors of American history and the tremendous bravery, heroism, and industry of African American people. As someone who didn't appreciate American history until her mid-twenties, I knew that the subject had often been taught in a way that omitted, distorted, and sometimes intentionally misrepresented the experiences of Indigenous, Black, Latinx, Asian, and other Americans of color. I wanted to help fill some of the holes in the narrative.

Upon reading the adult edition of the book, I immediately developed a deep respect for the author, Tim Madigan, with whom I hadn't yet spoken. I discovered that Tim, a White male journalist, had stumbled across the story and was astounded that he'd never heard of it. He then dedicated years of his life to researching and writing about the massacre, helping to bring this momentous historical incident to both the public's attention and, vividly, to life.

As a writer, I was blown away by both the quantity and quality of Tim's research. I could see how carefully he'd pieced his investigation together, his attention to detail, his craftsmanship in constructing the story, and his skill and artistry as a writer.

At the same time, as an African American, as a woman, as a person with deep family roots in the Midwest—and as one who has researched her own ancestry to better understand herself and her own family story—I saw that I'd have the opportunity to add some additional context and a new perspective. I wanted to frame the story a bit differently—to look at that same world through a Black woman's eye—as best as I could from a distance. I wanted to provide some additional insight into the experiences Black people had endured during Reconstruction and the Nadir of American history, a time period that includes the eras often described as the Gay Nineties and the Roaring Twenties. Gay for whom? Not for Black people.

As I read Tim's work, it dawned on me that the early chroniclers of the event were mostly White, male, and in positions of power. And as I read about all the accomplished men of Black Wall Street, knowing the role Black women have played in Black life and liberation and the unfolding of American democracy, I wondered—what was going on in women's lives? What were the women's contributions to Greenwood in general and Black Wall Street in particular? Though my primary job was to make the book shorter, I attempted to weave in a few new narratives.

COPING WITH HARD HISTORY

Going into the project, I had what I'd believed to be a decent amount of knowledge about the Tulsa Race Massacre. But the more I read, the more I realized how much I didn't know. Though I'd read about White-on-Black mob violence and had studied several recent reports about lynching published by the Equal Justice Initiative, I realized that I'd never read about White mob terrorism or an attempted lynching in detail. As a writer I often have a somewhat vivid imagination, but I could never have imagined such astonishing hatred, depravity, and cruelty. Shock, anger, hopelessness, despair, powerlessness, and grief coursed through me—sometimes all at the same time.

These stories certainly were not the ones I'd learned in history class that emphasized continuous racial progress. This is hard history, and it's important to learn and talk about. But to be honest, some days I felt a little numb. Some moments I struggled to continue reading; others I found myself staring at the ceiling, trying to take it all in. Sometimes, I felt tightness in my throat and chest and queasiness in my stomach. Other times, I felt tingling in my legs, as though I needed to stretch or run. When I felt this, I would do yoga, allow myself to go for a walk or go swimming. Still other times, my neck and shoulders tightened up as I took in the information. And on a few occasions I wanted to close my eyes and go to sleep. Several times I cried. That said, some of my tears mourned the horror that many of my ancestors endured, while others praised their amazing vision, resilience, endurance, commitment, patriotism, and ingenuity.

So if you feel sad, or confused, or angry, or shocked, or powerless, or any of the infinite combinations of emotions one may experience upon learning about a tragedy, you are perfectly normal. Our emotions are part of what make us human. Expressing rather than suppressing them helps to keep us healthy—spiritually, mentally, and emotionally. In fact, all the emotions and physical sensations you may experience while reading this book are completely normal. If it's appropriate, dance around, look for the room's exits, shake your body out, do some jumping jacks, go for a walk, put your head down, close your eyes. You may even need to take a nap. It's all normal. If you're reading this in school, you may want to ask your teacher if you can have a moment to shake it out.

Importantly, the discomfort that difficult emotions create can cause you to understand yourself and the world differently. Our uncomfortable emotions can help us open the door to new possibilities. You may be inspired to learn more about a particular aspect of this history. I found myself consumed with Reconstruction, an era I hadn't found particularly interesting before. I wondered about my ancestors' experiences and began to research them more deeply. You may want to ask your parents or grandparents about their family stories. However these stories affect you, I hope that after learning more about what Black Americans have faced—and continue to face to this day—you'll commit yourself to racial justice and anti-racism work.

A WORD ABOUT VIOLENCE

A lynching is a savage act. Mob violence is barbarous. This massacre, the largest act of homegrown terrorism ever perpetrated in the United States, was extraordinarily, horrifically, more violent than I had even imagined. In this adaptation I've attempted to find a balance between overly sanitizing what happened and lingering needlessly on gruesome acts. Though you undoubtedly have seen lots of violence in movies and on various media—I worried about how the details of Black people being so brutally victimized might land on Black children and parents, who already face an uphill experience of life and so much death in the media. I worried about how the reality of such pervasive White violence might impact White readers, most of whom have likely been taught a sanitized version of their role in American history. Since the story is about the often unspoken narrative of White vigilante violence, I also wondered how teachers would prepare to discuss it in class.

But the fact that something is upsetting to us doesn't mean that we should not engage it. Facing the truth empowers us to understand ourselves, our neighbors, and our world more accurately; to make appropriate choices and decisions; to heal our past and present and build a more promising future.

Together.

Ultimately, for our multiracial democracy to thrive, we must learn about and reckon with the reality that Black people, Indigenous Americans, and other people of color face experiences that contradict the stories of the "American dream," "equal opportunity," and "pulling yourself up by your bootstraps," that so many White Americans, in particular, have experienced and believe in.

It's important to note as well that the history in this book is not all violent. Also here is the remarkable story of the rebuilding of Black Wall Street, a comeback story for the ages that far too few people of any race know. Indeed, the story of the Tulsa Race Massacre is not merely about the vicious and inhumane acts of a mob of racist White people, but also about the brilliance and almost unimaginable imagination, genius, creativity, strength, resilience, and bravery of African Americans. Black people built Greenwood from nothing, transformed it into a prosperous community, fought back against its destruction, and immediately built it back. We hear far too few stories of Black industriousness and heroism.

FEELING UNCOMFORTABLE

There are many reasons the Tulsa Race Massacre can be difficult to look at. But it is only by facing the difficult things—by looking our worst human impulses in the eye, by asking what could be different and how we can be more equal and free—that we create the possibility of change. Our willingness to be comfortable with feeling uncomfortable—whether because we've learned about an ugly incident or are courageous enough to engage our difficult emotions—opens the ability to imagine ourselves in another person's shoes; to experience the beauty of our shared humanity from another person's perspective; to engage thoughts, feelings, and experiences that vary from our usual ones; to reach greater understanding of one another.

Uncomfortable feelings produce new truths, and with them, new possibilities. They also help to empower us to address unresolved issues. This is the path to a more equitable society, in which Black lives matter, in which people of color are safe, have the opportunity to contribute their gifts and talents to the world, and are empowered not merely to survive, but to thrive.

—Hilary Beard
December 2020

PROLOGUE

LIKE
JUDGMENT
DAY

For the rest of her life, and she lived a very long time thereafter, Eldoris Ector McCondichie remembered the exact words of her mother.

"Eldoris, wake up! We have to go!" Harriet Ector called to her daughter on that beautiful spring morning of June 1, 1921. "The White people are killing the Colored folks!"

The cloudless sky outside was still pink from the dawn, but with those words, Eldoris's drowsiness was gone in a blink, rendering her fully awake and trembling by the time she tossed aside the covers. The nine-year-old girl threw a dress over her head as her mother rushed her along, with scarcely time for shoes and socks, and followed her parents and older brother as they hurried toward the front door of their small home on Iroquois Avenue.

White people? Killing the Colored folks? Eldoris waited to shake free from the nightmare, but she couldn't. She turned her mother's words around in her young mind, trying to fit them together in a way that would make sense, but that didn't happen, either. The days before had been so peaceful, boys and girls antsy because the end of the school year was just a few days away, but nothing else seemed amiss whatsoever.

And White people? Eldoris's parents carefully sheltered her from some of the indignities and violence of the Jim Crow era. So, she hadn't yet discovered that there were some White people whom she had reason to fear. Instead, every morning since she could remember, her father had set out to clip White folks' lawns and weed their gardens, walking south through the Black quarter where her family lived, the Greenwood district, in Tulsa, Oklahoma. Downtown Greenwood consisted of sturdy brick drugstores, beauty parlors, newspaper offices, meat lockers, doctors' offices, restaurants, jewelry stores, upscale hotels, law offices, jazz joints, barbershops, skating rinks, and pool halls, all of them owned and run by Black people. In the evenings, the heavenly aromas of barbecue ribs and collard greens wafted in the air, blending with the notes of jazz and blues. A self-sufficient community, Greenwood was a celebration of what seemed possible for Black people in America less than sixty years after slavery's end.

Indeed, Greenwood's citizens, probably more so than Black people in any other place in the nation, had created and built everything they needed in their own neighborhood, a remarkable thirty-five-block city within a city, on the north side of the Frisco railroad tracks. As far away as Chicago, Black folks saw Greenwood as the top of the mountain, and for decades celebrated it as the "Black Wall Street of America." Within this vibrant and promising community, Black people could almost forget about the new brick skyscrapers, fancy cars, and big homes that belonged to the White people on the south side of the tracks. That is, until many made their daily sojourn crosstown for work, as Eldoris's father did.

But the moment they crossed the Frisco tracks that separated their community from downtown Tulsa, Greenwood's Black residents stepped into a world where their sweat was welcome, but their humanity was not. In 1907, as its first act after Oklahoma became a state, the all-White legislature passed laws preventing Black people from riding in the same streetcar or rail car as White people. Before long, Tulsa's Black residents could not work in or even enter many of the buildings downtown, or shop in the big new stores, or go to the movies, or attend the huge new modern schools whose textbooks were paid for with public dollars, or purchase a home in the neighborhoods where White Tulsans lived. Jim Crow conventions even prohibited Black people from using the state's public telephone booths. So, though everything may have seemed peaceful on the surface, to maintain their advantage, many White Tulsans held the threat of harm over Black people, as Eldoris was about to learn.

On that rosy dawn of June 1, 1921, Eldoris's innocence disintegrated with her mother's early-morning words. *The White people are killing the Colored folks!* And in the second that Eldoris poked her head out the front door, she knew it was true.

She turned her head south as she stepped outside looking toward Downtown Greenwood. A massive black cloud of smoke billowed there now, nearly obliterating the rising sun.

As her father pulled her from the house by the hand, she heard a terrible noise from the sky and looked up to see airplanes buzzing low. The little girl had seen the flying machines only a time or two before, and they were ominous creatures even then, but now as they roared above them, she heard the dull thuds of bullets hitting the ground around her feet like fat raindrops, and she realized that she and her family were being shot at from the air. She yanked free from her father then, racing in panic to a nearby chicken coop and pulling open the door. Several terrified adults already crowded inside stared back at her from the shadows. Chickens cackled nervously at the intrusion. Eldoris pushed her way through the grown-ups and crouched in a corner of the coop and would have stayed there forever if her father hadn't appeared at the door, pulled her back outside, and dragged her off to the north to join other Black folks fleeing town.

For her family was certainly not alone in their flight. A great column of Black people was racing north with them along the Midland Valley Railroad tracks that ran past her house, a despondent procession of thousands that stretched as far as Eldoris could see. Parents dragged their children along after them, just as Howard Ector now dragged his daughter. The old people shuffled along as best they could. Many of them were old enough to remember slavery, but nothing from those times compared to the horror of what was happening on this morning.

The planes disappeared from the sky after a few minutes, so now and then someone in the procession took a moment to ponder the growing wall of smoke to the south. Beneath that cloud, their homes and all their other earthly possessions were being incinerated. Why? The question hung over the procession like the smoke from the fires behind them. All anyone knew was that a few days before, a young White woman had accused a young Black man of assault. However suspicious the police had found her accusation, it had caused White people to swallow

Greenwood up with rage, as if every ounce of enmity that had been building up in the White people since the Civil War had exploded on their doorsteps. An angry White mob clamored at their heels. So Eldoris and her family and the rest of the people fled for their lives up the Midland Valley tracks toward the wooded hollows and rolling hills to the north of town, where they might finally be safe.

Looking around at the others, at the horror etched on the refugees' sunken faces, at the smoke behind her, Eldoris was reminded of something she had learned about in Sunday school. This was like Judgment Day! As she stumbled north with her family, she expected to see Jesus appear on his throne at any second, come to set everything right. But she never did.

Each member of Eldoris's family survived that day, but so did the horror—her mother's chilling words in the morning, the smoke, the crowds, the planes, the death and grief and destruction her family saw when they were allowed to return home a few days later. Somehow, their little house on Iroquois had survived, but most of the other buildings for thirty-five square blocks— almost every business, church, hospital, school, and home in Greenwood—had been reduced by the mob to ash and rubble. A few days after the burning, Eldoris walked to Detroit Avenue on the shoulder of Standpipe Hill, where so many of the Black doctors and lawyers and businessmen and schoolteachers had their large, beautiful brick houses. Now only an occasional wall or chimney still stood. On one surviving wall, a wisp of white curtain dangled from a window, tossing in the breeze. Eldoris somehow took that as a sign of God's love and hope.

But the memories always stalked her, God's love and hope or not. The memories stalked everyone. In the decades to come, few Tulsans on either side of the tracks spoke out loud of the great burning, as though the catastrophe was a secret that both Black and White people conspired to keep, although for different reasons. Indeed, people who moved to the city only a few years later might never have known that it happened at all. But whether it was discussed or not, no one who witnessed the events of those historic days in Tulsa could ever forget.

CHAPTER 1

What Do You Say Now?

In the spring of 1957, Don Ross was daydreaming at his desk during the first meeting of his high school yearbook committee. Until Mr. Williams began talking about the burning.

Ross, a sophomore that year, had flunked most of his classes at Booker T. Washington High School so far, preferring to flirt with girls and play pool after school instead of doing homework.

History courses were the exception. Captivated by the past, Ross, a Black American with Native American ancestry, usually aced them. He was particularly interested in the Civil War. Ross also had a way with words. That's one of the reasons he showed up at the first yearbook meeting. The other was that he had a crush on a girl on the yearbook staff.

The faculty adviser for the yearbook that year was a history teacher named Bill Williams, a graying Black man about fifty years old, who had been around Washington High longer than dirt. The students knew him as Mr. W.D.

Mr. W.D. began the meeting that day with a speech. He said something about the class yearbook being more than a chronicle of one year in a school. A yearbook should also describe the community at that time because school and community went together like mother and child.

"When I was a junior at Washington High, the prom never happened because there was a riot, and the Whites came over the tracks and wiped out Greenwood," Mr. W.D. told the students, using the name of the neighborhood in Tulsa, Oklahoma, where the school was located, and where most of the Black students lived. "In fact, this building was one of the few around here that wasn't burned, so they turned it into a hospital for Colored folks. In those days, there were probably Negroes moaning and bleeding and dying in this very room. The Whites over yonder burned Greenwood down, and with almost no help from anybody, the Negroes built it back to like it was. That's one of the things I mean when I say, 'the story of a community.'"

That got Ross's attention.

His older relatives had never said a word about anything so terrible, and there was nothing in Ross's experience that would make him believe that such carnage had taken place.

In the 1950s, people on both sides of the railroad tracks, the dividing line that segregated Black from White Tulsa, seemed to be prospering.

Though Ross's family was one of many that struggled to make ends meet, other Black residents of Greenwood owned skating rinks, drugstores with soda fountains, a social club, Jarrett's grocery store, Carver's and Farley's cleaners, Madison's and Isaac's shoe stores, Jackson and Jack's mortuaries, the Royal Hotel, and four movie theaters: The Peoria, Regal, Rex, and Dreamland.

Some of the world's finest blues and jazz musicians performed in the neighborhood's clubs. The nightlife at Greenwood and Archer was celebrated in song. And there were Spann's and Big Ten's pool halls, which is where Ross learned to love the game and often hung out.

So why would this teacher tell such a ridiculous lie?

Before he could catch himself, Ross leaped from his seat.

"Mr. Williams, I don't believe that," Ross said. "I don't think you could burn this town down and have nobody know nothing about it. My people have been here since 1924 and they never said a word about no riot."

"Sit down and shut up," Mr. W.D. responded.

Ross immediately did as he was told, regretting his act the minute his behind touched the seat.

Mr. Williams glared at him but didn't say a word when the teenager left the classroom that afternoon.

I DON'T THINK YOU COULD BURN THIS TOWN DOWN AND HAVE NOBODY KNOW NOTHING ABOUT IT

But the next day, after another yearbook meeting, as students started to file out, Mr. W.D. spoke to him.

"Fat Mouth," the teacher said. "You stay here."

Ross's heart started pounding, thinking that he was about to be reprimanded or punished. Instead, Mr. Williams pulled a thick scrapbook from the top drawer of his desk and handed it to him.

"Take a seat and see for yourself."

Ross sat down at a nearby desk.

From the moment he opened the book, his head began to spin.

The first picture showed White men standing over a charred body lying facedown in the dirt.

The next photograph was just like it.

Then came a picture of Black corpses stacked on trucks.

Then another of Black men being marched down familiar

streets with their hands in the air, guarded by armed White men wearing street clothes.

Next, one of flames shooting out of little homes and from big brick businesses along Greenwood Avenue.

And still another of a huge wall of black smoke.

Ross saw dozens of images, each worse than the last. His stomach began to turn somersaults.

"What do you say now, Fat Mouth?" the teacher asked.

For maybe the first time in his life, Ross was speechless.

That night, after supper, Mr. W.D. picked Ross up in his car and drove him to the Greenwood home of another Black man, Seymour Williams, a longtime history teacher and the Washington High football coach.

"So, this is the boy who doesn't believe in the riot," Seymour Williams said, smirking.

"Says it never happened," Mr. W.D. replied. "Says nothing like that could have happened because he'd never heard about it. Ain't that right, Fat Mouth? You hear about everything around here."

GREENWOOD WAS ONCE SO PROSPEROUS THAT IT WAS KNOWN AROUND THE NATION AS BLACK WALL STREET

Ross shrugged.

"Well, sit down next to me on this porch swing," Seymour Williams said. "And we'll tell you about something that never happened."

On the porch that night, Ross got a schooling that changed his life as the men shared painful secrets that made them rock on the swing faster and faster.

Stunned by what he heard, Ross wanted to learn more. So he began asking questions of the older people in his family and the community. They confirmed what he was learning from Mr. W.D. and Mr. Williams. That Greenwood was once so prosperous that it was known around the nation as Black Wall Street, as one of the most successful communities of Black Americans in the country—full of Black-owned restaurants, hotels, barbershops, hairdressers, legal offices, mechanics, clothing stores, shoe stores, clubs, movie theaters, beautiful homes, and a high-performing school system. Six Black residents even owned their own airplanes.

But on one morning in 1921, a mob consisting of thousands of racist White Tulsans had swarmed the neighborhood, shooting Black people, looting their homes, and torching their properties until the entire thirty-five-square-block area had been demolished. Airplanes even shot at them and dropped firebombs from the sky.

But Mr. W.D. and Mr. Williams also spoke with pride about how they themselves and their parents and neighbors defended their homes and businesses. They spoke of how, after the burning, the community rebuilt Greenwood so that it was better than ever.

What Ross learned began to crack open the door to a story so shameful that Tulsa's residents had conspired for more than thirty years to keep it secret, and the horrors of which have still been only partially revealed, even today, a century after the incident.

As he interviewed his elders,

AFTER THE BURNING, THE COMMUNITY REBUILT GREENWOOD SO THAT IT WAS BETTER THAN EVER

Ross began to change. The story ignited a passion that would fuel him for the rest of his life.

Here are some of the stories he and others have uncovered about the Greenwood District—about Black Wall Street—in Tulsa, Oklahoma.

CHAPTER 2

Beyond
Hatred's Reach

On a warm May night in 1913, in the shadowy lamplight
of Greenwood's First Baptist Church, Black men wearing
expensive suits and white gloves and Black women in their finest
white dresses waited expectantly.

Scarcely a spot in the pews was empty, for the main speaker of
the evening was Captain Townsend D. Jackson, a man whose life
experience was unique among Black Americans. Townsend had
lived through a time when many White Americans in the North,
as well as the overwhelming majority in the South, refused to
accept that Black people were fully human. Even though they
could witness with their own eyes that Black people could think
for themselves, experience and express feelings, and profess their
spirituality, racist White people pretended they could not see
Black people's humanity. Instead, they told themselves and each
other that Black people were "things," that Black adults were
like children, or that people who were clearly, well, people, were
instead animals or beasts.

The belief that White people, and their ideas, thoughts, and
actions, are better than and should dominate people of other
races or ethnicities, is known as White supremacy. Historically,
vast numbers of White people in the United States believed in

White supremacy—virtually all White Southerners and many Northerners as well. For a long time, these beliefs were the norm, and racists could insult, use, abuse, beat, whip, assault, neglect, molest, rape, and even terrorize Black people. And because these practices were so widespread and accepted, they would rarely face repercussions or punishment.

White supremacist beliefs grew out of the history of American slavery

These White supremacist beliefs grew out of the history of American slavery. In the United States, racists forced Black people into chattel slavery, the most vicious type. Chattel slavery meant the enslaver actually owned people and owned them forever. One of its most heartless aspects—one that made it tremendously profitable for the enslaver—is that any baby born into slavery was also owned perpetually by the enslaver. That child would then be forced to work for free for their entire life. Under chattel slavery, an enslaver could buy and sell people whenever they wanted to, just as if the people were property. And they did. They broke families apart and sold children away from their parents.

White supremacists practiced chattel slavery primarily within the eleven Confederate states that attempted to withdraw, or secede, from the United States during the Civil War—Alabama, Arkansas, Georgia, Florida, Louisiana, Mississippi, North Carolina, South Carolina, Tennessee, Texas, and Virginia—and the five states that bordered the Confederacy—Delaware, Kentucky, Maryland, Missouri, and West Virginia. By the time of the Civil War, slavery was practiced less frequently in the North; however, both indentured servitude and chattel slavery had been practiced there during the colonial era, when European colonists enslaved both Native Americans and Africans. Unlike chattel slavery, indentured servitude allowed a person to work down their debt—often a loan a European had taken out to migrate to the United States—in order to achieve their freedom. Indentured servants were subject to far less violence, and their children weren't born enslaved. Human beings enslaved under chattel slavery had no rights. No rights to be safe; no rights to the money they ought to have earned from the labor they were forced to do; no rights to earn their freedom by working off debt, as indentured servitude permitted.

By 1913, when Captain Townsend spoke with the people of Greenwood, fifty years had passed since the Emancipation Proclamation ended enslavement in the Confederate states. He was among the dwindling number of survivors of chattel slavery. The following describes the kind of world that the captain and other formerly enslaved people endured, resisted, and even thrived in. These conditions were also the historical foundation of what happened to Tulsa's Black Wall Street in 1921.

AN ERA OF PROMISE

In the years after Emancipation, the United States entered a period known as Reconstruction. During Reconstruction—which lasted from 1863 to 1877—the nation attempted to rebuild itself following the Civil War. In the aftermath of war and the abolishment of chattel slavery, the goals of Reconstruction included reuniting the country, rewriting its laws and Constitution, and taking the first steps toward creating a multiracial democracy.

Anti-racist ideas—ones that challenged the oppressive system that treated White people as superior and Black people as inferior—slowly began to circulate throughout the nation. For the first time in U.S. history, notable numbers of White Americans began to participate in efforts to transform the United States. Perhaps this would no longer be a nation that merely professed that "all men were created equal"—even as it counted Black people as three fifths of a human being for the purposes of assigning states political power and slavery existed in fourteen states. Thus began the long, and ongoing, journey to becoming a nation that sought to treat people of all races fairly.

THE LONG, AND ONGOING, JOURNEY TO BECOMING A NATION THAT SOUGHT TO TREAT PEOPLE OF ALL RACES FAIRLY

Beginning in 1865, the U.S. Constitution was amended to abolish slavery, to grant full citizenship and equal application of the law to the formerly enslaved, and to grant voting rights to Black males (back then, no women of any race could vote). Together, the Thirteenth, Fourteenth, and Fifteenth Amendments formed a second Bill of Rights for Black Americans. The Freedmen's Bureau was also established to protect formerly enslaved people from violence and aid the transition to a life of freedom.

As these laws and other societal changes slowly began to unfold, Black men, women, and children began to experience the chance to live as free and independent human beings—many for the first time. Though desperately poor and on the verge of starvation, many Black people—particularly those in the South—embarked upon costly, difficult, and dangerous travels to safer locations, relocating to hamlets, towns, and cities all over the country.

Black women, men, and children sought basic liberties, such as to be their own person, to not be controlled by a White person, and to not be subject to White supremacist violence. Many freed men and women dreamed of owning a small farm or business in order to provide for their family. They wanted to spend their time taking care of their own children rather than being forced to take care of White people's children. They aspired to help other Black people build new lives and create caring communities where they could actively participate in the new society.

Throughout the South and around the nation, Black people founded churches, started schools and colleges, taught each other how to read and write, and educated one another about the Constitution, all the changing laws, and their human rights. They created organizations to support the elderly, widows, orphans, and other vulnerable people in their communities. All of these activities would have been illegal during slavery.

Black people also began to exercise their right to vote, ran for political office, and actively engaged in creating laws and governments in cities and states around the nation. During Reconstruction, more than 1,500 Black men ran for and won federal, state, or local office in the South, including sixteen who were elected to Congress.

No longer restricted by enslavement, Black people in Southern states began to secure a wide variety of jobs as ministers, railroad workers, postal carriers, blacksmiths, sheriffs, and teachers. Black educators were a courageous lot. During slavery, it was illegal to teach a Black person to read, and enslaved Black people who learned to read risked extreme violence or even death. After Emancipation, large numbers of freed men, women, and children desperately wanted to learn to read, write, and further educate themselves so they could take charge of their lives, enjoy their freedom, and engage actively as American citizens. A large number of Black educators were women.

Black people hoped the nation might live up to its promise of being a land where all humans were created equal and deserved rights to life, liberty, and the pursuit of happiness.

PROGRESS?

But creating an equitable society is unbelievably difficult work.

The Freedmen's Bureau was underfunded, and federal troops were soon withdrawn from the South, leaving Black people defenseless against White Supremacist violence. Southern states implemented Black Codes, discriminatory criminal laws designed to control Black people and force them back into work relationships with White employers that were as close to slavery as possible.

CREATING AN EQUITABLE SOCIETY IS UNBELIEVABLY DIFFICULT WORK

Time and time again, Black people were left behind, abandoned, manipulated, and even betrayed by White people—sometimes intentionally, other times unintentionally.

Large numbers of White people, both in the South and elsewhere in the nation, refused to accept the idea that Black people deserved equality and rejected Constitutional Amendments and new laws promoting equality. Most were enraged that Black people were no longer enslaved, that the federal government had confiscated Southern land during the war—had even given some of it to free Black men—and that federal troops had been deployed throughout the South to help enforce the new laws that made Black people their social equals.

During the Civil War, Northern troops had destroyed many White-owned Southern farms and businesses, and without Black people's free labor, countless more fell into ruin. How were they going to make as much money and maintain their superior social status if they could not force Black people into slavery, Southern White supremacists asked? Furious that the federal government now recognized Black men and women as human and that Black people were voting, electing people to represent their interests, and making progress toward greater equality, most Southern White people didn't accept this new democracy.

UNBRIDLED TERROR

Overwhelmingly, racist White people used violence to control and stop Black people's progress. Furious that the same people whom they had previously enslaved were legally now free and equal, White supremacists—many of whom still possessed their Civil War weapons—rained down unbridled terror upon Black people.

Beginning in 1865, a handful of defeated Confederate soldiers founded the Ku Klux Klan, which became a White supremacist terrorist organization. Tens of thousands of Confederate soldiers joined it and other terrorist factions. Defeated and enraged, these insurrectionists would abuse, torture, terrorize, and lynch Black people; burn their homes and barns to the ground; torch their newly formed schools; and run people out of town at gunpoint. To mask their identity, exaggerate their height, and appear more frightening, members of the Ku Klux Klan would wear a white sheet or gown over their body and a pillowcase or cone-shaped hat over their head. Klan gang members would ride horseback and carry torches through Black communities at night, pretending to be the ghosts of dead Confederates as they terrorized people. From time to time, these gangs also attacked other Southerners whom they believed sympathized with Black people, such as union members, Catholics, and Jews. In April 1871, President Ulysses S. Grant signed a bill that attempted to halt the Klan's reign of terror. But White supremacists had many means of impeding Black people's progress.

HORROR AND DOMINATION

During the Klan era and beyond, White supremacists increasingly used mob violence to keep their Black neighbors in fear. The number of racial terror lynchings—the public murders of Black men, women, and children—skyrocketed. These horrific acts of terrorism usually involved some combination of whipping, beating, hanging, burning alive, and shooting the victim. The person was typically tortured for hours, with mob members often cutting off pieces of the victims' bodies, which the public then took home as souvenirs. Any perceived violation might result in a lynching, including attempting to vote, tipping (or not tipping) their hat to a White woman, or failing to observe the "rituals of deference and submission," as one writer later put it.

WHITE SUPREMACISTS INCREASINGLY USED MOB VIOLENCE TO KEEP THEIR BLACK NEIGHBORS IN FEAR

Some, but not all, lynchings took place under cover of darkness. Most public spectacle lynchings took place in broad daylight and often in the middle of the town's public square. It wasn't unusual for White students to be given the day off from school, for people from neighboring towns to take the train in to watch, or for these gruesome displays to begin in the morning, pause for church, and resume after services ended. Indeed, tens, hundreds, or even thousands of members of a community might gather to watch a Black person be tortured for hours. In 1893, a mob of ten thousand White people from all across the state gathered in Paris, Texas, to watch as a seventeen-year-old Black boy was tortured and killed. Also in Paris, Texas, almost thirty years later in 1920, a mob of three thousand watched another torture lynching. A wide spectrum of White society would participate, whether as eyewitnesses alone, as citizens, or as leaders who looked the other way or failed to hold the terrorists accountable. Black people couldn't even count on law enforcement to protect them. White lawmen often took part in these crimes. Indeed, it wasn't uncommon for the mayor, police, or sheriff to refuse to safeguard a Black person from the mob, to allow a raging White mob to remove their Black victim from legal custody, or even to join with the mob itself. Lynchings not only sent a message to Black people that they could be next but also that the White people around them celebrated their domination and control.

Between the Civil War and World War II, White mobs lynched thousands of Black Americans and terrorized countless others. Today, we know these thugs lynched at least 2,000 Black people between 1865 and 1877 alone and no fewer than 6,500 Black men, women, and children between 1865 and 1950. Millions of Black people migrated from the Southern United States to the North and West to flee these and other horrors. The era became the most violent in American history.

A TURN FOR THE WORSE

Once the federal government backtracked on its commitments to Black people, Southern state legislatures rapidly went to work to ensure that Black citizens would not experience democracy.

State after state effectively stole the vote back from Black people by implementing requirements that most people of any race had no hope of meeting. What person of any race or educational level knew how many jelly beans were in a large full jar, or how many windows there were in the White House for that matter? Yet these were the types of irrelevant questions White poll monitors would require Black people to answer in order to cast their vote. Strategies used to keep people from voting are known as voter suppression, practices that remain common even today.

In 1866, Tennessee passed the South's first "Jim Crow" statute intended to force newly freed Black people back into subordinate relationships and to separate, or segregate, themselves from White people in almost every facet of social and public life. Other states quickly followed suit. For nearly the next 100 years, White supremacists in the South passed state and local Jim Crow laws and engaged in practices intended to keep Black people subordinate to White people.

THE NADIR

The Nadir, or low point, of American race relations began in 1890 and lasted, some say, until 1950. By 1890, every state in the South as well as the North had retreated from their earlier efforts to create an interracial democratic nation. By that time, even Northern lawmakers began to pass Jim Crow laws and demand that Black people abide by racist customs. Most of White society abandoned Black people's fight to avoid the violence of racist White people and achieve the rights to life, liberty, and the pursuit of happiness, which the founders had declared were essential to American society.

Black people considered various strategies for participating in American society as well as protecting themselves. Beginning in the 1880s, many Black people embraced the teachings of Booker T. Washington, the famous educator and businessman who preached that White people would eventually respect Black people and see them as equals if Black people educated themselves and provided a useful service to society. In his attempt to avoid antagonizing White people, he advocated for Black people to pursue an industrial education or one that prepared them to do manual labor—as farmers, repairmen, cooks and house servants to White people, and so on—in their Southern communities.

Washington said in 1865, "To those of my race who depend upon bettering their condition in a foreign land or who underestimate that importance of cultivating friendly relations with the Southern White man . . . I would say, 'Cast down your bucket where you are'—cast it down in making friends in every manly way of the people of all races by whom we are surrounded. Cast it down in agriculture, in mechanics, in commerce, in domestic service, and in the professions."

Though Washington ultimately supported freedom, he encouraged Black people to find dignity in work rather than through pursuing positions of power or fighting for civil rights.

"I would set no limits on the attainments of the Negro in arts, in letters or statesmanship, but I believe the surest way to reach those ends is by laying the foundation in the little things of life that lie immediately about one's door. I plead for industrial education and development for the Negro not because I want to cramp him, but because I want to free him. I want to see him enter the all-powerful business and commercial world."

However, decades passed with little change from White America to show for Black people's heroic effort. By the turn of the century, many Black citizens—including some of Greenwood's residents—had begun to shift their opinion and embrace a different philosophy.

A graduate of Fisk University and Harvard University, W. E. B. Du Bois, who was biracial, believed that a generation of well-educated Black people—a group he called the Talented Tenth—could fight for civil rights, assume positions of power, and engage in intellectual scholarship by assimilating into White society. He strongly disagreed with the ways that Washington minimized Black people's ambitions to participate in the nation's civil and political life.

DECADES PASSED WITH LITTLE CHANGE FROM WHITE AMERICA

Du Bois said in 1903, "If we make money the object of man-training, we shall develop money-makers but not necessarily men; if we make technical skill the object of education, we may possess artisans but not, in nature, men. Men we shall have only as we make manhood the object of the work of the schools—intelligence, broad sympathy, knowledge of the world that was and is, and of the relation of men to it—this is the curriculum of that Higher Education which must underlie true life." Notice that women were not included in these conversations.

White people generally preferred Washington, who they believed supported the type of education that would limit Black people to inferior roles in Southern society, over Du Bois. In 1909, Du Bois joined with a group of Black and White people to found the National Association for the Advancement of Colored People (NAACP) to fight for Black people's civil rights and to stop lynching. As the years passed and so many White people continued to embrace violence, Du Bois gradually reached the conclusion that Black people must be prepared to protect themselves.

"We have cast off on the voyage which will lead to freedom or death," Du Bois wrote. "For three centuries we have suffered and cowered. No race ever gave passive resistance and submission to evil [a] longer, more piteous trial. Today we raise the terrible weapon of self-defense. When the murderer comes, he shall [no] longer strike us in the back. When the armed lynchers gather, we too must gather armed. When the mob moves, we propose to meet it with bricks and clubs and guns."

Nowhere in America had the decades-long discussion about the philosophies of Washington and Du Bois gone on longer than in the community on the north side of the railroad tracks in Tulsa, Oklahoma. As one of the most affluent Black communities in the United States—one that contained many well-educated people—this debate took place every day in Greenwood barbershops, jazz joints, and confectioneries, as it did across Black America. What else could Black people possibly do to win White people's respect? Could Black people ever prove themselves good enough—whether by hard work or academic education? Would Black people have to resort to bricks, clubs, and guns for protection? Was Booker T. or W.E.B. correct?

Not even a new century brought an end to the backlash

COULD BLACK PEOPLE EVER PROVE THEMSELVES GOOD ENOUGH?

and the violence. In 1906, a White mob turned on Black Atlanta residents for two straight days, killing as many as one hundred Black people and wounding many more. Both the Atlanta police and the Georgia National Guard participated in the attacks. Later that year, White terrorists turned on Black people in Wahalak and Scooba, Mississippi. Newspapers around the country reported that more than twelve Black citizens were killed.

Not surprisingly, Black people lived in fear of such violence. The brutality was becoming so barbaric and widespread that many thought perhaps the time had come for them to arm and look after themselves.

SUNDOWNER LAWS AND GRANDFATHER CLAUSES

Unlike during the Reconstruction Era, during the Nadir, White supremacist violence was no longer primarily confined to the South. In 1908, for instance, White rioters torched a Black neighborhood in Springfield, Illinois—the hometown of President Abraham Lincoln, who had issued the Emancipation Proclamation.

During this era, White gang violence was also on the rise in the territory that would, in 1907, become Oklahoma. Groups of hoodlums had attacked the Black residents of Berwyn in 1895, Lawton in 1902, and Boynton in 1904.

In 1907, when it was transformed from the Oklahoma Territories into a state, Oklahoma permitted men of all races to vote. However, Senate Bill Number One was a Jim Crow law that segregated travel. That same year, White marauders burned down the entire Black residential district of

Henryetta and then passed a "sundowner" law—one that required that any Black person leave the city before sunset. White Oklahomans lynched nine Black people between 1908 and 1916 alone. And those were just the episodes that made the newspaper.

Then, in 1910, Oklahoma lawmakers imposed a voter suppression strategy known as a "grandfather clause" to keep Black males from voting. In a nutshell, if you lived in Oklahoma—or in Alabama, Georgia, Louisiana, North Carolina, or Virginia, the other states that implemented grandfather clauses—and if your grandfather couldn't vote, you couldn't vote either. Most Black people's grandparents had been enslaved, so they couldn't vote. In fact, of the fifty thousand Black people who lived in Oklahoma in 1900, only fifty-seven had come from states that allowed Black males to vote in 1867. Once grandfather clauses were in place, the Fifteenth Amendment's promise became irrelevant. In Oklahoma, laws similar to this grandfather clause stayed in place until 1939. "Sundown towns" existed all throughout the United States, and sundowner laws remained commonplace until the 1960s with the informal rule still in effect in some places today.

HOPING TO ESCAPE

Around the turn of the century, newspapers owned and run by Black people were flourishing in Oklahoma. When someone was lynched, these papers spread the word far and wide. So did the legions of Black people who fled, relocating from town to town on the run from thuggish White people. Indeed, many of the Black people who migrated to Greenwood arrived hoping to escape White violence—first in the South but often more recently in Oklahoma.

By the 1910s, when Captain Townsend D. Jackson arrived, White-on-Black mob violence had again become so widespread that—after decades of trying to prove themselves worthy of White people's respect to little avail—Black people had begun questioning their previous assumptions that working hard, being good citizens, demonstrating humility, and accommodating White society were key to changing hearts and minds.

CHAPTER 3

A Promised Land

The Greenwood residents sitting in the audience at First Baptist Church that spring night in 1913 were well aware that Black people's advancement had ground to a halt. A few had been born into slavery themselves, and all had experienced racism at the hands of White people as they stymied the promise and progress of Reconstruction. Many were the children or grandchildren of people who had been enslaved, and they still experienced subordination and fear just as their ancestors did.

Captain Jackson had moved his family to Greenwood just a few months earlier. By now, his neighbors all knew that he had been born enslaved, and in the years after he had been emancipated, he had become a well-respected Black lawman and militia leader in Tennessee as well as Oklahoma. Rumor had it that Captain Jackson was a man who looked Oklahoma's White governor straight in the eye without blinking—an act of great bravery during an era in which a White person might kill a Black person for violating even the most minor Jim Crow custom. So they were anxious to hear his opinions and advice about the great racial issues of the day. As one of the few Black lawmen in the nation, perhaps he would help them strategize about how to keep

THE AUDIENCE INCLUDED GREENWOOD'S PROMINENT LEADERS AND MOST SUCCESSFUL ENTREPRENEURS

themselves and their families secure from the ever-present threat of White violence.

Surely, as a participant in the criminal justice system, he would have insights to share on these very pressing matters. Just where would the great Captain Jackson stand, they wondered?

A stately, six-foot fellow whose short, dark hair had gone mostly gray, Captain Jackson rose to the pulpit, stepping away from his wife, Sophronia, and youngest son, the handsome young physician Dr. Andrew Jackson. The audience included Greenwood's prominent leaders and most successful entrepreneurs.

ANDREW J. SMITHERMAN

As editor of the *Tulsa Star*, Greenwood's leading publication and its most authoritative public voice, Andrew J. Smitherman removed a piece of paper and pencil from his breast pocket and leaned forward, poised to capture Jackson's every word. Until that spring he'd worked in Muskogee, the state's Black newspaper publishing center. He had moved to Greenwood and founded the *Star* in 1913.

In the eight years between that night in the church and the terrible burning to come, Smitherman doggedly chronicled all the local news. He was a staunch supporter of Black voting rights and became the city's first Black elections inspector. Like so many of his peers who wrote for Black newspapers, he never missed a chance to rail against injustices White people perpe-

trated against his people. In fact, he demonstrated unbelievable courage by personally intervening in lynching attempts in
neighboring towns. In 1917, he personally investigated a mob of
lawless White people who torched the homes of twenty Black
families in Dewey, Oklahoma. Smitherman believed that, rather
than accommodating racism or praying that racist White people would not turn on them and rather than neglecting to an-
ticipate and protect themselves from lynch mobs, Black people
should arm themselves proactively to defend themselves and the
community. In 1919, the governor selected him to be among
the handful of Oklahomans—and the only Black person—to be
invited to meet President Woodrow Wilson when he traveled to
the state.

JOHN B. STRADFORD

Seated next to Smitherman was John B. Stradford, a short, dap-
per, mustachioed man, who had been born enslaved in Versailles,
Kentucky. J.B.'s father, J.C., had been taught how to read by their
enslaver's abolitionist daughter. Once he could read and write,
he forged his enslaver's name on a pass and escaped to Ontario,
Canada. There he earned enough money to return to Kentucky,
before Emancipation, and secure his own freedom and that of
his family.

J.B. earned degrees from Oberlin College and Indiana University Law School. He married and, determined to work only
for himself, became an entrepreneur, opening rooming houses,
bathhouses, shoeshine parlors, pool halls, and a hotel. His journey had taken him from Kentucky to Ohio, to Missouri, and to
Kansas with danger and hardship stalking him and his family at
every stop.

Stradford heard that economic opportunities existed in Tulsa and relocated there in 1905. When he arrived, the town was in the midst of a remarkable transformation from a tiny village in what was then still called "Indian Territory" to one of the world's most vibrant petroleum capitals. First incorporated in 1898, Tulsa's population at the time of the 1900 census was just thirteen hundred people and the town still resembled the 1830s Creek village its name was derived from. *Tulsa* came from the Creek word *Tallasi*, meaning "old town."

THE TRAIL OF TEARS

Oklahoma had been the end of the Trail of Tears, the deadly journey the federal government forced approximately one hundred thousand members of, primarily, the Cherokee, Chickasaw, Choctaw, Creek, and Seminole Nations—often called the Five Tribes—to take after President Andrew Jackson signed the Indian Removal Act in 1830. The Indian Removal Act empowered the United States to forcibly seize Native American lands east of the Mississippi and violently relocate thousands of Indigenous people from the South to the geographical areas that would eventually become Oklahoma, Kansas, Nebraska, and part of Iowa, then known as "Indian Territory." The government did this to make room for the expansion of chattel slavery. Indeed, the relocation of Indigenous people occurred as the nation was importing more than one million Black people into the Deep South.

Though six different nations fought back—the Potawatomi, Cherokee, Seminole, Kickapoo, Shawnee, and Eastern Cherokee—U.S. soldiers strong-armed the Native Americans and forced them to move at gunpoint, as they carried out the White supremacist theory of Manifest Destiny: the belief that White Americans were divinely ordained to expand the United States. Racist White people convinced one another that the nation had grounds to remove Indigenous people from the homelands that they had resided upon for thousands of years so White people could inhabit and cultivate those lands, primarily through the highly profitable capitalist system of slavery. Racist White people believed that Indigenous people's semi-nomadic lifestyles, communal approaches to growing crops, and hunting traditions didn't use the land as efficiently as White enslavers and settlers would and were, therefore, inferior. The pressure was particularly great in the southeastern and midwestern United States, where White enslavers often encroached upon Indigenous tribal lands. So, racist White people proclaimed it their duty and destiny to seize, settle, cultivate, and expand slavery in these lands.

Fifteen thousand Native Americans died along the Trail of Tears as a result of the difficult journey itself, illness, and the fact that the government neglected to provide the food and supplies it had promised. Most of the Indigenous people who survived arrived in "Indian Territory" in terrible physical and emotional condition and lacked resources except their horses, mules, a handful of implements, and household goods. The territory to which they had been relocated was already occupied by the Wichita, Plains Apache, Quapaw, and Caddo people, and ten additional tribes regularly migrated there.

After the forced exodus, the various Native American nations had Oklahoma largely to themselves until 1870, when the railroad arrived in that section of "Indian Territory" and the first permanent White settlers arrived. In 1887, the federal government dissolved its previous agreements with the Native Americans living in "Indian Territory" and offered between forty and one hundred sixty acres of land to individual tribe members instead.

Between 1889 and 1895, the government held a series of land openings, or "land runs," during which it offered settlers free or low-cost land, some of which was surplus land it had taken back from the Native Americans. These land runs attracted tens of thousands of new people to the region, including many Black people. Black families arrived in search of a "promised land," where they could live safely away from vigilante violence, establish communities, and raise their families. But after 1889, Black people living in Oklahoma Territory faced the same discrimination they faced everywhere else.

When Stradford arrived in Tulsa, the town wasn't segregated yet, but life had taught him that Black people stood the best chance of protecting each other from violence and succeeding by pooling their resources and supporting each other's businesses. Imagining an eventual neighborhood there, Stradford purchased property north of the Frisco railroad tracks. He also built a house and rented rooms to Black people who were migrating to Tulsa. He built more homes that people could rent and sold land to other Black people so they could build their own houses and businesses.

It didn't take long until he was one of Black Tulsa's most successful entrepreneurs. In 1918, he would open the famously luxurious, fifty-four room Stradford Hotel on Greenwood Avenue, which rivaled the finest White hotels and was one of the few Black-owned hotels in the nation. He built the first library in Tulsa for African Americans, since Jim Crow laws prohibited Black people from using the main library downtown. Like Smitherman, Stradford worried about Black people's plight in America, and he wasn't shy about saying so.

JOHN AND LOULA WILLIAMS

John and Loula Williams owned a drugstore, an auto shop, and a movie theater, and were the first Black people in Tulsa to purchase an automobile.

Born in Pittsburgh, John had moved to Memphis as a teenager to work as a fireman on the Illinois Central Railroad, where he married his wife, Loula, a college graduate and teacher. The couple soon moved to Arkansas and Mississippi, where Loula taught and John worked on steam engines, until racist White people drove them out of the Deep South to Oklahoma, where they arrived in 1903.

Williams worked on a paving crew when he arrived in Tulsa, then as a boiler operator for the White-owned Thompson Ice Cream Company, earning a salary large enough to buy a new Chalmers automobile—a purchase that caused his new neighbors to take notice. But John Williams not only managed to buy the car, he also taught himself to repair its engine, a skill that quickly attracted White Tulsans desperate for help with their own new automobiles. The engine business was so profitable that he opened Williams' One Stop Garage on Archer Street. Tulsa's leading White entrepreneurs and oilmen lined up to become his customers. John repaired engines and sold gas to the White people and their chauffeurs who waited outside his shop every day.

The couple built the three-story Williams Building at the prime corner of Greenwood Avenue and Archer Street. John, Loula, and their son, Bill, lived on the second floor and rented the third to an office of Black attorneys.

Loula left teaching to establish the Williams' Confectionery on the ground floor, which went on to become the heart of Greenwood's social life. The confectionery was a spacious place with a towering soda fountain situated amid twelve tables with four chairs each. An advertisement in the *Tulsa Star* boasted that it was the "headquarters for sweets, candies, nuts, fruits in season, ice cream, cold drinks, cigars, tobacco, and fresh butter every day."

> **Williams' Confectionery went on to become the heart of Greenwood's social life**

"Don't get disgusted because the warm weather is here," read another newspaper bulletin in 1913. "Remember Williams' Confectionery is a good place to keep cool. All the latest drinks sold daily."

Young Greenwood suitors made more marriage proposals at Williams' Confectionery than anywhere else in Black Tulsa. To celebrate, those engaged couples often stepped out of the confectionery and pushed their way through the happy crowds, then walked north along Greenwood Avenue to the Dreamland Theatre. The Dreamland's brightly lit palace provided yet another example of the Williamses' golden touch, and particularly Loula's knack for business. From the time the theater opened in 1914, almost every Greenwood family built a fifteen-cent movie ticket into their weekly budget.

The Dreamland's eight hundred seats were generally all filled as audiences watched silent movies accompanied by a live band, Black vaudevillian acts, or musical groups passing through town.

With two shows a night, Loula Williams typically locked more than a thousand dollars into the theater's safe each week. On Tuesdays, Loula and John drove across the railroad tracks dividing the Black and White sides of town to deposit their earnings at the White-owned Exchange National Bank. In the *Tulsa Star*, Andrew Smitherman hailed Loula as one of Oklahoma's most proficient businesswomen.

BARNEY CLEAVER

Barney Cleaver, the towering fellow seated near the back, was Tulsa's first Black sheriff's deputy. Consistent with the Jim Crow norms of the day, Cleaver had been assigned to patrol Greenwood's streets. Born to Virginian parents who had been enslaved, he had worked on a steamboat on the Ohio River between Charleston, West Virginia, and Cincinnati. Next he'd toiled in the West Virginian coal mines before his odyssey eventually landed him in Oklahoma.

O. W. GURLEY

Of all the tales of the townspeople in the audience, few reflected more ambition, luck, and timing, if not outright peril, than O. W. Gurley's.

Born on Christmas day in 1868 to parents who had recently been freed from chattel slavery, his parents relocated from Alabama to Pine Bluff, Arkansas, where he studied in a public school and worked on his father's farm. He taught as a young man, then obtained a position with the U.S. Post Office—a very rare and coveted position for a Black man of that era.

But young Gurley was restless, his dreams alternating between financial wealth and political ambition. That hunger led him to Oklahoma. On September 16, 1893, he participated in the Cherokee Outlet Opening of the Oklahoma land rush, which attracted approximately one hundred thousand people. Gurley literally raced fifty miles by foot before laying his stake, with his wife, Emma, to a plot of land in what would eventually become the all-Black town of Perry, Oklahoma. Gurley ran for county treasurer in Perry and became principal of the town's school. Ultimately, he and Emma opened a general store.

PLESSY VS. FERGUSON

As Gurley was getting on his feet, a White mob ran the Black residents of Lexington, Oklahoma, out of town. In 1893, a White gang threatened the Black people living in Blackwell with violence, causing them to leave; White people "hounded" Black people out of Ponca City; and masked raiders attacked Black people in Lincoln City.

White towns that were unable to rid themselves of Black people forced the Black people who remained to live in segregated communities. As these and other such events were occurring, a biracial man named Homer Plessy was taking his legal case to the Supreme Court. In 1892, Plessy purchased a train ticket from New Orleans to Covington, Louisiana. He took a seat in a Whites-only car. Just two years earlier, the state had begun to separate Black railway passengers from White ones. But Plessy refused the conductor's demand that he move, so he was arrested and put in jail. He filed a claim that this Louisiana law violated his Fourteenth Amendment right to equal protection. In 1896, his case finally reached the Supreme Court, which handed down the landmark decision Plessy v. Ferguson. In it, the Court established that racial segregation on intrastate railroads was constitutional as long as the facilities were "separate but equal." Of course, nothing during that era that was racially separate was also equal. But with the Supreme Court essentially declaring segregation constitutional, racist White communities around the nation began to segregate Black people from White people. Racial segregation would be legal across the South and beyond for another fifty years.

Though Gurley experienced considerable success in Perry, he began to envision even greener pastures for himself in a town fifty miles away. On November 22, 1905, wildcat oil drillers, working the land of a man named Ida E. Glenn, hit the first gusher of what became the Mid-Continent Oil Field. It would be the most bountiful producer of petroleum in the nation for years to come. Glenn Pool No. 1 gushed only twelve miles south of Tulsa, almost instantly transforming the town into an oil capital. White oilmen and speculators flocked there by the thousands, many becoming millionaires overnight. Like J. B. Stradford, Gurley rightly reasoned that somehow, Black people could also cash in. So the Gurley family moved to Tulsa.

With profits from Perry, O. W. Gurley, too, bought land—forty acres—and laid out the plans for a neighborhood. Back then, when Black people owned land it was noteworthy. O.W. and Emma opened a general store along a muddy country road that cut through empty rolling prairie north of the city limits. But neither the prairie nor the Gurleys' pockets remained empty for long. Black people looking for better lives poured off train cars at the Frisco depot by the dozens every day. Some had heard of the Tulsa boom and were hoping to capitalize on it themselves. Others were fleeing the South in hopes of finding a "promised land" free from the everyday violence of White supremacists and one that offered them the opportunity to make a decent life. Like J.B. Stradford, the Gurleys sold land to other Black people, many of whom built wood shanties and bought groceries from the couple who had been there first. And as landowners with a vision for a Black community, Gurley and Stradford collaborated and made a mint by selling and renting property.

Though they were locked out of society's larger opportunities, including most of the oil business, Gurley and other business owners nonetheless benefited in some ways when White Tulsans enacted Jim Crow statutes, which banned Black people from White stores and forced them to spend their money in their own neighborhood, strengthening the community's economy. Additionally, the oil business was profitable enough that, by 1910, virtually every White family middle class or above hired some combination of Black chauffeurs, maids, nannies, cooks, nursemaids, gardeners, or laundresses. Many of these service workers would live with their White employers during the week, returning to Greenwood to enjoy their Thursday night, which most employers allowed their domestics to take off. All-Black Greenwood became a town within a town. Its residents shopped in each other's stores and supported each other's businesses, creating an extraordinarily vibrant Black business community. With so many successful Black businesses located in the same community—and so much money circulating within the neighborhood because of the oil money that made its way into the hands of Black people, who then spent it with each other—Greenwood became one of the greatest concentrations of Black wealth in the United States. For that reason, the area would become known as Black Wall Street.

Greenwood became one of the greatest concentrations of Black wealth in the United States

The other prominent residents of Greenwood waiting to hear Captain Jackson speak included several lawyers and Dr. R. T. Bridgewater, Black Tulsa's first physician, and his wife, a teacher. Many schoolteachers sat in attendance that evening. Schools serving Black children had begun to open in Greenwood in 1908, teaching grades one through eight. By 1913, educators at the Dunbar School taught Black children in a high school setting. Booker T. Washington High School was built the same year, and consistent with Du Bois's school of thought, Black students there studied subjects like Latin, trigonometry and algebra, history, and literature, from the finest teachers anywhere. When he was still living in Memphis, that school's first principal, E. W. Woods, read an ad for Black teachers in Greenwood and walked the difficult and dangerous four hundred miles to apply.

E. W. Woods may have been Booker T. Washington High School's principal, but Black women took the lead in educating the Black children of that era. They included Lula Sims, Marie Martin, Jane Johnson, Birdie Farmer, and Mrs. R. T. Bridgewater, all of whom sat in the audience. Back then, Black educators did far more than teach. Most Black women instructors saw education as their mission. After slavery, legions of Black women answered the call to educate newly freed people, most of whom were illiterate, since educating Black people had been illegal. By 1868, fifteen Black colleges had been formed to train educators, who were often socialized to believe that serving their community was their highest calling.

"You can do much to alleviate the condition of our people," the famed Black educator Fanny Jackson Coppin, the commencement speaker for the 1879 graduating class of the Institute for Colored Youth, charged the graduates. "Do not be discouraged.

The very places where you are needed [the] most are those where you will get [the] least pay."

Black educators sought to educate newly freed adults as well as their children. Their efforts extended far beyond the walls of the school and included raising money to build the school buildings themselves; teaching moonlight school so parents could learn how to read and write; writing letters for community members; explaining contracts, including those covering the work agreements White employers offered, which often attempted to exploit Black people; and leading discussions about issues affecting the community. Teachers would educate the public about the endless whirlwind of changing rules, laws, and statutes that governed Black life. These Black women demonstrated leadership to our nation at a time when society undervalued the humanity and rights of American women in general—and Black women in particular.

Their work was utterly exhausting, yet they undertook it with pride even as White supremacists around the South terrorized, intimidated, and even killed countless Black teachers and learners of all ages. Because education paved the path to greater freedom and empowered participation in American society, Black schools always carried the risk of being vandalized or of being burned to the ground by a terror organization like the KKK.

Black communities idolized their teachers and saw them as heroes, the pioneering educator Mary McLeod Bethune among them. Born in 1875, the daughter of enslaved parents—and the fifteenth of seventeen children—Mary McLeod grew up in South Carolina picking cotton with her sharecropper parents and siblings for the same planter, and on the same land, that they had worked back during slavery. Eventually her mother saved enough money to purchase that land. Mary began school at age ten and was a voracious learner, who felt the world open up to her once she learned to read. She would come home from school and teach her siblings and other children in her community. As a young woman, Mary graduated from the seminary and obtained additional religious education, but after no religious organization would support her desire to be a missionary, she decided to become a teacher. She married another educator, Albertus Bethune, and had a son in 1899. The marriage ended in 1904. Determined to support herself and her son, she founded the Daytona Beach Literary and Industrial School for Training Negro Girls. In 1929, she transformed her school into Bethune-Cookman College, which began offering degrees in 1943 and operates even today as a historically Black college.

Indeed, to visit First Baptist on the night of Jackson's speech was to observe Greenwood's upper class—educated, literate, and prosperous. The community's elite packed into the sanctuary, curious about Captain Jackson, his just the latest in a series of remarkable success stories that continued to unfold in the community called Greenwood. Whether an educator or entrepreneur, each of the members of Captain Townsend's audience had, in her or his own way, proven false the widely believed lies about Black people that so many racist White people championed to justify their cruelty. Some no doubt shared the more confrontational beliefs that Smitherman and Stradford held about race relations. Others tended to speak less forcefully about the community's need to arm itself and engage in self-defense. Certainly everyone recognized the precarious position the Black community found itself in—vulnerable at any moment to White racists' intimidation, mob violence, or worse.

NATIVE AMERICANS AND SLAVERY

When the government forced Cherokee, Choctaw, Chicka-saw, Creek, and Seminole tribes from the South into "In-dian Territory" along the Trail of Tears, they brought both free and enslaved Black people with them. Some of these Black people had escaped from their White enslavers to the Creek, Seminole, and Cherokee communities, which accepted them as free people and protected them. However, a handful of affluent and powerful members of the Creek, Cherokee, and other nations purchased and enslaved Black people. By the Civil War, more than eight thousand Black people lived among these tribes.

The slavery practiced by these Native Americans was both similar to and different from slavery practiced by White Americans. Though most tribes considered Black people to be property, they allowed Black families to live together and did not separate family members to sell them. Only rarely did Native Americans subject enslaved Black people to violence, and they did not regard them as animals or beasts of burden. In fact, Native American planters typically labored alongside the Black people they enslaved as they grew enough food to live on. They also permitted enslaved people to learn to read, to write, and to gather for their own religious services.

Though the slavery might not have been as violent, it was slavery nonetheless. In 1842, Black people enslaved within the Cherokee Nation attempted to flee to Mexico, where slavery had been abolished. In 1850, the Seminole leader Wild Cat established a settlement in Mexico with about three hundred Black people. Many Black people living among the Seminole Nation lived in their own communities. Some intermarried with Seminoles and several Black men became leaders in that nation. After the Civil War, the United States entered new treaties with each of the Five Tribes that abolished slavery, extended citizenship to freed men and women, and gave them rights to land. Some of these new landowners were Black or biracial Black and Native American. Some of them relocated to Tulsa, already landowners and possessing financial and other material resources.

CHAPTER 4

A Perilous Position

Though, on this night, he stood before the audience a revered Black lawman, Captain Jackson had been born enslaved. His final days of enslavement did not occur on his owner's Georgian plantation. They occurred instead on the smoky, mist-dampened battlefield of Lookout Mountain near Chattanooga, Tennessee. The husky biracial boy—the son of his White plantation-owning father and the Black woman he raped—was only seven when his father first hauled him into the Civil War. Two years later, in the fall of 1863, his father's Confederate regiment withered beneath the assault of Union forces and was forced to retreat.

There's no telling what happened during the Confederates' defeat. Did Union soldiers save the boy from the Confederate army and his father? Seeing his chance to dash for freedom, did the nine-year-old run away and escape? Did his father free him intentionally? Did genuine affection exist between the White enslaver father and biracial son whom he'd enslaved? Did the father offer his son any advice, any money? Did they hug each other goodbye?

All that we know for sure was that nine-year-old Townsend Jackson was free.

During the decades afterward, Jackson often downplayed the dangers and difficulties he'd faced as a young boy as well as the strength and resourcefulness he had to demonstrate to survive. The nation was still at war, and his people would remain in bondage for two additional years. Yet somehow Jackson was free.

During these terrifying times, this nine-year-old child was alone.

An account of Captain Jackson's life was published in the *Tulsa Star* years later, based on an interview with him, and described those postwar years in just two sentences: "Secured his discharge after the battle of Mount Lookout, and went to Memphis a short while thereafter. Through correspondence, he found his mother at Trenton, Tenn., to which place she had immigrated after the war."

Emancipation was a terrifying and confusing time—and it must have been even more so for a nine-year-old. After the war ended, thousands of newly

EMANCIPATION WAS A TERRIFYING AND CONFUSING TIME

free Black people traveled from plantation to plantation, from town to town, from city to city—homeless and one step ahead of starvation—as they searched for their children and family members whom their enslavers had sold away or took with them when they had moved West. Some freed men and women hunted for loved ones throughout their entire lives.

Others sought out a safe place to live and a way to earn a living so they could eat and put a roof over their head. Countless Black men had been killed during the war and many women and children were forced to fend for themselves, as Captain Townsend had been. Terrorized by local White people who wanted to keep

Black people under their control, or even just needing to eat and lacking better options, some Black people stayed on or near the land where they'd been enslaved. Others headed to cities and congregated there. Many depended on what little help the Freedmen's Bureau offered both Black people and vulnerable White people.

At some point after reconnecting with his mother, Jackson found work in Memphis as a waiter at the famous Gayosa Hotel. There, he served food and drinks to rich White men. Another Black waiter taught him to read. That prepared him to attend night school, where he studied math and history, literature and Latin. This education situated him to participate in the growing community of affluent Black Memphians. This group would have included Robert Church, a biracial man whom a mob of White people had attacked and left for dead during the 1866 Memphis Race Massacre. On that date, a horde of racist White people killed more than forty-five Black people, injured seventy-five others, and robbed and burned down almost one hundred homes, churches, and schools. Somehow, Church survived. After the 1878 yellow fever epidemic—during which White people fled the city in droves—Church smartly purchased real estate at fire-sale prices. Eventually he would become what many believe was the South's first Black millionaire. (For much of United States history, Jim Crow laws dictated that if you had even a single "drop" of Black blood, you were considered Black.) During Reconstruction, many of Church's buildings became home to all sorts of Black businesses that blossomed along Beale Street, a neighborhood that became famous and in which many Black musicians would bring the blues and jazz to life.

But Jackson didn't aspire to be a businessman. Perhaps because he remembered military life during his youth—or maybe because the South was incredibly violent, and he was so young and felt vulnerable and wanted to protect himself and others—Jackson dreamed of being a lawman. In fact, he helped to recruit and organize a Black militia. In 1878—when he would only have been in his mid-twenties—he and his officers maintained public order as the yellow fever epidemic killed thousands in the city. Once the epidemic ended, the bravery of Jackson and fourteen of his militiamen earned them permanent positions on the Memphis police force.

However, racist White people struggled to accept Black people's success, becoming jealous and fearful of losing any of the advantages that being born White provided. This included the right they believed they had to set aside the best and most high-paying jobs for themselves. Jackson and his Black officers lost their positions to a group of racist Irishmen. Many White people viewed Jackson as being "uppity," a term racists often used to describe Black people who refused to behave as though they believed they were inferior, as Jim Crow and White supremacy required.

CHALLENGING THE OPPRESSIVE ORDER

During the years that he lived in Memphis, Captain Jackson would certainly have known of a Black schoolteacher-turned-journalist named Ida B. Wells, who by then had become editor and co-owner of a Black newspaper called the *Free Speech and Headlight*. Born enslaved, Wells had educated herself at Shaw University. She took classes at Fisk University, another historically Black university, as well.

When Wells was just twenty-two, she had made a name for

herself among Black people nationwide. After a conductor on the Chesapeake & Ohio Railroad removed her from the first-class seat she had purchased and then attempted to force her to sit in the segregated car, Wells not only sued the railroad company, she actually won her case, and the judge said the railroad should pay her five hundred dollars, about thirteen thousand dollars today. A Black woman winning a lawsuit against a White company was unheard of then. Not surprisingly, to maintain White supremacy, the Tennessee Supreme Court overturned the verdict.

These injustices sparked Wells to write about racial injustice and Southern politics in newspapers owned by Black people. Writing under the pen name Iola, she became well-known by Black Americans far and wide. In one of her editorials, Wells criticized the inferior quality of Memphis's segregated schools. Rather than improving them, the school system fired her. A Black woman courageous enough to stand up to powerful White people without mincing her words was uncommon. Her following exploded. Rather than bend to an employer, the incredibly courageous Wells supported herself by selling subscriptions to the newspaper she co-owned.

Early in 1889, a mob of White people felt threatened by Captain Jackson because he bought and smoked a cigar in a White store. Envious of his success and outraged that he'd challenged the oppressive social order, they set out to lynch him. A few years earlier, Jackson might have stood up to the horde out of principle. As a Memphis policeman, he had done so many times before as he protected Black people accused of various false and exaggerated charges. But a decade earlier, he had gotten married. Now he and his wife, Sophronia, were raising two boys and a girl. He would not risk the lives of his family members. So when the mob arrived at their home on that night in 1889, they found it empty. The family had hidden themselves in the homes of friends. A few days later, they headed west aboard a car of the Rock Island Railroad. Captain Jackson's descendants would pass the story of his escape down through the family for generations.

On April 22, 1889, Captain Jackson joined the land rush in the territory that eighteen years later would become the state of Oklahoma. For weeks, thousands of settlers had amassed at the boundary of the Southwestern wilderness. At exactly noon on that date, U.S. Cavalry troopers sounded bugles and fired their guns into the air. Some fifty thousand people set off on a mad dash—racing by foot, on horseback, in wagons, and by railroad car—to claim the forty acres of free land the federal government was offering to settlers. Captain Jackson staked his claim in an area that became the town of Guthrie, which sprang up almost overnight.

Before long, large numbers of Black people fleeing the South began to settle there. At first, the town's new arrivals were too caught up in their hopes for the future—whether the chance to own land, instant wealth, or just a place they could safely raise their family—to think much about racial bigotry. In fact, Black people were able to assume important positions in Guthrie's new territorial government. Captain Jackson became its jailer and was elected justice of the peace. He was also appointed to the Guthrie police force and organized the territory's first Black militia, as he had back in Memphis. Along the way, he became well-known both to White and Black politicians. After statehood, in 1907, the White governor of Oklahoma even appointed Captain Jackson to serve as an Oklahoma delegate to an important national conference on Negro education.

Captain Jackson's family flourished as well. His daughter, Minnie Mae, met and married a bright young lawyer, H. A. Guess, who would soon become one of the most respected Black attorneys in the region. But he was especially proud of his youngest child, Andrew, who earned a spot in the freshman class at Meharry Medical College, the nation's finest for Black doctors.

Predictably, White people in Guthrie also became jealous of Captain Jackson. In 1912, the mayor ordered him to limit his policing to the Black sections of town. Jackson resigned immediately, but having survived slavery, the Civil War, and the dangerous years afterward, he wasn't discouraged. He remained stubbornly hopeful that his resourcefulness would triumph over hatred. He'd heard that one hundred miles east, in the booming oil town of Tulsa, Black people were becoming even more prosperous than they had been back in Memphis. It appeared that, there, industrious Black people had figured out a way to protect themselves from White people's hatred.

HAVING SURVIVED SLAVERY, THE CIVIL WAR, AND THE DANGEROUS YEARS AFTERWARD, JACKSON WASN'T DISCOURAGED

In Memphis, as well as across the South, Black people began to see the newly opening frontier—and particularly Oklahoma—as a possible "promised land." Desperate to be safe and eager to support each other in getting on their feet, many Black people imagined creating all-Black cities. In time, they founded approximately fifty such cities. Some even envisioned an all-Black state, although that never came to pass.

THE NATION'S FIRST INVESTIGATIVE REPORTER

While Captain Townsend was settling into his new life, back in Memphis, Ida B. Wells's life changed forever when a White mob lynched her dear friend Thomas Moss, in March 1892. Moss and two friends, Calvin McDowell and William "Henry" Steward, had opened People's Grocery Store, which had attracted Black customers away from the White-owned establishment where they previously shopped. Furious that Black businessmen had cut into business the White shopkeeper inaccurately believed he had a right to, he and his friends threatened the Black men. But men in the Black community came together to support Moss and his co-owners. When a White gang showed up, intending to burn down the building, they encountered armed Black men, who shot three White people in the process of defending the establishment. The police then arrested one hundred Black people, including Moss, McDowell, and Steward, and charged them with conspiracy.

The White press whipped up a frenzy, claiming the Black men had victimized innocent White people. The newspaper warned that if the White men died, mob violence would follow. The White men recovered, but still a mob gathered outside the jail. Black people stood guard to prevent the terrorism.

After the Black defenders left, the police allowed the mob to break the businessmen out of the jail in order to lynch them. The judge ordered the sheriff to shoot any Black activist whose demonstration seemed to be causing trouble. He also prohibited anyone from selling guns to Black people.

When the mob asked Moss if he had anything to say before they killed him, he said, "Tell my people to go west, there is no justice for them here."

Moss's murder was one of two hundred twenty-five lynchings White thugs perpetrated that year.

Afterward, the mob broke into People's Grocery, ate the food, and then destroyed the store. Shortly thereafter, more than six thousand Black Memphians left the city and headed to places like Kansas and Oklahoma—so many people left that White store owners worried whether their businesses would have to close.

Heartbroken and infuriated by the murder of her friend, Wells immediately focused her reporting on lynching. She invented the career of investigative journalism as she interviewed people and pored over the details of these vicious assaults. Later that year, she published an exposé called Southern Horrors: Lynch Law in All Its Phases. *The story shined the light on the practice of lynching, challenged the truthfulness of many of the stories White people told to justify murdering Black people—namely by alleging that Black men were sexually assaulting White women—and launched her on a national (and eventually international) speaking career raising awareness about lynching's horrors.*

In sum, Wells wrote that nobody believed that Black men were assaulting White women and that lynching was merely a tool that racist White people used to keep Black people subordinate. That claim infuriated racist White folks, who weren't used to a Black woman standing up to them. While Wells was visiting Philadelphia, White terrorists burned down her printing press and threatened to hang her from a lamppost. So Wells moved to New York and later Chicago, where she continued her career and later married, becoming Ida B. Wells-Barnett.

In 1912, Townsend Jackson and his family boarded the train once more, this time for a short trip to Tulsa. And now, on a warm May night just one year later, Captain Jackson's heart swelled as he stood in the pulpit addressing new neighbors—many of whom had endured odysseys and survived treacherous struggles similar to his and whose optimism remained just as strong.

Jackson greeted his audience and began speaking. But much to the disappointment and even consternation of his new neighbors, he did not speak about the role that lawmakers should play in protecting Black communities, or about the ways members of the criminal justice system often participated in lynchings, or about whether he thought Black people should take up arms to defend themselves against the risk of mob rule. Instead, he reminded his neighbors to be modest and humble, reflecting upon Jesus's instructions that people should be "like little children" in order to enter God's kingdom. In fact, Captain Jackson complimented Black people who "by his silent example gives light to those who sit in darkness."

Just imagine such words coming from a man who had spent the better part of his life as a law officer facing down White mobs—a person whose own family had been run out of Memphis by one.

"If the time shall ever come when we possess in the [Black] people of this country a class of men noted for enterprise, industry, economy, and success, we shall no longer have any trouble in the matter of civil and political rights," he said. "The battle against the popular prejudice shall have been fought."

Perhaps Captain Jackson believed the life of his son, Dr. Andrew Jackson, who by then was known as one of the nation's finest Black surgeons, proved his point. Even White people came to the young Dr. Jackson for help. Perhaps a part of Captain Jackson did believe that high achievement could help shield Black people from at least some White violence. That's what Captain Jackson seemed to be saying, though his own experience suggested that this approach hadn't worked in his own life. His firsthand experience with racial hatred's bitter realities had nearly killed him.

Quite likely, he understood what was at stake. He saw all that his neighbors

HIS FIRSTHAND EXPERIENCE WITH RACIAL HATRED'S BITTER REALITIES HAD NEARLY KILLED HIM

had accomplished—how many prosperous businesses they had created from so little. As a member of law enforcement, he certainly knew just how perilous their position was. He grasped what Black people would risk if they stood up to the already violent White people who surrounded and outnumbered them. He likely understood the dangerous dilemma that this accomplished and materially wealthy community faced—that they stood between the devil and the deep blue sea. They would be in trouble if they did stand up for themselves against any White mob and in trouble if they didn't. That night, he was clearly opting for the more conservative approach.

Yet his speech left the more activist members of the audience feeling bitterly disappointed. In the end, the most militant crowd members would be right. No amount of Black achievement could assuage White hatred and jealousy. His words would seem so naïve just eight years later, on the terrible spring morning when White Tulsans torched Greenwood. Indeed, in the great catastrophe of 1921, no one would lose more than Captain Townsend D. Jackson himself.

CHAPTER 5

May 30, 1921: The Incident

Nineteen years old, Dick Rowland shined shoes at the Drexel Building downtown. A handsome, muscular young man with a charming personality, he had been adopted by his mother, Damie Rowland, back in 1905. He'd shown up on the doorstep of her grocery store in Vinita, Oklahoma, an orphan whose name was Jimmie Jones, charming and talkative even as a young child. Damie had fed Jimmie and taken him in.

Barely able to make enough money to feed themselves, Damie and Jimmie moved to Tulsa, where she'd heard Black people were getting rich.

When he started elementary school, Jimmie decided that he wanted to be called "Dick." That's when he started developing a mind of his own. In his first years of school, Dick brought

Black people were getting rich

home very good grades, and Damie fantasized that he might become like one of the Black doctors, lawyers, or businessmen in Greenwood. As he grew older, however, Dick became less interested in hitting the books. Instead, he became drawn to Greenwood's jazz joints, where he often went dancing and chasing young women. A good football player, he dropped out of school two years in a row as soon as the season was over.

Having had to quit at about the fourth grade herself, Damie would beg her son to go to class. Greenwood was filled with Black businessmen, teachers, and newspaper editors, each living examples of the treasures an education might provide. Damie dreamed of the day when Dick might have a high school diploma of his own. Maybe he could even attend college and become a doctor. But he would never listen.

GREENWOOD WAS FILLED WITH BLACK BUSINESSMEN, TEACHERS, AND NEWSPAPER EDITORS

"Why should I, Aunt Damie? Look at this," he'd reply, pulling out a roll of bills.

Most were ones but some were fives and tens; that astounded her. She could not believe Dick made that kind of money shining shoes.

"With the oil and all, these White folks go to bed poor and wake up as rich as country butter," Dick told her. "They'll tip you five dollars for a fifteen-cent shine just because the guy before tipped you four!"

Then Dick would peel a five-dollar bill from his roll and hand it to her. "Treat yourself to something nice," he'd say, smiling as he trotted out the door of her boardinghouse.

Yet Damie worried, as any mother would. Every week he seemed more flamboyant than the last. She wondered what all he was involved with. Then, one year, Dick bought himself a diamond

"TREAT YOURSELF TO SOMETHING NICE"

ring as a birthday present. His friends started calling him "Diamond Dick," which pleased him greatly. Damie knew that he had started drinking and had fallen in with the wrong crowd, but he laughed when she told him how worried she was about him.

Sarah Page was a White, seventeen-year-old young woman living in a rented place on North Boston Street. Though two years younger than Dick, she'd already been married and divorced. Rumor had it she'd ditched her husband in Kansas City and come to Tulsa to live with a relative. That spring, Tulsa's sheriff had served her with divorce papers. Back then, being a divorced woman was considered scandalous.

Sarah operated an elevator in the Drexel Building. Her path crossed with Dick's after his employer at the building's shoeshine stand arranged for the bootblacks to use the fourth floor restroom. It was a dirty little cubicle marked COLOREDS ONLY, but Dick didn't complain. He got to ride Sarah's elevator several times a day.

Today, the accounts of what happened in the elevator that day vary widely. But Damie knew from the gleam in Dick's eye that he found Sarah attractive. She never knew for sure whether the relationship went beyond being acquaintances, but his aspirations were clear.

Of course, Dick was aware of the danger faced by a Black man who had eyes for a White woman. It seemed that every other day brought a story about White mob violence somewhere in the country or about another Black man being lynched. Often the claims of a White woman triggered a chain of violence.

In 1917 and 1918, large mobs had attacked Black people in

Houston, in Philadelphia, and in East St. Louis, Illinois, allegedly because they posed an economic threat. In 1919, the year Black troops returned home from World War I, in Oklahoma alone, groups of White attackers lynched six Black men. That summer, mobs were known to have attacked Black people in Longview, Texas; Chicago, Illinois; Knoxville, Tennessee; Omaha, Nebraska; and Elaine, Arkansas.

The summer of 1919 became known as the Red Summer because so much Black blood flowed in the streets. In response, poet Claude McKay wrote "To the White Fiends":

> Think you I am not fiend and savage too?
> Think you I could not arm me with a gun
> And shoot down ten of you for every one
> Of my black brothers murdered, burnt by you?
> Be not deceived, for every deed you do
> I could match out-match: am I not Africa's son,
> Black of that black land where black deeds are done?
>
> But the Almighty from the darkness drew
> My soul and said: Even thou shalt be a light
> Awhile to burn on the benighted earth,
> Thy dusky face I set among the white
> For thee to prove thyself of highest worth;
> Before the world is swallowed up in night,
> To show thy little lamp: go forth, go forth!

That same year, the NAACP published a report called *Thirty Years of Lynching in the United States: 1889–1918*, one of the most comprehensive studies of lynching ever written. Later that year, the organization began to press for a federal law against lynching. In fact, in 1921, the NAACP held more than two hundred meetings around the country to promote anti-lynching measures.

Many times, the trouble had started with a White woman screaming "rape" if a Black man had merely smiled at her, had not stepped off the sidewalk, or had violated any one of Jim Crow's arbitrary and endlessly shifting social conventions. Nearly a quarter of lynchings of Black Southerners were based on a White person's allegation of sexual assault. Even crying rape without naming a perpetrator could trigger racist White folks to become violent. Black men had been lynched for entering a room where White women were sitting, asking to marry a White woman, knocking on the door of a White woman's house, and inviting a White woman to have a cold drink.

BLACK MEN HAD BEEN LYNCHED FOR ENTERING A ROOM WHERE WHITE WOMEN WERE SITTING

In reality, the NAACP's report showed that only twenty-five percent of lynchings involved an actual sexual assault. Those cases should have received due process and been tried in a court of law rather than by a mob of White vigilantes.

Damie knew that White Tulsans had even lynched their own. Why, in 1917, about fifty men in black robes and black masks, the "Knights of Liberty," had kidnapped seventeen White Industrial Workers of the World union members from a police caravan taking them to jail on trumped-up charges. They stripped them, tied them to a tree, whipped them, poured hot tar on their bodies, and then coated them with feathers.

"The number of blows was regulated by the chief of police himself, who was easily recognizable [beneath his robe] by six of us at least," one tortured union member later said. "It was all prearranged. The police knew where we were going."

When their torment was over, the attackers used gunshots to run the seventeen men off into the Osage hills. That same night, placards were posted at prominent public places around Tulsa: NOTICE TO I.W.W.'S. DON'T LET THE SUN SET ON YOU IN TULSA.

The incident became known as the "Tulsa Tar Party," and the Black people in Greenwood took notice.

In 1920, the Tulsa police arrested an eighteen-year-old White man named Roy Belton for murdering a cab driver named Homer Nida. Belton had confessed to shooting Nida but told police that his gun had discharged accidentally. Belton should have had the chance to take his case to court, but shortly after Nida's widow called for revenge in the newspaper, a mob of White thugs gathered outside the courthouse. Mob members insisted that the sheriff, named Wooley, turn Belton over.

"Let the law take its course, boys," Sheriff Wooley replied. "The electric chair will get him before too long, but you know this is no way to interfere with the law."

The vigilantes disarmed the sheriff and forced him to release Belton. In a caravan stretching for more than a mile, the mob then drove Belton to where Nida had been shot.

The Tulsa police helped direct traffic.

Then, with a huge crowd of White spectators roaring in approval, the vigilantes led Belton underneath a large billboard, threw a rope from a nearby farmhouse around his neck, allowed him to smoke a cigarette, and lynched him.

When Belton was cut down, "Sudden pandemonium broke loose," the *Tulsa World* reported. "Hundreds rushed over the prostrate form to get bits of clothing. The rope was cut into bits for souvenirs. His trousers and shoes were torn into bits and the mob fairly fought over gruesome souvenirs. An ambulance finally pushed through the jam of automobiles. The body was carried to the car, late arrivals still grabbing for bits of clothing on the now almost nude form."

Tulsa Police Chief John Gustafson said afterward that while

he didn't normally condone mob violence, the lynching "will prove of real benefit to Tulsa and vicinity. It was an abject lesson to hijackers and auto thieves, and I believe it will be taken as such."

Such sentiments were echoed on the editorial pages of the city's dominant White newspaper, the *Tulsa World*. The only public protest of Belton's murder came from the Greenwood side of the railroad tracks.

"There is no crime, however atrocious, that justifies mob violence," Andrew Smitherman wrote in the *Tulsa Star*, giving voice to the fears roiling in so many Black souls. "The lynching of Roy Belton," Smitherman wrote, "explodes the theory that a prisoner is safe on the top floor of the Courthouse from mob violence."

Dick Rowland was just a teenager when all of this occurred. He may not have understood the grave danger an interracial friendship or flirtatious relationship posed, but Damie certainly understood the peril her son would be in. If this was what White folks occasionally did to each other to enforce the community's unwritten rules, a Black man who violated Jim Crow's conventions didn't stand a chance.

Damie believed that Dick's crush on the girl had washed away his better judgment.

A BLACK MAN WHO VIOLATED JIM CROW'S CONVENTIONS DIDN'T STAND A CHANCE

On the morning of May 30 and of the Memorial Day parade, Dick had gone upstairs to drop off some shoes he'd polished and to use the bathroom. He then waited for Sarah's elevator to take him back downstairs.

When the elevator door opened, Dick smiled at Sarah. It's

not completely clear what happened next; however, both Sarah and Dick gave similar accounts to police. Apparently, he bumped into her as he walked in, likely because he tripped and stumbled, perhaps accidentally stepping on her toe and maybe grabbing her arm. Dick tried to apologize, but Sarah pounded him over the head with her purse, hitting him again and again, hard enough to snap the purse's leather handles.

When the elevator reached the ground floor, Sarah opened the door and screamed, "I've been assaulted!"

A clerk came running out from Renberg's Clothiers right next to the elevator.

Dick outran him and got away.

CHAPTER 6

Dick Rowland Runs

I t was about noon when Dick appeared at Damie's boarding-house on Archer Street. He almost never came home at mid-day, when Tulsa's oil executives poured out of the tall buildings downtown for lunch and to get their shoes shined. But on that day, Dick raced home. When he arrived, sweat was pouring down his face, and he couldn't speak for several seconds.

Immediately, Damie suspected that the Page girl was at the center of Dick's troubles.

"I reached up to hold her arms back and keep her from pounding my head, and held them there," Dick told his mother. "When the elevator reached the ground floor, Sarah screamed, 'I've been assaulted!' A clerk came running out from Renberg's Clothiers right next to the elevator shaft and tried to catch me. But I outran him and came here."

Dick looked like he was about to cry. Damie hugged him.

"I've got to hide until tomorrow," he said.

"What do we do then?" Damie asked.

"I don't know."

Damie lowered the blinds of the boardinghouse, but she and Dick both knew that there would be no hiding. Innocent or not, no one would believe him. Sooner or later, he would have hell to pay for touching a White woman.

The first night passed quietly. All night long, they waited for a knock at Damie's front door but none came, and their spirits lifted some. In fact, Dick snuck out the next day to see his friends.

But police spotted him on the street, handcuffed him, and hauled him to the jail.

Dick called Damie in tears, pleading with her to get him an attorney.

Damie promised to help him as best she could, her own heart breaking and her body trembling with fear. She was crying as she left her boarding-house, crossed the Frisco train tracks to the White side of town, and headed up Boulder Avenue toward the county courthouse.

> **POLICE SPOTTED HIM ON THE STREET, HANDCUFFED HIM, AND HAULED HIM TO THE JAIL**

She couldn't help remembering the skinny little boy who had appeared on her doorstep when he was just six. Now, though guilty of nothing but being naïve and demonstrating bad judgement, she wondered whether Dick would live to see his twentieth birthday.

Once she arrived at the courthouse, Sheriff William McCullough invited her into his office. A tall, kind man with a thick handlebar mustache, he made her feel a little better.

McCullough said the Page girl was nothing but trouble and that Tulsa detectives were already skeptical of what she'd said. When questioned by detectives, Page's account of the elevator incident had varied little from Rowland's. The young woman said he had grabbed her arm, but whether it was to brace his fall or an act of assault was not clear. It could very well have been an accident, as Rowland had claimed. He was uncertain that the case against Rowland would ever be prosecuted. At that point, his incarceration was as much to protect him from the possibility of White mob violence as anything else.

In any event, Sheriff McCullough promised Damie that Dick would get his day in court.

He arranged for Damie to contact a prominent attorney, a White man named Washington Hudson. Hudson was the best lawyer in Tulsa and knew all the right people, the sheriff told her.

Within a few years, in fact, Hudson became the Democratic floor leader in the Oklahoma State Senate.

What McCullough didn't tell her, and what Damie couldn't have known, was that Hudson would also soon become a leading member of Tulsa's Ku Klux Klan.

The Klan had been gaining a foothold in Tulsa, with the first Tulsans swearing the Klan oath as early as 1918. Some joined for what they claimed were legitimate reasons. To them, the oil boom had turned the city into a cesspool of bootlegging, gambling, drugs, prostitution, robbery, and murder. So many thefts and burglaries were taking place and vehicles being stolen that insurance companies no longer covered many Tulsa businesses. Robberies were a nightly occurrence in the most affluent neighborhoods. Weary of its inept and corrupt police department, White citizens of all statures often looked to the KKK as a means of restoring order. Indeed, by 1921, outlaws in Tulsa, both White and Black, had to fear floggings by white-robed vigilantes as much as they did arrests by uniformed officers.

THE KLAN HAD BEEN GAINING A FOOTHOLD IN TULSA

Yet hundreds of others were drawn to the Klan as a means of vigilante violence that expressed hatreds in the most forceful of terms. In Tulsa, those hatreds simmered as intensely as anywhere in America, particularly toward Black people, as well as Catholics and Jews.

Adding to the incendiary atmosphere, many White veterans had returned from the Great War armed with caches of smuggled weapons. Worse, their jobs had evaporated as the demand for oil tanked following the end of the war. Towns like Tulsa plunged into a deep, though temporary, recession, during which many White men found themselves unemployed. So idleness, combined with bootleg whiskey, fanned the veterans' collective rage.

But nothing inflamed them more than what they saw on the Black side of the railroad tracks—the sturdy brick businesses along Greenwood Avenue, the fancy homes, the cars, and the gold pieces flashed around by bootblacks like Dick Rowland.

To most White people, in the hierarchy of Black sins, "uppityness"—doing better financially, knowing more intellectually, or having more cultural exposure than White people— was second only to engaging in a behavior that was perceived as offensive to a White woman.

So the grumbling intensified in the Tulsa speakeasies where White veterans, oil-field roughnecks, cab drivers, and construction workers bought their illegal Prohibition liquor.

Drunken White ruffians groused about Black men riding in limos while White men walked. They grumbled about the new styles of music, jazz and blues, that they found so vulgar and that wafted toward them from Greenwood at night. They grumbled that the "choc beer" sold in Greenwood was cheaper than their own bathtub gin.

They grumbled about the Black veterans who showed up in uniform on Memorial Day, insisting on their place in the downtown parades.

And it wasn't just the White people who were down on their luck that felt this way. Many who made up Tulsa's White gentry—politicians, professionals, even the ministers—endorsed the racist vitriol of men like *Tulsa Tribune* publisher Richard Lloyd Jones.

To them, the best Black people were subservient and childlike beings, dependent on the White man. They were worthy of cooking White people's dinners, washing their floors, doing their laundry, even breastfeeding their children, but not much else.

And the worst Black people, they told themselves, were the depraved, lusty men who, they believed, coveted White women.

The mere existence of Black Wall Street—a place filled with so much Black success, even wealth, that many White people looked like failures by comparison—forced White people to face their own lies and false beliefs about their superiority, as well as their limitations.

Greenwood undercut the idea that White people were the superior race.

To these believers, White supremacy must be enforced at all cost.

GREENWOOD UNDERCUT THE IDEA THAT WHITE PEOPLE WERE THE SUPERIOR RACE

So, in Tulsa each month, dozens of new KKK initiates would swear on the Bible, promise to study the Kloran (the handbook of the Klan), learn the secret handshake, prick their fingers and sign the Klan oath in blood, pay their dues, and receive the familiar white regalia. Klan members organized picnics, took up collections in church, helped White widows, and distributed Klan literature. It was widely assumed in Tulsa that Klansmen, without their robes, were at the heart of the Roy Belton lynch mob in 1920.

More than a half-century later, on a hot summer day in 1972, a Klansman of that era, Andre Wilkes, shared that in 1918 he had been one of the first in Tulsa to promise his lifelong allegiance to the KKK. He added that, within a few years, he and virtually every other member of the landmark Majestic Theater orchestra downtown had white robes hanging in their closets.

Wilkes spoke of the blood oaths, the marches, and the special squads that undertook the whippings or worse. Though he denied participating himself, he said he had no doubt that the Klan in Tulsa had encouraged mayhem and engaged in murder. He had heard the following advice passed along to Tulsa Klan leaders from the national officers of the order:

"The best way to increase membership," Tulsa's Klan leaders were reportedly told, "is to have a good riot."

Dick Rowland's fate now likely rested in their hands.

CHAPTER 7

Lynching Tonight

On May 31, 1921, not one word in the *Tulsa World* newspaper mentioned Dick Rowland's arrest the day before or Sarah Page's accusation of assault in the Drexel Building elevator. The events' absence was probably explained by the skepticism of the Tulsa police.

But in the offices of the *World*'s competition, *Tulsa Tribune* publisher Richard Lloyd Jones saw an opportunity—another means of boosting the paper's circulation in his ongoing war with the *World*.

Thus, the racist and salacious headline that ran prominently on the front page: NAB NEGRO FOR ATTACKING GIRL IN ELEVATOR.

In the story beneath it, the *Tribune* breathlessly recounted Dick Rowland's arrest, identifying him as "Diamond Dick," a Negro delivery boy.

Sarah Page, the paper said, "noticed the Negro a few minutes before the attempted assault looking up and down the hallway of the third floor of the Drexel Building as if to see if there was anyone in sight. A few minutes later he entered the elevator, she claimed, and attacked her, scratching her hands and face and tearing her clothes. Her screams brought a clerk from Renberg's store to her assistance and the Negro fled."

The story concluded by describing Page as "an orphan who works as an elevator operator to pay her way through business college."

But Jones and his paper did not stop there. In a dehumanizing editorial, Jones claimed that Diamond Dick Rowland was certain to be one of those "bad Negroes," a beast. When finished, Jones's editorial diatribe ran beneath the famous headline that seemed to foretell Rowland's lynching.

The first edition rolled off the *Tribune* presses and into the arms of the paperboys at about three o'clock on that warm, sunny Tuesday afternoon.

At each downtown street corner, the *Tribune* paperboys, competing with those who sold the *World*, hawked their wares to passersby, taxi drivers, and businessmen, bellowing the most outrageous headline of the day: EXTRA! EXTRA! TO LYNCH NEGRO TONIGHT! READ ALL ABOUT IT!

EXTRA!
EXTRA!

The few hundred copies of that edition were snapped up in minutes and passed hand to hand across Tulsa.

Some citizens tossed the paper away in disgust, appalled by such irresponsible journalism that intentionally played into racial stereotypes and could result in a lynching.

But many other White people took the headlines as a call to arms.

Only minutes after the *Tribune* hit the streets, the first members of the Tulsa mob headed for the county courthouse, where Dick Rowland was being held. The horde grew even more as White men and women got off work and rushed from their downtown offices to the courthouse.

The lynching talk spread to the upper floors of the *Tribune* Building just as quickly.

Its editors pleaded with the publisher to recall the edition and

Jones finally relented. Copy boys were sent scurrying into the street to attempt to retrieve the offending papers, but by then, most of them had vanished into history.

Jones's editorial was pulled from subsequent editions and torn out of any papers that could be located but to little avail; it was too late. The paper had cast a match to the dry kindling of racism in Tulsa. The machinery of catastrophe had been set in gear.

THE MACHINERY OF CATASTROPHE HAD BEEN SET IN GEAR

Sheriff William McCullough's stomach tightened when a deputy brought him a copy of the *Tribune*. He had a profound distaste for vigilante violence, particularly hanging, and had been appalled when his predecessor had so meekly surrendered Roy Belton.

For safety's sake, McCullough ordered Rowland be transferred from the municipal jail to the county lockup, a fortress-like building that occupied most of a city block and sat upon a high embankment at the corner of Sixth Street and Boulder Avenue. A facility where officers were better situated to protect prisoners.

Sheriff's deputies hustled Dick Rowland through a basement entrance into the county courthouse and took a short elevator ride to the sheriff's office on the first floor. The nervous Rowland dutifully signed the documents booking him into jail.

Then came the longer trip up, past the four courtrooms on the second floor, past the jury room and the law library on the third, to the jail on the fourth floor.

Other than the elevator, only one other entrance opened into it: a reinforced steel door with steel bars at the top of a steep flight of steps wide enough to accommodate only one person at a time.

Here, McCullough believed that Rowland would be safe.

Rowland's cell was the same place Roy Belton had awaited the lynch mob only seven months earlier. That afternoon, based on what he could hear from the streets below, Rowland could have had no doubt that the same fate was in store for him.

Beginning about four o'clock, he heard the buzzing of the crowds on the terrace below, a noise that grew louder by the hour. Members of the White throng began to taunt him. He surely feared it was just a matter of time before the steel door to the jail would swing open and he would be handed over to the vigilantes—the latest guest of honor in what had become known locally as "a necktie affair."

McCullough knew from personal experience that hanging a man was ugly enough when it was done legally—the sort of thing that tended to linger in a man's thoughts and dreams.

On March 1, 1911, he had led a heavily shackled prisoner from jail, shuffling through a taunting crowd toward a crude gallows that deputies had built in a nearby vacant lot the day before.

The court had said that the tall, skinny young Black man had killed a deputy in nearby Dawson. McCullough supposed that was true. But he also knew it was common enough for White law officers to abuse Black people for the sport of it. In fact, he couldn't help wondering whether the White officer might somehow have deserved his fate.

The young man didn't seem the murderous type.

He had requested oysters for his final meal, so McCullough had ordered a heaping plate of fried oysters from a restaurant across the street. When he delivered the food, he found the boy sitting on the floor of his cell, his back to the cold wall, an old Bible open on his lap.

"This is a good book, isn't it?" the young man said, smiling.

"Yes," McCullough replied. "It's a pretty good book."

The young man's face then turned serious.

"Don't you think it's bad to take my life?" he asked.

"Yes, but it's a job that I have to do," McCullough replied.

The sheriff saw moisture gather at the corners of the young prisoner's large eyes. His stomach tumbled, and he felt a burning in his own cheeks. He'd been tempted to ask his prisoner why he had killed the deputy but didn't.

"Thank you for the oysters," the young man said after a minute.

"You're welcome," McCullough replied.

"You seem like a nice fella. Not like the rest of them."

"That's kind of you to say."

"I wish someone else would do my hanging, to spare you from having to do it," he said.

"Thank you again," the sheriff replied. "But it's my duty."

"I suppose it is."

"You might want to eat those oysters before they're all cold," McCullough said.

"Yes, sir. Thank you again. And good night."

McCullough had tried to sleep on a cot in his office but couldn't. He'd looked in on the boy several times as the hours passed. The half-eaten plate of oysters sat next to him on the floor of the cell as he read the Bible in the dim light cast from one naked bulb outside. His lips moved silently as he read.

The horde began milling outside before daybreak.

As the sheriff walked his prisoner down a short hall to the front door, he saw tears fall down the young man's cheeks.

Outside, the crowd, loud and angry, parted as McCullough, the young man, and a few deputies with rifles inched their way toward the scaffold.

The prisoner climbed the four steps of the gallows one halting step at a time and stepped slowly to the place where the noose hung waiting for him. A deputy handed McCullough a black hood, and the sheriff slipped it over the young man's head.

"Sheriff, if you would take this up for just a second, there are a few words I'd like to say," the young man said.

"Okay," McCullough replied. "But just for a second."

The sheriff removed the hood, and the rabble fell silent. The prisoner cleared his throat and spoke in a loud voice.

"Now I want to say that all people should tell the truth when they come to the courthouse," the condemned man said. "And I hope God Almighty blesses each and every one of you."

I HOPE GOD ALMIGHTY BLESSES EACH AND EVERY ONE OF YOU

Then he looked toward the sheriff.

"Now I'm ready," he said.

McCullough slipped the hood back over the man's head. He dropped the noose around his neck and tightened it.

For a few terrible seconds, McCullough thought he might

vomit in front of all those people who were shouting for the young man's blood.

But then he gently nudged his prisoner off the edge of the gallows, and the rope snapped taut.

For the rest of his life, McCullough saw the young man's face in his dreams.

Every day, when he went to work, he remembered him.

So he had meant every word he'd said to Damie Rowland. He knew what it was like for a man to hang. He was determined that no lynch mob would undertake that task.

Dick Rowland would live to have his day in court.

Soon after McCullough moved Rowland to the county lockup, the Tulsa police commissioner, J. M. Adkison, called. He had seen the *Tribune* article and knew the mayhem it was bound to incite.

By then, of course, crowds already stood in the streets surrounding the courthouse.

Adkison suggested it might be best to hustle Rowland out of town right then. McCullough decided to wait, a decision he would soon come to regret.

The mob outside the courthouse grew larger. The chants intensified.

Give us the [n-word]! Give us the [n-word]!

But by then, the sheriff began to realize that his promise to Damie Rowland would not be easy to keep.

CHAPTER 8

Fear in Greenwood

The lynching talk spread just as quickly on the north side of the Frisco tracks.

Within minutes of the *Tribune*'s publication, E. W. Woods, the principal at Booker T. Washington High School, received an anonymous telephone call from what sounded like a White man, warning of the movement to lynch Dick Rowland. Woods immediately excused his students, who hurried home to their parents with the horrifying news.

Porters and shoeshine boys had rushed north across the Frisco tracks with copies of the *Tribune* as soon as it hit the streets. Now, small crowds huddled together on Greenwood Avenue, looking over each other's shoulders at the front page, aghast.

Within an hour, word of Dick Rowland's predicament had horrified Greenwood.

Most were at least faintly familiar with the young man whose life now seemed threatened.

They were terrified for the safety of this teenager and for the well-being of their community, which suddenly seemed very precarious.

What would angry White Tulsans do? And at what point would they stop?

Dick Rowland was a flashy mischief-maker. Hopeless as he may have appeared, he certainly didn't deserve to be lynched.

Young Robert Fairchild knew Rowland better than most. To him, Rowland was a friend of sorts, a colleague. Only sixteen, Fairchild was still a student at Booker T. Washington High. But almost every day after school, he hurried to the eight-chair shoe-shining parlor at the corner of Second and Main, where he worked side by side with Rowland for tips that put fat rolls of cash in their pockets.

What hogwash! Fairchild thought.

Rowland flirted with that girl like he flirted with any other. Dick was a harmless, happy sort and was in no way stupid enough to attack a White girl that way.

Yet there it was in newspaper black-and-white: His friend was in a real mess and the White people were ready to string him up by the neck—probably some of the same ones whose shoes they shined every week.

Or maybe, Fairchild thought, *they wouldn't get the chance. Maybe the Black people in Greenwood would make a stand.* Many had just come home from the Great War, bringing hellish tales of combat. Among those was the grocer O. B. Mann.

Customers of the Mann Brothers Grocery Store had brought him the first word of the mess that Dick Rowland was in.

In 1918, Mann had shivered in the muck of the trenches of France's Argonne Forest with the rest of the Black men of the U.S. Army's Ninety-Second Division. He had seen firsthand what a bullet or mortar round did to a soldier if it caught him just right. What bombs and poison gas did.

But those weren't the only weapons the Germans had used. Their planes swooped low over the soldiers and dropped leaflets of paper almost as defeating as bombs.

"[Hello], boys," one of the leaflets began. "What are you doing over here? Fighting the Germans? Why? . . . What is Democracy? Personal freedom, all citizens enjoying the same rights socially and before law! Do you enjoy the same rights as the White people do in America, the land of Freedom and Democracy? Or [are you not] treated over there as second class citizens?"

The questions kept coming.

"Can you get into a restaurant where White people dine, can you get a seat in a theater where White people sit, can you get a . . . berth in a railroad car or can you even ride, in the South, in the same street car with White people?

ARE YOU NOT TREATED OVER THERE AS SECOND CLASS CITIZENS?

"And how about the law? Is lynching and the most horrible cruelties connected therewith a lawful proceeding in a democratic country?" the propaganda asked. "You have been made the tool of the egotistic and rapacious rich in England and in America, and there is nothing in [this] whole game for you but broken bones, horrible wounds, spoiled health [and] death. No satisfaction whatever will you get out of this unjust war. You have never seen Germany, so you are fools if you allow people to teach you to hate it. Come over and see for yourself . . . Don't let them use you as cannon [fodder].

"To carry a gun in the service is not an honor but a shame. Throw it away and come over to the German lines. You will find friends who help you along."

The words had echoed in the hearts and minds of Mann and his Black comrades, who were risking their lives for democracy—even though they could not vote, they were not seen as citizens, and many White people didn't even believe they were human.

Amid the smoke and blood and horrible death, the German propaganda tempted many of them to defect but few gave in. Almost none of them deserted because the Black soldiers had optimistically believed that White Americans back home would recognize their sacrifices for the cause of democracy and treat them more humanely as a result.

They thought they had proved to their White commanders what good soldiers they were. They thought they had shown their fellow White soldiers that they were, in fact, human beings.

They returned home believing that Black life would finally be different—that the nation would see them as loyal Americans worthy of equal treatment and full citizenship.

Emboldened with this new identity as loyal soldiers, they would insist on it.

Indeed, the great intellectual and leader W. E. B. Du Bois spoke for Mann and most returning Black veterans when he wrote: "Under similar circumstances, we would fight again. But by the God of Heaven, we are cowards and jackasses if now that the war is over, we do not marshal every ounce of our brain and brawn to fight a sterner, longer, more unbending battle against the forces of hell in our own land."

THE BLACK SOLDIERS HAD BELIEVED THAT THEIR MILITARY SERVICE WOULD PROVE THEY WERE WORTHY OF EQUAL TREATMENT

The Black soldiers had believed that their military service would prove they were worthy of equal treatment, voting, and full citizenship.

And for a brief moment, they had been cheered.

On February 17 in New York City, the Seventeenth Regiment, an all-Black Army corps, returned home and approximately one million people witnessed them parade from Lower Manhattan up Fifth Avenue to Harlem. On March 12, the Ninety-Second Division, another Black brigade, had returned to a warm welcome in Hoboken, New Jersey, right across the river.

And that year on May 21, the Nineteenth Amendment to the Constitution had passed, extending the right to vote to White women. Certainly, the Black vote taken away by Jim Crow restrictions such as literacy tests, poll taxes, and the grandfather clause couldn't be far behind, they imagined.

But those Black soldiers found so much disappointment when they returned home. If anything, the Red Summer showed them that the plight of Black people in America had worsened after the war. For it seemed that, day after day, another Black veteran was strung up by White people someplace in America.

In downtown Tulsa, store signs read that Black people were not welcome. Black soldiers were shunned as they tried to join in Tulsa's Memorial Day parades. Instead, they were forced to march by themselves as White people jeered at them. Indeed, during the Memorial Day parade one day earlier, Black veterans of the Great War had put on their old uniforms and marched down Tulsa's rain-slickened Main Avenue as White folks wearing red poppies pinned to their lapels taunted them with racial slurs.

What else could they do? If neither the courts, nor police, nor mayors, nor civic leaders would protect them from lynchings, mob violence, and everyday acts of intimidation intended to demean, intimidate, threaten, and convince them that White people were superior, who would?

Black people hoped their national campaign against lynching would help.

THERE SEEMED TO BE NO OTHER OPTION BUT TO BEGIN TO DEFEND THEMSELVES

But in some quarters, Black people had reached the conclusion that there seemed to be no other option but to begin to defend themselves.

In 1919, poet Claude McKay had penned, "If We Must Die."

```
If we must die, let it not be like hogs
Hunted and penned in an inglorious spot,
While round us bark the mad and hungry dogs,
Making their mock at our accursèd lot.
If we must die, O let us nobly die,
So that our precious blood may not be shed
In vain; then even the monsters we defy
Shall be constrained to honor us though dead!
O kinsmen! we must meet the common foe!
Though far outnumbered let us show us brave,
And for their thousand blows deal one death-blow!
What though before us lies the open grave?
Like men we'll face the murderous, cowardly pack,
Pressed to the wall, dying, but fighting back!
```

Ready to protect himself and his community, that afternoon Mann removed his store apron, jumped onto his horse, and galloped deeper into Greenwood, where worried crowds had gathered. He grabbed a copy of the *Tribune*, his blood quickening as he read the front page.

People were saying that the Ku Klux Klan was plotting an assault on the jail to get Dick Rowland and lynch him.

Mann pushed his way through the largest crowd, the one outside the *Tulsa Star*, where Greenwood's elders had gathered to discuss the crisis and how to handle it.

Smitherman, who, in his role as editor of the *Tulsa Star*, had been reporting on lynchings and even traveling across the state in a heroic attempt to stop them in progress; the businessmen John Stradford, John Williams, and O. W. Gurley; the lawyer named Spears; and the deputy Barney Cleaver.

Though worried, that afternoon the Greenwood elders were preaching calm and patience until they could determine the extent of the threat to Rowland.

THE GREENWOOD ELDERS WERE PREACHING CALM AND PATIENCE

Predictably, Smitherman and Stradford were doing most of the talking.

Let's not take leave of our senses, they were saying. *Calm heads are required.* But if the White mob so much as touched a fingernail on that boy in jail, well that was a different matter.

But Mann had a distinctive perspective. Though his grocery store had flourished in the years after he returned home from war, his money had done nothing to tamp down his rage.

None of these men had seen what he had seen.

None of them had read those insulting German leaflets that dropped at his feet while Black soldiers were cut down by bullets and choked by gas.

Now the battle to which Du Bois referred was at hand. Mann was sure of it. It was time to "marshal every ounce of our brain and brawn to fight a sterner, longer, more unbending battle against the forces of hell in our own land."

With White mob violence threatening from every direction, to Mann it had only been a matter of time before Tulsa's White racists followed in the ruthless footsteps laid down in so many other communities.

This younger generation—those whose sweat and ingenuity had built a Black Wall Street and championed democracy by serving in the war—was not as fearful or easily intimidated as previous generations had been. They deserved their rights and wanted to stand up for what the nation owed them and their community.

THE TIME HAD COME FOR THEM TO DEMONSTRATE THEIR RESOLVE

The time had come for them to demonstrate their resolve, just as they had against the Germans across the Atlantic.

It was a Greenwood physician, Dr. Gentry, who called O. W. Gurley with the news in late afternoon, and Gurley's stomach sank the moment he heard it.

The Greenwood pioneer knew that if White Tulsans dared to try to lynch Dick Rowland, they had a heck of a fight waiting for them. Too many militant men like Smitherman and Stradford had been advocating for self-defense for too long not to back up their words now.

On top of that, Black soldiers like O. B. Mann had come

home from the war with ideas about equality that Gurley believed were unrealistic, thinking they could whip the world.

If the White racists thought they could lynch Dick Rowland and not pay for it with their own blood, they had another thing coming.

And that meant only one thing to Gurley: a race war, a conflagration that could wipe out, in an hour, the accomplishments and riches the Gurleys had spent their last fifteen years in Greenwood trying to accumulate.

Was any racial justice worth that?

Back then, the term "race war" was often used to describe a conflict between White police and Black military veterans. Consistent with the White supremacist propaganda of the era, the media would typically portray the White officers as innocent and Black vets as armed and drunken. Dating back to the Civil War, racist White people saw Black people who owned guns as a threat to White supremacy.

Gurley threw a jacket over his bow tie and starched white shirt and rushed into the street, where he ran into the deputy, Barney Cleaver. Cleaver said he had just come from the courthouse, where the sheriff assured him that no harm would come to Rowland, no matter what the paper had said. There would be no lynching in Tulsa that night, Cleaver promised.

"You'd never know it by the looks of this street," Gurley replied, hurrying past the deputy and through the crowds to the *Star*'s front door.

Men nodded at Gurley as he entered, and they continued their debating. At one point, Stradford got worked up.

"The day a member of our group is mobbed in Tulsa, the streets will be bathed in blood," he roared.

He promised to be the first to avenge Rowland's lynching, if it happened. "If I can't get anyone to go with me, I will go single-handed and empty my automatic into the mob and then resign myself to my fate."

Men around the room nodded.

A few shouted "Amen!"

Stradford clearly would have plenty of company if such intervention was necessary.

In fact, looking around the room, it seemed like many of the men actually spoiled for a fight, a chance to vent their rage. Some were itching for a reason to strike back at their White oppressors.

But some of the anger was actually false bravado. Everyone knew that Tulsa's Black community was outnumbered. The population of Tulsa at that time was made up of about eleven thousand Black residents and roughly one hundred thousand White residents.

There was no denying just how vulnerable they were, but sometimes it's easier to express anger than fear or vulnerability, particularly when you fear you may be annihilated. Especially when you're in a group.

It was then that Gurley finally spoke up. He, too, urged calm.

"We need more information," he argued, volunteering to drive downtown himself and speak to the sheriff, then to report back on the state of things there.

After heated discussion, the others eventually agreed, and Gurley set off in his car with a man named Webb for company.

As word traveled like wildfire across the town and tensions mounted on both sides of the Frisco tracks, some Tulsans attempted to maintain the appearances of normalcy by clinging to the rituals that normally marked the end of the school year.

On the south side of the tracks, Catholic mothers dressed their daughters in white and ran brushes through their hair to prepare them for the graduation pageant at the Holy Family Catholic School, which would be held that evening at Tulsa's Convention Hall.

In Greenwood, Bill Williams, the son of the famous entrepreneurs John and Loula, joined his junior-year classmates in the luxurious ballroom of the Stradford Hotel, placing flowers on the tables and hanging colored paper from the ceiling for Booker T. Washington High School's junior/senior prom, scheduled for the following night, June 1.

It was close to suppertime when he left the Stradford for the short walk south down Greenwood Avenue to his home on the second floor of the Williams Building.

By then, cars full of yelling young men raced up and down the street, and hundreds of people talked urgently in small groups.

To Bill Williams, the activity made it seem like a Thursday night, like the maids' night off. He could not imagine what was behind the strange uproar.

He found out when he climbed the steps to his family's apartment and his mother handed him a copy of the *Tulsa Tribune* with a look of concern on her face.

His father, the ace mechanic and crack-shot hunter, was busy cleaning his guns.

CHAPTER 9

Tuesday, May 31:
The Sheriff's Promise

When Gurley and Webb arrived at the courthouse, the scene was worse than either could have imagined. Hundreds of White people had gathered outside the south and west entrances, and even from two blocks away, the men could hear their angry shouts.

Gurley parked his car, and he and Webb tried to skirt the mob as best they could, hurrying up the courthouse steps. They found Sheriff McCullough pacing inside on the first floor. Clearly worried, the tall lawman repeated what Cleaver had told the two earlier.

"There won't be any lynching if you can keep your people away," Sheriff McCullough told Gurley.

"How can we be sure of that?" Gurley asked.

"Well, maybe you can't be sure," McCullough said. "But anybody who gets to Rowland up in the jail will have to kill me first. If I need more help, I'll give you a call but just sit tight until then."

Sheriff McCullough had the reputation of being a man of his word.

And Gurley agreed that the worst thing at the moment would

be armed, angry Black men arriving at the courthouse, which would stir things up even more.

The Greenwood entrepreneur promised the sheriff he would try to calm things with his people. He and McCullough shook hands and bid each other good luck and good night.

In the meantime, O. B. Mann had angrily left the *Star* and strode north through the crowds for a short distance to the Dreamland Theatre.

There, he climbed onto the stage, where his body was caught in the projection lights, casting a massive shadow on the screen behind him.

"Turn up these lights!" O. B. Mann yelled. "The movie's over 'cause I got news! The Whites are getting ready to hang a Negro boy downtown, and I say Black Tulsa ain't about to let that happen. We're going to go down to stop it, and if you want to join us, come on."

TURN UP THESE LIGHTS!

With that, Mann leaped from the stage and raced up the aisle toward the doors.

The Dreamland Theatre, full that night as always, emptied within five minutes, the audience pouring out into the mounting chaos of the street.

By the time Gurley returned, the worry and outrage had escalated beyond anything one man could hope to diffuse.

Greenwood's leaders had dispatched messengers to every corner of the community, putting out the call for men and arms. Volunteers arrived every minute, individually and in groups, carrying rifles, pistols, shotguns, garden hoes, rakes, and axes.

As he turned onto Greenwood Avenue, Gurley dodged a succession of speeding touring cars with Black men packed inside or hanging from running boards, yelling and firing their weapons into the night.

The *Star* office was no less volatile.

Gurley began by repeating what the sheriff had said.

"You're a liar!" a man named Anderson screamed.

Anderson leveled his Winchester rifle toward Gurley, aiming straight between his eyes.

"The mob took a White man from that same jail and lynched him just a few months ago. So what makes you think the sheriff will lift a finger for a Negro boy!"

There was no arguing with his point. Roy Belton's ghost lingered about the room like the thick blue smoke from the men's cigars and cigarettes.

If Tulsa's sheriff couldn't or wouldn't protect a White man from the mob, how could he promise to protect a Black boy?

The answer was obvious: He couldn't.

As the brilliant afternoon turned into an equally gorgeous evening, the White crowds outside the courthouse grew steadily, clogging the street around the courthouse and causing a traffic jam. The gathering seemed almost festive, as men taunted Rowland in the jail above, some of their words prompting loud laughter from the crowd. Children dashed happily among the ankles of the adults, as if they were attending an innocent event like a church picnic.

Every few minutes, Sheriff McCullough checked on the crowd through the windows of his first-floor office. Each time he looked, the horde of people had grown larger. Most, especially the women and children, were probably just curious or had come simply to be entertained. But McCullough recognized a few as members of the Belton lynch mob. At least some of those folks carried pistols in their overalls or the jacket pockets of their Palm Beach suits.

AT LEAST SOME OF THOSE FOLKS CARRIED PISTOLS

As time passed, McCullough increasingly wished he had snuck Dick Rowland out of town while he still had the chance.

At this point, he believed that his only option was to hunker down, wait, and hope. Neither he nor the police chief made any serious attempt to disperse the crowd; nor did he command his deputies to disarm it.

Repeatedly, McCullough rehearsed in his mind what he would say or do if any members of the mob approached the courthouse seeking his prisoner.

How would they react when he refused? he wondered. Would they dare shoot a lawman?

At seven o'clock, Barney Cleaver arrived at the courthouse and reported to Sheriff McCullough that hundreds of armed Black men on Greenwood Avenue were poised to come charging to Rowland's defense.

McCullough briefly considered that possibility and assumed that the Tulsa police would be of little help. The chief detective was rumored to be a high-ranking Klansman, and Police Chief Gustafson, if not a Klansman himself, had let his position be known when he allowed Belton to be lynched the previous fall.

Maybe a few squads of armed Black men might actually help protect Rowland, McCullough considered. But he quickly rejected the idea, recognizing the explosive potential of a courthouse confrontation.

McCullough instead dialed up one of the few local men he trusted, his friend Ira Short, who had just been elected county commissioner. Short immediately agreed to assist in any way he could. In fact, he had just arrived at the courthouse when three well-dressed White men stepped out of the crowd, confidently climbed the courthouse steps, and walked through the west doors.

The men were strangers to Sheriff McCullough, but other people had seen them in various places downtown earlier that the afternoon, though not before.

Obviously, they had just arrived in Tulsa. It was a safe bet they were Klan organizers who had picked a particularly fortunate moment for a recruiting mission. Whoever they were, McCullough cut them off before the first could finish a sentence.

"If anybody tries to harm my prisoner, someone is going to get killed," the sheriff said, his hand resting on his holstered revolver. The men sensed immediately that McCullough was not bluffing. They smiled politely, nodded, then left without saying a word.

Once outside, as the crowd gathered around them, the strangers rediscovered their voices.

The honor and purity of White women everywhere is at issue right here in Tulsa! A young orphan girl has been horribly violated! Can Tulsa stand by for that? Does her pain not deserve avenging? What Tulsa court is sufficient to deal with a Negro beast such as the one who sits behind bars in the jail right up there, just across the street?

The crowd cheered, voices rising in unison.

Sheriff McCullough's own words to the crowd a few minutes later were no match.

The sheriff seemed pathetic as he stood on the courthouse steps, yelling to be heard over the jeers, insisting that there would be no lynching, pleading with good Tulsans to ignore the strangers and disperse before things got out of hand. Go home to your families, he told them, before it was too late and everyone was real sorry.

Disregarded by the throng, McCullough finally gave up. He shook his head and stepped back inside the courthouse. Then he rode the elevator to the fourth floor and disabled it there.

Next, he gathered his six White deputies and made sure each was heavily armed.

McCullough then ordered that anyone fool enough to climb the narrow staircase, the only other route to Rowland's cell, should be shot on sight.

CHAPTER 10

Down the Road to Apocalypse

Back in Greenwood, the community leaders decided that they could not leave Rowland's fate to chance.

They must act before the mob had a chance to storm the courthouse; they couldn't let Rowland swing from the same billboard sign where Roy Belton had met his death.

The crowd cheered as the men crowded into the cars for the short drive south. Stradford and Smitherman, both armed with pistols, led the group. The businessman John Williams drove one car, his shotgun sitting at his side. Jake Mays drove his crowded taxi. O. B. Mann was there with several of the toughest Black veterans.

The men arrived at just after nine o'clock.

A hush fell over the throng as the short convoy of cars approached the courthouse from the west, driving down Sixth Street.

The idea that Black people would stand up for themselves sent shock waves because it defied every norm of White supremacy. Rarely did Black people stand up for themselves in the face of White power. Being perceived as uppity or insolent could cost a Black person their life.

So, the sight of the Greenwood entourage—Black people

who refused to conform to White supremacy's painful pecking order—terrified several White people, sending them dashing into the night.

The rest of the White mob in the street silently parted to let the Greenwood vehicles through as they turned right from Sixth onto Boulder in front of the courthouse. The caravan came to a stop in front of the west entrance, and the vehicles' somber occupants stepped down from the cars' running boards or out of the seats, brandishing their weapons and courageously returning White glares.

"Get the [n-words] out of here!" one White man called.

MOST HELD THEIR TONGUES

But most held their tongues. The White mob had a huge advantage in sheer numbers, but the Black men clearly held the edge in firepower. Many in the mob sidled away to the south side of the court-house, away from the Black men's weapons.

Inside the courthouse, McCullough heard the crowd go quiet.

His heart sank when he saw the armed men from Greenwood approach.

"Lord, would you look at this," he said. "Barney, I think we better get out there."

McCullough and Deputy Barney Cleaver hurried down the courthouse steps to meet the men, who immediately made their resolve known. They insisted they would stay until satisfied that Rowland was safe, and there was no way any reasonable man could be sure of that as long as this lynch mob surrounded the courthouse.

If the sheriff could not protect his prisoner, Dick Rowland's own people would take care of the job for him, the group promised.

Sheriff McCullough instructed Cleaver to explain.

No matter how bad the situation looked, a group of deputies waited at the top of the courthouse stairs for anyone who made trouble, Cleaver said. Short of setting fire to the courthouse, there was no way a mob of even a million men could get its hands upon Dick Rowland, the deputy assured his Greenwood neighbors.

"Boys, you are not doing right," Cleaver concluded, bowing to the White supremacist pressures of the era. Indeed, the idea of a White mob attacking a Black man falsely accused of sexual assault had become a norm in White society. "There isn't anybody going to get that boy tonight. He is perfectly safe here," he continued. "You shouldn't have done this thing, for it only stirs race trouble. Now go on home and behave yourselves."

Cleaver succeeded in convincing the men, who surely knew the dangerous risk they had taken and what was at stake.

The men promised to return if events warranted. Then they piled back into their cars, glaring again at the White mob surrounding them, and slowly headed north on Boulder for the short drive back across the Frisco tracks.

Sheriff McCullough had no such success with the White horde. Noting the peaceful departure of the Black men, he renewed his pleas for the throng to disperse, but their hooting and jeering only intensified.

The fact that the Black men had shown up to protect one of their own had the White mob on the verge of hysteria.

To their minds, it was bad enough that a young Black man had attacked a young White woman in Tulsa, but now that crime was compounded by the fact that carloads of Black men had come to his defense. And they'd dared to show up with guns, which, at that point, most of the White mob did not have.

White supremacist beliefs had erroneously taught many White people that they were superior to Black people and that Black people did not value themselves or each other. These Black men had defied the ideology that demanded they subordinate themselves to White people and cower under the fear that a White person could annihilate them at any moment. And they were doing so in spite of the reality that no White person was likely to be arrested, charged with a crime, tried in a court of law, convicted, shamed by their family, censured by their pastor, or ostracized by the mainstream White community for committing a crime against a Black person.

The Greenwood men's brazen and infuriating show of racial solidarity, force, and determination fed White racists' most visceral fears—hatreds dating to slavery—when uprisings of enslaved people were the White South's greatest dread.

"The armory!" a man yelled.

Within seconds, hundreds of White people began running east on Sixth Street. The first to arrive after the mile-long sprint pounded at the bolted doors of the National Guard Armory. Others tried to break in by detaching the iron grating from around the windows.

Hearing that commotion, National Guard Major James A. Bell rushed from his home across the alley and found himself confronting an angry crowd of four hundred.

"What do you want here?" Bell asked.

"Rifles and ammunition," a leader of the mob replied.

"You won't get any of those things here," Bell told him.

"We don't know about that," someone else shouted defiantly. "We guess we can."

"I'll tell you again," Bell repeated. "Not one bullet leaves this armory without orders from the governor. In the name of the law, I order you to disperse at once."

The mob ignored him and instead, pressed forward.

Major Bell drew his revolver.

"I've got men in the armory armed with rifles with ball ammunition, and they will promptly shoot any unauthorized person who goes through the front door," Bell threatened.

THE MOB IGNORED HIM AND INSTEAD, PRESSED FORWARD

With that, the mob was finally convinced. After some defiant shouting, the crowd gradually retreated. Scores of men hurried back toward the courthouse.

Where weapons were concerned, many of the others had better luck. They had scattered to their homes and businesses across Tulsa, grabbing pistols from their drawers or rifles and shotguns down from their walls.

Over the next hour, the courthouse horde continued to grow.

By ten o'clock, an electrified mob of more than two thousand White people had amassed. Hundreds now bravely brandished weapons in one hand and bottles of whiskey in the other.

"See how brave they will be the next time they dare show up," emboldened mob members said to each other.

Tensions escalated with every tick of the clock.

Occasionally, carloads of Black men sped past the courthouse, likely on reconnaissance missions, then turned back toward Greenwood, which incensed the White mob.

It was a night of rumors, most of them untrue.

IT WAS A NIGHT OF RUMORS, MOST OF THEM UNTRUE

Back in Greenwood, speculation began to circulate about ten o'clock that could not be ignored. Too many Greenwood residents seemed to be saying the same thing: The White mob had finally launched an assault on the courthouse to get Dick Rowland.

As it turned out, someone had probably confused the assault on the armory with the supposed attack on the courthouse. But Dick Rowland's defenders could not afford to wait to sort out the discrepancy. Grim faced, they piled back into their cars, about seventy-five men in all—more than twice the number of the first trip—and once again headed south across the Frisco tracks.

Additional groups headed over on foot, shouldering their rifles, shotguns, and garden tools as they marched in military formation toward the courthouse.

A White college student named Mary Jo Erhardt encountered one such cadre marching west on Sixth Street. Years later she would reflect upon what she saw.

"All were armed," she wrote. "Army rifles seemed to predominate, then hunting rifles of various caliber, then handguns. Were I an artist, what graphic studies I could still paint of the faces of those men—anger, resentment, fear, desperation, despair—all were there, and on each face, dogged determination. A dangerous army of men who would be extremely hard to stop if one wrong move or word occurred."

The Greenwood contingent courageously entered into what had become enemy territory. The men driving cars parked near the courthouse and marched single file to the west entrance, weapons over their shoulders.

Once again, Sheriff McCullough met them at the steps and assured them that he had the situation in hand. The White mob was heavily armed as well, but it was obvious that no assault on the jail had taken place.

At least not yet.

So again, the men agreed to return to Greenwood.

But at ten fifteen, the night's violent passions finally boiled over.

An old White man, short and frail, went after the largest man in the Greenwood group, the war veteran O. B. Mann.

The old man barely came to Mann's belt buckle.

"What are you going to do with that pistol, [n-word]?" the old White man demanded.

"I'm going to use it if I need to," Mann replied.

"No, you give it to me," the White man said.

"Like hell I will."

The old man lunged for Mann's pistol, which discharged in their brief tussle.

I'M GOING TO USE IT IF I NEED TO

Within seconds, a hundred other shots rang out, sending the panicked mass of men, women, and children fleeing in all directions at once. People dove into or behind empty cars, hid behind oak trees and shrubbery, or pounded furiously on the doors of nearby homes, begging for shelter from the flying bullets. Scores of others, finding no sanctuary, fell to the street and buried their heads beneath their arms. Hundreds attempted to escape in their cars, which then careened wildly down the streets, narrowly missing fleeing pedestrians.

Within seconds, the Greenwood group sprinted toward home on foot, most of them dashing up Main and Boulder Avenues toward the safety of the Frisco tracks that divided the town.

Behind them, at least twenty people, both White and Black, lay dead or wounded. The old White man who had confronted O. B. Mann was among the first to die. A stray bullet killed another White man who had been observing the melee from a block away.

After the first shot, Sheriff McCullough took cover, rushing into the courthouse and sprinting up the stairs, expecting the White mob to immediately launch an assault up the narrow staircase leading to the jail where Rowland was held.

McCullough would remain in the jail for the rest of the night. *At least he could make good on that much of his promise. He would protect Rowland*, he thought, *or die trying*.

Sheriff McCullough's deepest fears had been realized. The nation's worst race war had begun, and neither he nor anyone else had the power to stop it.

CHAPTER 11

The Apocalypse

At the Majestic Theater, in downtown Tulsa, a White man burst through a door into the theater, yelling racial epithets and shouting that a race war had begun.

Within seconds, the audience emptied into the street.

At almost the same moment, the students of the Holy Family Catholic School were lined up across the stage of Tulsa's Convention Hall, youngest student to oldest, preparing for the graduation pageant.

Young Ruth Sigler, dressed in white like all the girls of the Catholic school, had just delivered the line that had been assigned to her in the program.

Father John Heiring, the Holy Family pastor, rushed onto the stage.

"I'm sorry, but everyone must take their children and return home immediately," the priest said to his startled audience. "A vicious race riot has erupted. Your lives are in great danger. When I am through with this announcement, please go straight home."

On the Greenwood side of the tracks, John Williams's son, Bill, knew his father had joined Greenwood's leaders on their first trip to the courthouse around nine o'clock. He had been greatly relieved to see the party return just a few minutes later.

But only an hour after that, John Williams and an even larger group of men had set off on another mission. Within minutes,

Bill Williams heard loud popping noises from the south, as if every jalopy on the White side of the tracks had backfired at the same time. The boy recognized the sounds from hunting trips with his father. It was gunfire that filled the night, and Bill shuddered when thinking that his father might be in the middle of the fusillade.

Henry C. Sowders had never seen Greenwood like this.

For several years, he had worked for Mrs. Loula Williams at her Dreamland Theatre as a projectionist. As a White man toiling each day in a Black theater, never once had he felt threatened—at least not until that night.

Earlier, a large fellow had barged in and made an announcement about White people trying to lynch that Rowland boy downtown. That had pretty much cleared the place out.

Then, at about ten or ten thirty, the Dreamland's manager, Mr. Cotton, poked his head into the projection room. Cotton was a quiet, peaceable man who always seemed happiest with eyeglasses sliding down his nose, working on the Dreamland accounts for Mrs. Williams. But now Sowders saw that Cotton had a .45-caliber pistol strapped to his thigh.

"What are you doing wearing that gun?" Sowders asked him.

"Looking out for number one," Mr. Cotton replied before disappearing again.

With that, Sowders figured enough was enough. He shut down the projector and made his way downstairs to the front door.

That's when he saw the crowds in the street, brandishing every manner of weapon, some firing blindly into the night air as if whatever had made them so angry was flying someplace among the stars.

He heard people chanting, "It'll never happen here!" like a battle cry. He heard one fellow breathlessly describing, to a group of others, the terrible gunfight that had broken out just a few minutes earlier at the courthouse, a war between an army of White racists and a few Black men who had gone to save that boy from being lynched. Now there was blood on the streets and Black people lying dead on the White side of town, and the White folks would pay, wouldn't they?

"It'll never happen here!"

The crowd seemed more frenzied with each passing minute and, in his estimation, more likely to turn its rage against the only White person handy: him.

IT'LL NEVER HAPPEN HERE!

So Sowders pushed his way toward his car, which he had parked a few doors down Greenwood Avenue. No one had laid a finger on it on any night before, but now he was stunned. Someone had turned back the convertible's top, and his car was full of people—about nine of them.

"Let's go!" one shouted to the fellow behind the wheel. "Let's get on downtown."

"Hold them horses," the other man said. "Didn't you hear what happened? You wanna get us all killed?"

Sowders had saved for years to buy that car, and his anger got the better of his good judgment. He walked right up and insisted they step out immediately so he could drive home. The men in the car laughed and playfully pointed their guns in Sowders's direction, then laughed some more as the projectionist threw up his hands and took a few frightened steps back.

Just then, Sowders felt a huge hand take hold of his shirt collar from behind. He felt like he was lifted off his feet by that one large hand and deposited in the flatbed of an old Ford truck parked a few yards away. The hand belonged to the same man who had created the ruckus on the Dreamland stage earlier that night: O. B. Mann.

Mann had managed to retreat back across the railroad tracks after the shooting at the courthouse. Now, as much as anyone, he seemed to be calling the shots with the Black mob on the street.

"If you know what's good for you, Mr. Sowders, you'll sit right here, nice and quiet," Mann told him.

Mann then approached another man, handing him a dollar bill.

"You better hurry up and get this fellow to the other side," Mann said. "This is no place for a man of his color now."

HURRY UP AND GET THIS FELLOW TO THE OTHER SIDE

The second Black man nodded and climbed into the cab of the truck, fired up the engine, and began to inch through the people. As Sowders looked down, every last man seemed to brandish a gun. He recognized almost all of the faces. Friendly, peaceful people for the most part. But now they yelled up at him, menacingly waving their weapons because Sowders was a White man and a race war was on.

The truck turned right off Greenwood Avenue onto Archer Street, heading west past the small wooden homes and the neat brick buildings that contained the Black dry cleaners, lawyers' offices, blacksmith shops, and restaurants.

As the sound of gunfire grew louder, Sowders had the feeling that he was a reluctant soldier moving toward the front lines of a great battle. On the south side of Archer, he recognized the Black police officer named H. C. Pack, who was pleading with another group of angry men, begging them to stay away from the Frisco tracks where bullets flew back and forth between the two worlds. But the young men swept by Officer Pack as if he were invisible; those boys wanted a piece of the fight.

At Cincinnati and Archer, the Ford truck nearly ran over a Black man in a starched white shirt and dark pants who was firing blindly toward the south with his rifle.

The sound of gunfire grew louder

Sowders noticed two other Black men, both in overalls, lying motionless in the street, blood staining the dirt beneath them.

"Afraid that's as far as we go, Mr. Sowders," the driver called out from the cab. "Off you go now."

Sowders jumped from the bed of the truck as it pulled away, crouching low as shots from both sides of the Frisco tracks thundered in his ears. The heaviest fighting was now just a few blocks away; two packs of Tulsans massed on either side of the railroad. He dashed from building to building, from tree to tree, timing his movements with brief lulls in the shooting.

He slipped around the Frisco and Santa Fe Passenger Depot and finally made it to First Street, where he saw a large mob of White men standing outside Dick Bardon's sporting goods store. Bardon's front door had been kicked in and all the windows were broken. Every few seconds, another man emerged from the store with a new rifle or shotgun or pistol and his pockets bulging with ammunition.

Some of the looters were uniformed Tulsan policemen.

As he observed the faces around him, Sowders saw that, if anything, the White men were more frenzied than the Black men had been. He left Bardon's and hurried around the corner to the police station at Second and Boulder, but virtually the same scene greeted him there. Just across the street from the station house, another group of White men had kicked its way into Megee's Hardware and were emptying the place of its guns and ammunition.

Rather than enforcing the law, arresting the looters, or re-establishing order, police officers had also joined in the mayhem at Megee's.

POLICE OFFICERS HAD JOINED IN THE MAYHEM

Sowders turned from the store and pushed his way inside the police station, where he was jostled around in the loud chaos until he found a man in uniform. He tried to tell the officer that his car had been commandeered by the people up in Greenwood and that he wanted to make a report. The cop laughed.

Just then another young man approached the officer, saying his name was Laurel Buck, a bricklayer who wanted to be deputized like the hundreds of other fellows now wearing special badges or ribbons.

"Get a gun and get an [n-word]," the police officer told him, and Buck disappeared into the crowd.

Rather than taking steps to protect Black people from the coming assault, the police were equipping White men to commit murder and other crimes against Black people.

Sowders forced his way back outside. He paused in the street, listening as another man spoke excitedly of White men who were chasing down any Black man they found downtown, whether he had been part of the fighting or not. The thugs had pursued one unarmed man down the alley between Boulder and Main, the man said, until he'd ducked into the rear entrance of the Royal

Theater—his final mistake. The White mob followed him in and shot him dead right by the orchestra pit. That must have been worth the price of a movie ticket, don't you think? Men roared with laughter.

Sowders started walking home, wondering about his car. Other autos, full of heavily armed White men firing into the air and yelling, careened past him up and down the street. He had never been so relieved to get through the front door of his house, where he lay on his bed the rest of the night, listening to the guns.

That night, W. R. Holway was attending the second show at the Rialto, watching *The House that Jazz Built*, which featured Wanda Hawley. Halfway through the feature, someone rushed in and shouted, "[N-word] fight! [N-word] fight!"

Women screamed, and people rushed for the exits like the place was on fire. By the time Holway made it outside, gunfire was echoing from all directions.

Seconds later, he witnessed a desperate young Black man sprint down an adjoining alley. A short, wiry fellow

PEOPLE RUSHED FOR THE EXITS

wearing a dirty denim shirt, denim pants, and work boots, the man panted as he stopped, looking both ways at the mouth of the alley.

But as he ran, a dozen guns fired as one, a barrage so thick it was a wonder the White gunmen didn't end up shooting each other.

The young man fell. He was still alive, clutching a pistol and writing in agony. A man in a bow tie and crisp straw hat approached and kicked the gun from the man's hand, allowing the hoodlums to surround him.

A White man in a dark suit, whom Holway supposed to be a doctor, approached with his medical bag and tried to push through to the wounded man. The crowd cursed him and pushed him back. The doctor shook his head, reconsidered, and continued walking down the street as the mob began to hack at the Black man with pocketknives.

Three ambulances roared down the street.

"Get the hell out of here!" one man yelled.

"Don't touch that filthy [n-word]!" another screamed. The stunned ambulance attendants shut off their engines and watched.

The crowd grew as blood pooled in the street around the young man, and he called for his mama as he died. White people fought their way through the mob to get a better look. Holway recognized many Klan members among them.

CHAPTER 12

May 31, 1921:
'Round Midnight

At midnight, a small White crowd gathered again at the steps of the courthouse. Still barricaded inside the jail, Sheriff McCullough and his deputies heard them screaming from the street.

"Bring the rope! Get Dick Rowland!"

McCullough and his men braced themselves once more, not knowing whether the danger was past.

Bring the rope!

But, by then, Rowland was an afterthought for most of the White mob, which grew to ten thousand men and boys and even included a few women.

After being terrified by the opening exchange at the courthouse, the racists in Tulsa had quickly recovered their wits. Once they'd pushed the Black men back to Greenwood, the White horde recongregated downtown. Dick Rowland—and whatever he might have done to some White girl on an elevator—was no longer their concern. The night had been transformed into something much larger.

THE NIGHT HAD BEEN TRANSFORMED INTO SOMETHING MUCH LARGER

White folks were dead. As sure as God was in his heaven, many vowed that the Black men would rue the day they spilled the blood of the "superior race."

In the eyes of many White people, this was war.

After the outburst of gunfire at the courthouse, the Black men had scattered in every direction. The angry White mob hunted many of them down, killing them before they could escape downtown Tulsa. Three more died in pistol duels at close range.

Other men from Greenwood made use of their military training and retreated in an orderly fashion. They knelt down and fired at the pursuing White men, laying down cover for their Black comrades who sprinted north toward the Frisco tracks.

But each Black man in this battle knew that their retreat would end at the tracks and that the Tulsa police would not attempt to protect them.

They would die before allowing the White mob to come charging into their beloved Greenwood, where their innocent wives, children, and family members fearfully waited at home. They would defend the dignified and prosperous Black Wall Street they had created in less than one generation, the place they had worked so long and hard to create, the world of which they were so proud.

Unlike in Europe—where Black men had been slaughtered for democratic principles that didn't apply to their lives once they returned home—on that night

THEY WOULD DEFEND THE DIGNIFIED AND PROSPEROUS BLACK WALL STREET

in Tulsa, the point of their sacrifices was clear. Three centuries of enslavement and abuse boiled up inside of them. Finally, they would defend and stand up for themselves, if not to save Dick Rowland, then to protect their families, homes, and businesses against the White marauders and the White supremacy that oppressed them.

The first major stand came on the northern edge of White downtown at the intersection of Second Street and Cincinnati Avenue. The Black men stopped and fired from alleys, from behind cars and trees, and from around the corner of buildings, unleashing a barrage at the White men hunkered down to engage them in bloody urban warfare. The battle unfolded just outside the luxurious Hotel Tulsa. White guests with rooms on the upper floors observed the fight below them—but not for long because every few seconds, bullets splintered another hotel window.

Spectators were much bolder two blocks away. About five hundred people, scores of them women in long dresses and Sunday hats, crowded along Main Street to observe the thrilling exchange, feeling safer because most of the bullets traveled north and south and the crowd stood a bit off to the west.

In the middle of the fray, shots ricocheted from the brick walls of the hotel and from other nearby buildings, such as the Axelson Machine Company, Right Way Cleaners and Laundry, Nixon and Nixon law offices, and the Manion Ness Piano Company. Late-night diners at the Carroll and Huddleston Restaurant dove for the floor as bullets shattered the café windows above them. Others scattered out the back door into an alley.

An innocent bystander was among the first casualties. A. B. Stick, a city clerk from the nearby town of Sapulpa, was a guest at the Hotel Tulsa that night, and he was loitering about the lobby when the battle broke out. Curious about what he thought were firecrackers popping in the street, he stuck his head out to investigate and was felled almost instantly by a bullet.

The battle on Cincinnati raged for more than an hour—until ammunition ran low for both sides. In the lull, the Black men, whose numbers were greatly reduced by casualties, sprinted toward the Frisco tracks, where hundreds of reinforcements awaited them.

Scores of armed White men pursued them, and the tracks became the new battle line. The two sides traded heavy fire along the tracks for the rest of the night. At one point, an unwitting passenger train pulled into Frisco Station. Bullet holes pierced both sides of the cars, causing the unsuspecting passengers to dive for the floor in terror.

Shortly after the courthouse shootout started, Tulsa-based National Guard members got involved in the fray.

National Guardsmen began to congregate at the Tulsa armory at about eleven o'clock, and just after midnight, crowds of Tulsans cheered as Lieutenant Colonel J. F. Rooney and his heavily armed, khaki-clad unit rumbled past the courthouse in an army truck on its way toward the police station.

LET THEM COME IF THEY DARE! "Now let them come if they dare!" one man cried.

The Tulsa police immediately deferred

to the National Guard commanders, who found a frenzied army of civilians in the street when they arrived.

Only hours before, many of those civilians had been part of the mob that had gathered to lynch Dick Rowland. Now, at least five hundred of them had been newly deputized as law officers with a legal mandate to "get a gun and get an [n-word]."

These were the same hoodlums who had armed themselves by looting Tulsa's hardware stores, sporting goods stores, and pawn shops—all of which had been ransacked and cleaned out by midnight.

The civilian brigade ranged from preteens to men in their eighties, from taxi drivers and oil roughnecks to entrepreneurs and the wealthiest oilmen, White people united in unruly passions that National Guard officers felt challenged to marshal to some lawful end.

One of the officers, Major Charles Daley, was also a commander with the Tulsa Police Department. With the authority of both positions, he stood on the steps of the police station shortly after midnight, pleading for quiet.

"If you wish to help us maintain order, you must abide by my instructions and follow them to the letter, rather than running wild," Major Daley yelled, and some in the mob seemed to nod their assent.

What he defined as maintaining order involved asking the same people who had just comprised the lynch mob, the same people who had looted businesses for weapons, to take charge.

Neither Tulsa's police nor its National Guard took steps to protect the city's Black citizens or the Greenwood neighborhood from the angry assault.

In fact, Major Daley recognized several war veterans among the crowd and enlisted them as his assistants. He further attempted to impose order by separating the men carrying pistols from those armed with rifles and by ordering that all boys twenty-one and younger be immediately disarmed—instructions that were promptly ignored.

Elsewhere in the city, to prevent Black people from entering the White sections of Tulsa, National Guard officers ordered roadblocks at all the major thoroughfares running in and out of Greenwood.

Units composed of volunteers and Tulsa police were dispatched to protect the public works plant on West First Street and the water works plant on Sand Springs Road. The National Guard assigned squads of White volunteers to patrol downtown Tulsa on foot, with instructions to preserve order, watch for snipers, and gather up any Black people on the street.

The patrols had orders not to fire unless fired upon, which they ignored as well.

A machine gun was dispatched with National Guard members to the top of Standpipe Hill, and other soldiers established a skirmish line just west of Detroit Avenue, thus sealing Greenwood off in that direction. Triage stations were organized at the police department and at the National Guard Armory, where the wounded of both races were ordered taken for medical treatment.

A MACHINE GUN WAS DISPATCHED

But whatever the intentions of the local National Guard officers, keeping order was the last thing on the collective mind of the mob now so loosely under their command.

Sheriff McCullough remained locked in at the top of the courthouse stairway, protecting Dick Rowland in the jail.

Every few minutes, another voice would call up to him, desperately yelling about papers he needed to sign so the governor would send in the National Guard from Oklahoma City.

To McCullough, that sounded like the ruse of a desperate mob, whose members knew that its only way to Rowland would be to overpower or trick the sheriff.

But then he heard a familiar voice yell, "Sheriff! It's me."

He recognized the sound of the cop reporter from the *Tulsa World*, a fellow he'd spoken with almost every day since taking office a few months earlier.

Finally, here was someone he knew.

It was well after midnight and now June 1, 1921.

Sheriff McCullough allowed the reporter to come up the steps to the door of the jail.

The reporter, who was White, slid a sheet of paper through the steel bars as McCullough kept his pistol handy. Sure enough, the sheriff recognized the signatures of the police commissioner and a state judge on a letter requesting troops be sent to assist the beleaguered Tulsa authorities.

McCullough added his name and handed the document back to the reporter, who dashed down the steps.

At 1:48 a.m., Tulsa authorities dispatched a telegram to Oklahoma Governor J. B. A. Robertson formally requesting National Guard assistance to put down what was later described in National Guard action reports as a "Negro uprising."

The telegram read: "Race riot developed here. Several killed. Unable [to] handle situation. Request that National Guard forces be sent by special train. Situation serious." It was signed by the chief of police, the sheriff, and a district judge.

By two thirty, a hundred cars, some of them luxury sedans driven by some of Tulsa's most prominent White citizens, raced through the city's streets. Some undertook wild sorties into Greenwood, firing indiscriminately into Black homes.

Others converged on White residences where Black domestic workers lived during the week. Dozens of Black people were pulled from their beds on the White side of town, dragged screaming in their nightclothes from the homes. Those who resisted were beaten severely. Other Black domestic workers were hidden by their White employers beneath beds or in cellars or attics, temporarily spared from the ugly passions that had taken over the night.

The heinous burning of Greenwood began well after midnight, long after the Black men had been pushed back across the railroad tracks and began to defend their community, and the first White gunmen had finally penetrated the area, routing people from homes and businesses along Boston Avenue and on the western end of Archer Street.

THE HEINOUS BURNING OF GREENWOOD BEGAN

Some White people would later claim that the first fires were set for tactical reasons, to flush Black guardians from buildings where they fired at the White mob.

But it soon became evident the White thugs would settle for nothing less than scorched earth. They would not be satisfied to kill Black people or to arrest them. They would also try to destroy every indication of Black prosperity.

It was in those early morning hours that White marauders first engaged in a ritual that would become increasingly common over the next several hours: the liberal spreading of kerosene or gasoline inside Greenwood homes and businesses and then setting them ablaze.

Fire department crews rushed north as the first fingers of black smoke stained the night air above Tulsa, but as had happened to the ambulances on Third Street, White hoodlums pulled guns on them and threatened them.

Tulsa Fire Chief R. C. Adler forbade the firefighters from dousing the flames.

It was probably during those first hours on Boston and Archer that one of the burning's most infamous atrocities took place.

An old Black couple refused to leave when the mob stormed down their street that night. In fact, when the White gangsters burst through their door, they found the man and woman kneeling side by side in prayer at the foot of their bed. The men immediately shot the couple in the back of their heads, looted their home, and set it on fire, incinerating the bodies of the couple inside.

By four o'clock, flames had consumed two dozen Black homes and businesses, including the Midway Hotel on Archer Street. In many of the homes, terrorists burned people alive and listened to their screams.

By dawn, the White invaders outnumbered Greenwood's Black defenders by ten or more to one. The White people also enjoyed an overwhelming advantage in weaponry and ammunition, and they made plans to exploit it. Casualties mounted as the night wore on, particularly among Black people.

Sometime that morning, a light-skinned Black man who could pass for white had mingled among the mob at the police department and learned what most in Greenwood already expected: The White perpetrators were discussing a full-scale invasion of the Black quarter sometime in the next few hours.

Elsewhere, some White teenagers heard a similar conversation. Scores of White men had gone home and put on their war uniforms. Some, who seemed to be the leaders, stood on cars and worked the crowd into a lather.

"Men, we're going in at daybreak," one man said as the crowd roared.

WE'RE GOING IN AT DAYBREAK

Another man ordered an ammunition exchange in preparation for the coming assault. "If any of you have more ammunition than you need, or if what you have doesn't fit your gun, sing out." The crowd buzzed as men checked their pockets for ammo and passed bullets back and forth.

Then a third man spoke. "Be ready at daybreak!" he yelled. "Nothing can stop us, for there will be thousands of others going in at the same time," and this time, the roar that greeted his words was deafening.

Elsewhere, at about five o'clock, five hundred White men near the Frisco Station engaged in a furious exchange with Black men positioned on the rooftop of a two-story building just across the railroad tracks on Archer. At least six Black corpses lay between the warring forces in the place that came to be known as "no-man's-land." White men cheered raucously as the body of a fallen Black defender was tied behind a car and dragged through downtown Tulsa. Over the next several hours, the corpses of dead Black men dragging behind the cars of White men became a common sight in the streets of the city.

As the insanity continued to escalate, the Black police officer H. C. Pack could not help but feel partly responsible. He had lived in Tulsa since 1916 and, for the past several years, had patrolled Greenwood as one of Tulsa's two Black officers, enforcing the White people's laws. Two days earlier, he and Officer Carmichael had arrested Rowland in the naïve belief that he would get a fair hearing.

Now, as dawn approached, Pack conceded the truth: Racist White people did not apply the law where Black folks were concerned. The Black men of Greenwood, whom he'd previously perceived to be hotheads, had been right all along. The only justice for Black people was the justice they would earn by fighting for it.

When he saw the fires, Pack knew it was just a matter of time before his home would go up in flames.

As the horizon lightened in the east, Pack found his way

down to Greenwood Avenue, where he saw people pouring out of the Stradford Hotel, scurrying north in flight.

Many homeowners in Greenwood had already fled, becoming part of a growing river of refugees stumbling north up Greenwood Avenue away from downtown and toward the country or down the Midland Valley Railroad tracks.

Maybe daylight would bring back a bit of sanity, Pack thought, but his better judgment told him that was not likely to be the case.

Sure enough, just before dawn, a small band of White sharpshooters hauled a machine gun and thousands of rounds of ammunition to the top of the granary of the Middle States Milling Company on First Street, which was located on the south side of the tracks. From there, they enjoyed a clear shot at most of Greenwood.

Also that morning, at five o'clock, more than one hundred soldiers piled into boxcars in the state capital of Oklahoma City for the hundred-mile journey east to Tulsa.

CHAPTER 13

Daybreak

People later disagreed about whether the whistle came from a steam engine parked in the Frisco rail yards or from one of the White factories on the south side. In any event, the shrill noise pierced Tulsa's predawn quiet at precisely 5:08 a.m. on June 1, 1921. And whatever its source, there could be no doubt as to its meaning: The whistle was the signal for the White invasion of Greenwood to begin.

A lusty cheer welled up among the thousands of White people poised at various locations on the edge of Greenwood.

Men poured out from behind boxcars and the freight depot.

"From every place of shelter up and down the tracks came screaming, shouting men to join in the rush toward the Negro section," one White man, Choc Phillips, wrote years later. "Mingled with the shouting were a few rebel yells and Indian gobblings as the great wave of humanity rushed forward, totally absorbed in thoughts of destruction."

Yet for all the planning and bravado, the White mob's initial advance was slow, especially as they attempted to attack across the Frisco tracks. Several White corpses from the night before attested to the fact that the Greenwood residents would not surrender meekly.

So, at the sound of the whistle, the terrorists operating the machine gun at the top of the Middle States mill laid down a withering barrage, firing north across the tracks onto Greenwood Avenue while White attackers on the ground opened up with their arsenal of stolen guns and ammunition.

Nevertheless, several White shooters fell.

Several White shooters fell

The others took to firing from behind the cover of trees, boxcars, locomotives, buildings, and automobiles, advancing yard by yard—if they advanced at all—absorbing heavy fire from Greenwood. The fighting was the most intense along the Frisco tracks and on the west side of Greenwood, where local members of the National Guard joined White civilians to fire down on the Black quarter from atop Standpipe Hill.

On Greenwood's east side, the Black residents offered only token resistance, allowing roving bands of White mob members to penetrate with near impunity.

It was there that the White boy named Walter Ferrell lived with his family.

The Ferrell house, in fact, sat right on the border of the Black community; it was so close that the Ferrells and other White families took up the east side of the street, and Black families lived on the west side.

White and Black adults exchanged neighborly pleasantries, calling greetings back and forth on warm evenings. And, almost every day after school, Walter played with the three Black brothers about his age who lived with their parents across the street and two doors down.

In Walter's mind, the children were perfectly acceptable companions. The color of their skin didn't mean a thing when you needed a few more boys to fill out the sides for baseball, when playing hide-and-seek, or when confronting the imaginary monsters while on youthful excursions into the hills and creek bottoms of the nearby countryside.

Each day, Walter and his friends marched off to their separate schools—Walter to study with the White children, his friends to learn with the Black children. But their segregation ended with the afternoon bell, when Walter and the three other youngsters joined up to play until their mothers called them in for supper, playing again afterward until dark.

At least, that's what they did until the morning the whistle awakened everyone in Walter's house. A spasm of gunfire followed, which the boy at first mistook for an approaching thunderstorm. His mother and father seemed nervous over breakfast, though they wouldn't tell him why. Shortly thereafter, as Walter stood outside, a big black sedan roared up the street and screeched to a halt in front of the house of his three friends.

The car was full of White men carrying rifles or shotguns. Walter watched two of the men kick in the front door. The first gunshot rang out seconds later, followed closely by a shotgun blast, then three more gunshots. His friends were somewhere inside that house, and he imagined how afraid they must be to have those gangsters busting through the door so early in the morning, then shooting off their guns in there.

Why would they do such a thing?

WHY WOULD THEY DO SUCH A THING?

Walter's frightened thoughts were soon interrupted by the men's reappearance. He thought he heard them laughing as they lit torches and splashed liquid on the wooden walls of the house, which exploded in flame when they touched it with their torches. Then the White thugs ran back to their car and sped off.

Walter felt the heat from the flames within seconds. He ran back inside his house, where he realized he had soiled his pants in his terror. He watched from a front window for the rest of the morning, praying and waiting for his friends to escape from the flames.

Walter waited at that window until the house was nothing more than a pile of smoldering cinder. His friends never came out.

Despite all the success he had in Tulsa, John Williams had never forgotten.

Despite the White men, the rich White men, lined up each day outside Williams' One Stop Garage in Greenwood, he never forgot.

Despite the fact he fixed the White men's cars and accepted their money, and even though Loula ran the Williams' Confectionery and the Dreamland Theatre just down Greenwood Avenue with two other theaters in nearby Muskogee and Okmulgee, he always remembered.

Even though he and Loula had become wealthy even by White standards, John Williams had not forgotten what had driven him to Oklahoma in the first place.

Bill Williams saw it in his father's eyes that morning as the sun came up.

The night before, his dad had finally returned home about midnight, after the shooting at the courthouse, unhurt but looking unusually weary and somber. He would not answer his son's questions about what had transpired downtown, insisting instead that the boy go off to bed.

But before dawn, Bill had heard the whistle. Immediately sensing it was a warning, he rushed out of his room on the second floor. He found his father crouched in the second-floor bathroom that faced south, still dressed in overalls stained with grease from his previous day's work. Only now, John held his prized Savage rifle in both hands like he did when waiting for pheasant to be flushed from the bushes or for geese to fly overhead.

Bill saw his father's shotgun leaning against a nearby wall and a pistol tucked into his father's belt. Ammunition was piled around him in boxes, on the commode, and lying loose on the floor. Every few seconds as he crouched there in the dark, John peered out the window toward what looked to be thousands of White people on the other side of the tracks firing wildly toward the north.

"Well, now they're shooting at us," John said, as if to himself, as he drew up the screen on the bathroom window.

He rested the barrel of the gun on the windowpane, squinting over the gunsight, and calmly squeezed off six shots, the noise echoing in the small room and causing Bill to throw his hands over his ears. Three White bodies fell in dark heaps near the railroad tracks, and when they did, a dozen others scurried for cover.

Bill crawled up next to his father as he shot, and he saw that John's jaw was grimly set. But when his father glanced over at him, Bill saw that his eyes were glinting. His dad emptied the spent cartridges onto the floor and loaded several more bullets into the Savage, sighted the rifle, and squeezed off six more shots.

Because he had not forgotten what had brought him to Oklahoma.

HE HAD NOT FORGOTTEN WHAT HAD BROUGHT HIM TO OKLAHOMA

John had swallowed his rage all those years—the rage of having his fate and that of his family depend on the dark whimsy of hateful White people, the rage that now poured out through the barrel of his expensive rifle.

Behind them in the hallway, Bill's mother and a teenager named Posey, who lived with the family, peeked around the corner as John took on the White pack.

Other Black gunmen fired at the White shooters from the windows and rooftops along Greenwood Avenue, but the Williams Building was at the intersection of Greenwood and Archer, the southern gateway to the Black quarter and therefore the closest to the advancing throng. This meant John's bullets were the most strategic in keeping Greenwood from being overrun, and he knew it.

"Bill, help me defend Greenwood," John said, holding the shotgun toward his son. "Grab some of that buckshot there on the floor. Loula, I think it's time you headed on off to your mother's."

Help me defend Greenwood

Loula nodded from the doorway. She crawled into the bathroom to hug Bill, who was still crouched next to his father at the window. She touched her husband's shoulder then crawled back into the hallway, where she hugged Posey and disappeared down the stairs. Posey stayed in the hall while Bill loaded the shotgun the way his father had taught him on lazy weekend afternoons when they hunted for Sunday supper. He handed his father the shotgun, grabbed the empty Savage, and loaded that too.

There was something thrilling about it, working with his father that way. For the first time in his life, Bill felt like a man. And for the rest of his life, he would wrongly believe that more White people than Black were killed that day because of all the White men he saw fall outside their bathroom window.

But the numbers arrayed against them were too great. And when the sun came up, the White people unleashed another weapon.

"My Lord, Bill, would you look at that," John said.

A biplane appeared from the east, circling high at first like a vulture surveying its prey, then diving low over Deep Greenwood, its engine a loud, terrifying moan. The plane roared close enough that John could see the man in the strange headgear and goggles in the plane's second seat, firing a rifle toward Greenwood Avenue.

A second plane followed soon upon the first, attacking in the same manner. Seeing their destructive intent, John fired several shots at the planes before they disappeared to the north, but for the first time that morning, Bill's father seemed unnerved, shaking his head and muttering to himself as his son handed him the loaded shotgun.

The appearance of the planes had the opposite effect on the White hoodlums. More cheers welled up among them, and dozens rushed over the tracks as John became distracted by the assault from the air. They managed to take positions within a hundred feet of the Williams Building, and a group of White gunmen trained its weapons on John's bathroom window, splintering the windowpane into a thousand tiny slivers.

"I guess we better get outta here now," Bill's father said. "Come on, fellas. Let's go."

He handed Bill the shotgun and carried the Savage himself. All three filled their pockets with bullets and shells. Then John, Bill, and Posey scurried down the stairs, out the front door of the Williams Building, and onto the sidewalk of Greenwood Avenue. They clung to the buildings on the west side of the street, inching their way north until another burst from the machine gun perched at the top of the mill on First Street caused them to duck into the Bell and Little Restaurant, which was deserted.

After a few minutes, John spotted a young Black man with a shotgun standing in the door of the pool hall across the street. John then dashed out into the street with Bill and Posey at his heels. Bullets zipped around their heads as they scrambled toward the pool hall and dove inside the door.

"Sure glad to have some company," the man with the shotgun said when they arrived. "I figure the best shot is from one of the windows upstairs."

John nodded. The four of them raced to the second floor into a bedroom with a window that looked out onto Greenwood Avenue. From there, it was a long but clear shot toward the top of the mill and the place around some boxcars where the White shooters were still pinned down by the Black defenders.

But now the White marauders were breaking into the buildings of Greenwood Avenue from an alley to the west.

White men's guns were soon poking out and firing back at John and the boys from windows of the Black-owned buildings across the street. John could even see White men in the windows of his own building on the corner.

Greenwood Avenue was lost.

"Well, let's go," he said, heading out the bedroom door and down the stairs.

Bill and Posey followed him into an alley behind the pool

hall. John tossed his Savage to the ground, pulled out his pistol, and did the same with it. He told Bill to drop the shotgun and told both boys to empty their pockets.

"It's probably best if we split up," Bill's dad said. "Head north and I'll meet you in the country. Hurry off now."

But Posey followed John, so Bill set off alone, running north up the alley. He stopped to rest after two blocks, looked around to see if any White people pursued him, and reached into his pocket for his handkerchief. To his alarm, he felt two shotgun shells hidden there and quickly tossed them into some nearby bushes, which was a good thing. A few seconds later, he and two White hoodlums arrived at the next corner at the same time, nearly bumping into each other. The White boys, who looked to be only a few years older than Bill, were dressed alike in denim shirts and denim pants soiled to the knees with dust. They both wore crisp, matching brown caps.

"Gotcha," one said, pointing a shotgun at Bill's head.

"Hold it right there."

Bill stopped and threw his hands 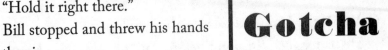 in the air.

"Where's that gun of yours?" one of them asked.

"Don't have no gun," Bill said.

"I know you do. I seen you throw something back in those bushes. Why don't we go have a look?"

One of the boys guarded Bill as the other trotted down the alley and poked around in the bushes. Bill knew he would be killed if the White boy found those shells, so he whispered the words of Psalm Twenty-Three:

"The Lord is my shepherd; I shall not want . . . Yea, though I walk through the valley of the shadow of death, I will fear no evil: for thou art with me."

In a few minutes, the boy returned from the bushes after a fruitless search, and Bill sighed with relief.

"You're lucky," the young hoodlum said to him. "Now march."

They herded Bill up the alley another block to Easton Street, where a handful of White men held about forty other Black men and boys captive beneath a stand of oaks. Bill recognized most of the hostages. They were customers from the confectionery, or classmates in school, or friends of his parents, but he was ashamed to see them in such a state of subjugation and despair.

He walked toward a tree without speaking or making eye contact and slumped to the ground. The White tormentors taunted their prisoners and prodded them with their guns. Bill was consumed by his own rage then. Angry tears spilled down his face. He wished he hadn't left his father's shotgun behind.

O. W. Gurley had tried to warn those folks.

He had argued the night before until he was out of breath: If they persisted in trying to help that Black boy in jail down at the courthouse, they might just get everyone in Greenwood burned out.

That should have been plain to everyone.

Those boys knew, as well as Gurley did, the fate of Black men labeled as uppity by White men in other American cities.

Had they forgotten East St. Louis, Chicago, Houston, D.C., Omaha, Duluth?

Didn't Deputy Barney Cleaver and the sheriff both assure them that Dick Rowland was safe behind bars? And even if he wasn't, was the life of one Black teenager worth all this?

Now they would see: The price of pride was fire.

Gurley stayed awake that night with his wife, Emma, sitting up in their rooms on the top floor of the Gurley Hotel.

The smell of smoke grew stronger by the hour. At daylight, flames had begun to spit from the roof of Sattie Partee's place only a few yards south, launching red cinders within a few feet of Gurley's doorstep. He ran downstairs and outside in his shirt-sleeves, hearing the crackling of the fire at Partee's place and gunfire booming all around him. The air was so filthy with smoke that he gagged and put a handkerchief to his mouth.

Six White men emerged like ghosts from one corner of this hell, walking toward Gurley through the smoke from the direction of Sattie's place. They carried shotguns and rifles, burning torches, and five-gallon containers. All of them wore khaki outfits, but Gurley couldn't tell if they were soldiers from the National Guard or White war veterans who had dusted off their old uniforms for that morning's attack on the Black quarter.

They marched up to Gurley when they saw him standing outside.

"You better get out of that hotel because we're gonna burn all of this goddamn stuff," one of the men said. "You better get all your guests out."

Then the thugs moved on to the next building, pounding on the doors of the restaurant, then to the pool hall next to the restaurant, screaming for anybody inside to get the hell out because those buildings were marked for the torch.

Gurley ran back inside and found his wife as he had left her, in a bedroom rocking chair, rocking furiously as she stared at the window, quaking with fear.

"We need to go, Emma," he said. "The fire's going to get us, too. The fire's going to get everyone."

"But where will we go if the fire is everywhere?" she asked.

"I don't know," he said.

As they stepped onto Greenwood Avenue and saw all the Black folks fleeing north, Gurley had an idea. He and his wife would run in the other direction and try to make it south across the tracks, back to White Tulsa, where he was known as one of the reasonable Black men and as a man of means.

He and Emma would be safer with the White people than with the Black people, he reasoned. So they rushed south on Greenwood Avenue to the corner of Archer, pausing at the Williams Building to look around the corner. It was then that Gurley learned that White Tulsans were in no mood that morning to make distinctions between Black people.

Two White men with pistols came around a building on Archer and fired at the Gurleys.

Emma moaned and fell heavily to the street.

"Emma!" Gurley cried as she fell. "Lord help us."

Her eyes were open as he bent over her, searching her body for a wound.

LORD HELP US

"Gurley," she said to her husband. "Don't worry about me. You need to run."

So he did.

He ran as fast as his fifty-three-year-old legs could carry him, back up Greenwood Avenue, running north now with the rest of the Black folks, passing women, children, and old people who were fleeing from the White terrorists and their torches and their guns.

Before long, he found himself panting at the playground of the Dunbar Elementary School.

That's when his age finally overtook his terror, and he could flee no more. He stumbled toward the school and slipped into the crawl space beneath the new wooden building, hiding there for what seemed like hours, silently panting and sweating, and weeping for Emma and for a life of dreams and hard work gone to ruin because Black people couldn't leave well enough alone in a world where White people could annihilate Black folks with no consequences.

Every so often in his distress, he peered out from his hiding place, and eventually he saw that the flood of refugees had trickled to nothing.

Now hundreds of White perpetrators filled the streets, all of them carrying guns and several wielding torches. He saw one White teenager point toward the school, and a group walked toward it.

"I swear I saw him go under the school right about there," the teenager said, standing only a few feet from where Gurley hid.

"Well, let's just see," a man replied.

The barrel of a rifle was thrust into the crawl space and it fired several times. Gurley nearly screamed with terror, clawing his way as far as he could beneath the building, the bullets missing him by inches.

"Ah, hell," the man's voice said. "He must have crawled out the other side."

Gurley then heard a pounding noise, glass breaking, and feet shuffling in the building above him. He smelled smoke a few seconds later and realized that they had set the school building on fire too.

HE KNEW HE WAS DEAD

He knew he was dead if he stayed beneath the school and dead if he didn't.

Smoke poured from the school's broken windows as he stumbled away from the building, but it was his great fortune that most of the White hooligans had been distracted by events farther north. The street in front of the school was almost quiet. Gurley walked to a place nearby where an old White man with an antique shotgun held fifteen Black men captive. Gurley threw up his hands and surrendered, telling the White man he meant him no trouble.

The White invaders detained thousands of Black people—men, women, and children of all ages and from every strata of Greenwood life—and marched them to Convention Hall, then, when the hall was full, on to the local baseball stadium called McNulty Park.

Young Bill Williams was forced into one of those humiliating processions. Sometime midmorning, White gunmen marched him and scores of other Black citizens back down Greenwood Avenue, as if to make them observe the consequences of their courageous stand.

He witnessed White men and women walking in and out of the Stradford Hotel as if they owned the place, one man stealing Mr. Stradford's Victrola, two others robbing it of a cash register, yet another looting a chair from the lobby.

The scene was the same at Mr. Ferguson's drugstore up the street, and Mrs. Walker's beauty parlor, and J. T. Presley's restaurant.

But of all the terrible things he witnessed that day, what he saw next remained his most vivid memory: a short White man with a dark mustache emerging from the Williams Building wearing his mother's leopard coat. Her matching leopard handbag was strung over his shoulder. A leopard belt dangled from the purse. Other White men whistled at him.

As Bill was marched past with his hands in the air, he tried to memorize the looter's face.

Eventually Bill arrived inside Convention Hall. Thousands of Black people sat silently in the artificial light, strewn about on the floors or slumped in folding chairs that had been set up for the Catholic school's graduation program the night before. The people wept softy or spoke quietly among themselves.

When Bill saw them, he thought of the determination on Greenwood Avenue just the night before, the resolve, the pride. Greenwood would not stand idly by while a Black boy was lynched in Tulsa. Now—huddled as they were in Convention Hall just a few hours later—Bill saw only their weariness and defeat.

During the fight for Deep Greenwood, O. B. Mann had killed several White attackers, which gave him a fleeting satisfaction. He'd killed German soldiers in the war, but then he was Private Mann under orders from White officers, and he'd had no particular beef with the fighters on the other side. But this enemy had tormented his people for centuries, and now it was launching an assault that rivaled the worst he had seen in France. Only now the attack was against the homes and businesses of the folks who bought their groceries from the Mann Brothers store on Lansing.

He had been born for this moment, all the ancient anger coiled inside, waiting for the time when he could strike back. Like many of the White Tulsan veterans, he, too, had snuck a rifle home from the war. And for a few minutes that early morning, Mann also enjoyed the illusion that he and John Williams and the other Black men fighting from the buildings along Greenwood Avenue would actually defeat the White mob or at least turn them back across the tracks.

HE HAD BEEN BORN FOR THIS MOMENT

The White aggressors took heavy casualties on their first push before sunrise, when a cloud of bullets greeted them and sent them scurrying in retreat. But Mann's hopeful illusions burned off with the morning sun when he could see that there was no end to the invaders.

Kill one White man and ten more sprang up in his place.

The Black men defending Greenwood also didn't have the luxury of looting a dozen pawn shops and hardware stores. Their bullets had been purchased for hunting, and that ammunition soon ran low.

Then the planes attacked when the sun came up, and the White terrorists began to break into buildings on the west side of Greenwood Avenue from alleys in the rear. When Mann saw them poking around inside Black property, the rage made him dizzy. He wanted to go after those fellows with his bare hands, which he might have done if the boy hadn't come up the stairs, breathless from the horror and his long run for his life, to say the men needed help at Mount Zion.

Mann was incredulous. They were attacking where?

"At Mount Zion," the boy said. "Hundreds of folks firing down at us from Standpipe."

So they would attack a church too. Mann squeezed off a few final shots at the White shooters across Greenwood Avenue and followed the boy down the back stairs, then out the door for the half-mile sprint.

CHAPTER 14

Attack on Mount Zion

In 1913, one particular group of Baptists bought a large vacant lot at the corner of Easton and Elgin, just below Standpipe Hill. Their intention was to build a sanctuary so imposing that the devil himself would cower when it was done.

Under the leadership of Pastor R. A. Whitaker, a gifted orator, they contributed in nickels, dimes, and dollars to the building fund of what would be called "Mount Zion Baptist Church." It took seven years and the ability to stave off frustration and doubt, but the flock held on to its dream of worshipping in the finest Black sanctuary in that entire part of the nation. Together, the Baptists saved forty thousand dollars, about half of what was needed to complete the sanctuary but enough to convince White lenders to kick in the rest.

Finally, beginning in 1920, the Mount Zion faithful watched as the beautiful red bricks mounted one atop another and marveled at the new bell tower that stretched toward heaven. They rejoiced at how sunlight played through the stained-glass windows. On the morning of April 10, 1921, 856 Greenwood residents crammed into the pews of the Mount Zion Baptist Church for the first time, along with the dozens who fanned themselves while standing in back because the pews were filled. That Sunday morning, the congregation knew the euphoria of Moses's people during their first glimpse of the Promised Land, for they had wandered nearly as long, and the fruit of their efforts seemed just as sweet.

On that spring morning, Pastor Whitaker's words first echoed from the rafters of the new sanctuary. His people clapped and swayed and raised their hearts and their hands to heaven, singing Negro spirituals and gospel music that wafted out onto Easton and Elgin every time someone opened the church door. Every last penny saved, every last day they had waited, had been worth it in the end.

PEOPLE CLAPPED AND SWAYED AND RAISED THEIR HEARTS AND THEIR HANDS TO HEAVEN

Less than two months later, the White mob massed on Standpipe Hill—which extended into Greenwood like a long, fat finger—and formed a skirmish line down the hill to surround the Black community on the west. Then they mounted a blistering attack from that direction, raining bullets down upon Mount Zion, Booker T. Washington High School, and all the nice homes of the doctors, lawyers, teachers, and leading Greenwood entrepreneurs. The dedication of Mount Zion had been a hint of heaven, but this morning was clearly a taste of hell. White bullets fell on that section of Greenwood like hail.

But at first, the White attackers couldn't advance down the hill into Greenwood so much as an inch. Someone counted more than fifty Black men guarding Mount Zion when the sun rose, several of them up in the bell tower, others stationed with rifles and shotguns firing out windows closer to the ground. Mount Zion's belfry offered an unobstructed line of fire at the invaders. For an hour or more, Black marksmen who were trained to fight Germans picked off any White hoodlum foolish enough to move forward. Many died trying.

The sanctuary smelled of gun smoke, and the stained-glass windows were shattered and lay around the Black defenders in large, colorful shards. But the men inside continued to fight ferociously to save the house of God for which they had waited so long.

Young Ruth Sigler had never seen a dead thing until that morning, not even a pet. But she had never witnessed open warfare, either, or an assault that approached genocide, or a whole community going up in flames. There were many things the first-grade girl had never seen until then, and many things she hoped to never see again.

She was a child of seven, the daughter of a man who'd become rich in oil and real estate before his death a few years earlier. Ruth had been raised in the cocoon of White privilege, a world of storybooks and new dolls and fancy ribbons for her hair.

She wondered in later years how she managed to fall asleep that terrible night. But she did. A loud bumping sound outside awakened her at dawn. When she looked out the window, she saw two slat-sided cattle beds inching down the street with dead Black bodies stacked up on them.

Her mind raced and her stomach tumbled. She had overheard previous conversations between Uncle Ross and Aunt Jessie about how the Klan hated Black people, so she naturally figured that the Klan had killed those people on the trucks. Indeed, while out on a drive one night the previous year, she, Uncle Ross, and Aunt Jessie had inadvertently witnessed a group of White-robed and hooded KKK members tar-and-feather a Black man during a hilltop cross burning right outside of the city. The Klan hated Catholics, too, didn't they? Might she someday end up on a pile of dead people?

Even when she had calmed down, Ruth had difficulty explaining what she had seen. She had so much trouble untangling her words that she began to wonder whether the dead bodies had been there at all. Auntie patted Ruth's head and dismissed her vision as a particularly bad nightmare. But then Uncle Ross came bursting in through the front door, holding a folded newspaper, looking like he hadn't slept.

"The *Tulsa World* says an army of Blacks are coming from Muskogee, and they're gonna burn the whole place down," he told Aunt Jessie, gesturing with the paper.

"My Lord," Auntie said.

"The *World* says those Negroes are gonna start at Central High School and work their way out from there," Uncle Ross said.

"But Ross, that's only a block away," Auntie said. "What will we do?"

"I'll tell you what we won't do," Ross said. "We won't stay here. You and the children get out to the car. We need to get to the country place. My guess is that we'll be safe there."

The four of them, Uncle Ross and Aunt Jessie, Ruth and her brother, Jack, rushed outside and climbed into the Ford. Ross fired up the engine and sped off east on Eighth Street. Suddenly, he turned north.

"What on earth are you doing?" Aunt Jessie said.

"I want to have a look at what's causing all that smoke," Jack replied.

I WANT TO HAVE A LOOK AT WHAT'S CAUSING ALL THAT SMOKE

"But what about the Negroes coming from Muskogee?" Aunt Jessie asked.

"It couldn't hurt to take a quick look, could it?" Ross said. "My God, I've never seen smoke like that. I'll just take a minute. Then we'll go. I promise."

Uncle Ross then drove up the backside of Standpipe Hill. He stopped the car, and they all sat speechless, struck mute, almost paralyzed by the otherworldly spectacle unfolding around them.

Dozens of other cars were already parked in the grass at the top of the hill. Some of the occupants were spectators, including several women who stood behind the thick trunks of oaks and cottonwoods to look down on what was happening in Greenwood.

But there was an army of terrorists up there too. Several men wearing the khaki uniforms of war veterans and other men in civilian clothes lay on their bellies at the crest of the hill, firing with rifles and shotguns into the Black neighborhoods below.

Ruth could look down into Greenwood from the backseat of the Ford. She saw the source of the smoke: orange flames flickering from dozens of homes and larger brick business buildings.

Groups of Black people dashed away from Standpipe through the dark haze, many of them adults dragging children along by their arms. Some fell as they ran and didn't get up. White puffs of smoke billowed repeatedly from the windows of a huge brick church at the bottom of the hill—smoke from the guns of the Black men who fired back up at the White shooters.

Then planes roared in from the east, circling over the church. Ruth was afraid the planes would swoop in their direction and shoot down at them, too, but in a few minutes the machines circled again and disappeared.

Several khaki-clad veterans manned the machine gun. One man aimed and fired toward the church while another fed a string of bullets into the gun. One of the veterans at the machine gun spotted Ruth and her family, still sitting stunned in their car, and broke away from the others, running toward them.

"Dammit to hell!" he yelled. "Get out of here! You're in the range of fire."

Then he dropped his shotgun, and a dark red stain sprouted on the left shoulder of his uniform.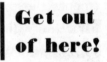

"Oh my God!" he cried. "Oh my God!"

He staggered forward and then fell over into the dirt.

Ruth lost it.

"Jack, slap her," Aunt Jessie yelled. "She's hysterical."

Uncle Ross drove off, and they raced toward the country as Ruth vomited out the window.

The standoff made the White mob around Mount Zion impatient and angrier each time one of their own fell dead or wounded. But the Black men defending themselves in the church still would not budge. The White attackers charged the church in a series of frontal assaults that were blunted before any of them could get near Mount Zion's front door. Many White men were killed in the attacks. Inside the church, as the battle wore on, Black casualties numbered seven men killed or wounded.

Then the White men turned to deception.

"Hey, fellas," one man shouted toward the church. "Enough blood's been shed here. Let's talk."

A few White men waved a white sheet, walking slowly toward the front door of the church, apparently unarmed and with their hands in the air. O. B. Mann immediately suspected a trick and kept his rifle trained on the men as they inched forward. But the Black men were desperately low on bullets and his comrades figured it wouldn't hurt to listen, so they held their fire until it was too late. Mann's suspicions had been correct.

ENGULFED IN FLAMES WITHIN MINUTES

While the Black defenders were distracted, White men snuck up to the sides of the church with kerosene and torches and set the church ablaze. The massive sanctuary was engulfed in flames within minutes. The battle for Mount Zion was effectively over, and with the church went the last great vestige of Greenwood life.

The Black men assembled in the sanctuary, choking from the smoke, holding handkerchiefs over their mouths while they considered their options. They could stay in the church and burn to death, or they could join ranks and dash for freedom out the front door and maybe kill a few more White men as they did, which was no choice at all.

The men loaded the bullets that remained. O. B. Mann shouldered one of the wounded Black men and moved toward Mount Zion's front door with the others who gathered in the thickening smoke. Hell itself could not have been worse than it was inside that church, so forty men went charging out the door, firing as they went. Mann and about thirty others somehow penetrated the White ranks, then raced north along Easton.

They fought final losing battles at a place farther north called Sunset Hill and then, about noon, at a Black-owned store on the northern boundary of Greenwood. After that, Mann and the few survivors fled into the hills.

Ten other Black defenders never made it off Mount Zion property. Smoke poured from the Mount Zion windows, and the belfry collapsed as the White mob cheered.

The Black battalions never arrived that morning from Muskogee or from anyplace else. The notion that they'd attack White Tulsa had just been wild speculation, White fear that had gone viral.

Black people never threatened either Central High School or any other White institution in Tulsa. In fact, classes at the sprawling school went on that morning as scheduled, though a sizable portion of the student body was absent because frightened parents kept their children home or because so many teenage boys had joined the White mob.

Not that the school day proceeded normally. A visiting professor from France was livid when, in the middle of her lecture on French poetry, her students insisted on rushing to the windows to watch trucks and wagons loaded with dead bodies rumble past. Several boys climbed to the roof of the high school to watch corpses trucked away, to get a better view of the explosions that erupted periodically in Greenwood, or to see the flames that shot up from the Black-owned buildings.

A history teacher named Mrs. Whitham discovered the boys on the roof and insisted they return to their rooms and study for final exams. The students reluctantly complied, then spent most of the morning at the windows anyway. Some of them became ill at the sight of the bodies and asked to be excused.

For others, the corpses and the sound of gunfire that lingered throughout the morning inspired a different reaction. A large gang of teenage boys decided they would like to join the action after all and headed down the halls toward the front door.

The principal intercepted them on the front steps, ordering them to go home immediately, but the boys ignored him and struck off down the street to the north. Most of the shops along the way were closed, and the boys encountered dozens of weary White men heading home after the events of the night. One of the men handed the delighted boys a new rifle with enough ammunition to fill his pockets.

"I've had enough shooting," the man said. "I'm going home and going to bed."

Then he shuffled off, and the boys raced happily in the direction of the smoke and the flames.

CHAPTER 15

Retrospective

On the night of May 31 and June 1, 1921, the White mobs had torched more than 1,115 Black homes (314 more were looted but not burned), five hotels, thirty-one restaurants, four drugstores, eight doctors' offices, the new Dunbar School, two dozen grocery stores, the Black hospital, the public library, and even a dozen churches, including the community's most magnificent new edifice, Mount Zion Baptist Church. White hoodlums burned or looted most of the Black families' personal belongings as well. All in all, White gangs torched thirty-five blocks full of buildings and killed as many as three hundred people.

Scholars and journalists attempting to reconstruct the great burning in the decades after it happened bumped up against an almost impenetrable conspiracy of silence among White Tulsans, who refused to talk about it. Within hours of the catastrophe, the members of the mob had disappeared back into the fabric of the White community, their atrocious tales to be whispered about in the secrecy of Klan meetings, bragged about in speakeasies when overly drunk, or recounted on deathbeds when the prospect of spending eternity in hell finally compelled the guilty to confess heinous sins.

As the years passed, great remorse did indeed plague some White participants. Two members of Tulsa's KKK conceded as much when talking confidentially to a magazine writer in the early 1970s. The wife of another man remembered the day, decades after the bloodbath, when she and her husband heard the tragedy briefly mentioned on a local radio station. The woman said that her husband, then an old man who once had spoken obliquely of a day he killed Black people, rose from his seat on a sofa, took down his hat and coat, and disappeared without a word into the cold outside for a solitary walk that lasted the day. He did not speak to his wife for days afterward, seemingly lost in the past.

Others regretted that more Black people weren't killed, that every last Black-owned building wasn't burned.

"I would do it again," one Tulsan Klansman, speaking confidentially, said a half-century after the event.

And though the worst culprits remained anonymous, there was no shortage of people making excuses about what White Tulsans had done in generations to come.

THERE WAS NO SHORTAGE OF PEOPLE MAKING EXCUSES

Most White people blamed the tragedy on the Black community, viewing their attempted defense of Dick Rowland as an unforgivable act of provocation. Many White Tulsans remained unable or unwilling to see how their racist assumptions that Black people should inhabit an inferior social position caused them to view human beings attempting to protect a teenager from being lynched as an outrageous act. They continued to believe that their intention to mete out vigilante justice upon Dick Rowland before the legal process played out was righteous.

For decades, the catastrophe was generally known as the Tulsa Race Riot, a gross misnomer.

Some White people blamed ruffians almost exclusively—oil roughnecks, cab drivers, bootleggers, and the like—the lower class of White people who poured from the boardinghouses along First Street to give their drunken hatreds free rein. But Tulsa hardly contained enough White rowdies to man an army of ten thousand. Photographs of the tragedy also showed that many in the White mob drove the most expensive cars and dressed in clothes beyond the means of the average person. Women who eagerly observed the fighting wore the finest floor-length fashions and the most stylish bonnets offered at Lerner's Department Store downtown.

Police commanders, local officers of the National Guard, and other authorities later insisted that their only purpose on the night of May 31 and the morning of June 1 was to protect White Tulsans from what they perceived as a Black uprising. Why was it not also the job of law enforcement to safeguard Dick Rowland from a lynch mob? Why was it not also to protect Black Tulsan residents from the White hoodlums who rained terror upon them? Why was protecting Black lives less important than protecting White-owned property?

While conceding that six two-seat war training planes had been dispatched from Curtis Field outside of Tulsa, leaders insisted that the aircraft were limited to reconnaissance missions over Greenwood. White newspaper accounts of the time, based on interviews with Tulsan authorities, reported that the aircraft were assigned to circle the embattled area and to note the spread of fires and the location of refugees.

But multiple accounts from Black residents identified that flaming balls of a substance—perhaps turpentine or kerosene—and bullets rained from above, igniting the roofs of buildings.

Tulsan authorities and civic leaders also denied organizing or otherwise encouraging the multipronged White attack that began before dawn and didn't end until the last Black defender had been either captured, killed, or driven north into the countryside and until the last Black family had been routed from their home.

That contention, too, was contradicted in several ways, among them the later testimony of Tulsan firefighters, who said Tulsa Fire Chief R. C. Adler forbade them from responding to calls in Greenwood, no doubt under orders from Tulsa's highest councils. Firefighters instead were ordered to protect White-owned homes and businesses located near the Black district.

A former Tulsan police officer, Van B. Hurley, described a downtown meeting between Tulsan authorities and its top civic leaders at the height of the crisis. This was where they made plans to dispatch the planes that scores of witnesses later insisted had fired down on Greenwood. Hurley added that the leaders "never put forth any effort at all to prevent [the burning] whatever. [And they] said if they [the Black community] started anything at all, to kill every damn son of a bitch they could find."

Others recalled that uniformed Tulsan police officers not only failed to prevent atrocities but also openly participated themselves. In the days after the burning, the daughter of a Tulsan detective passed out fistfuls of Blackjack chewing gum to her neighborhood friends, bragging that her father had snatched a quantity of it from one of the looted stores in Greenwood.

"I saw men of my own race, sworn officers, on three occasions search Negroes whose hands were up," said Thomas Higgins, a White resident from Wichita, Kansas, who was visiting Tulsa when the catastrophe broke out. "And not finding weapons, [they] extracted what money was found on them. If a Negro protested, he was shot."

A Black sheriff's deputy, V. B. Bostic, later testified that a

White police officer rousted his wife and himself from their home, poured oil on the floor, and set a match to it.

Another White policeman was known to have raced home at the height of the attack to change out of his uniform before hurrying back to Greenwood, where he led a group of looters through Black homes and businesses.

HE LED A GROUP OF LOOTERS THROUGH BLACK HOMES AND BUSINESSES

In yet another case, the young bricklayer, Laurel Buck, later testified that he had tried to join the assault on Greenwood early on June 1 but was restrained by a single policeman at the corner of Cincinnati Avenue and Archer Street. As Buck lingered there with several hundred others, he saw two uniformed officers walk up the east side of Cincinnati, breaking windows of the Black-owned buildings with pool cues. Smoke poured from the shattered panes seconds after the officers entered.

Yet an overarching mystery remained eighty years later. Who masterminded the attack that destroyed Greenwood, and who led the impressive mobilization of White Tulsans that preceded it? Who recruited mob members by the hundreds from Tulsa's homes, theaters, cafés, and businesses and so efficiently dispatched them to the most strategic points on the edge of the Black community? Was it the Klan? The police? Both?

WHO MASTERMINDED THE ATTACK THAT DESTROYED GREENWOOD?

Ultimately, only the participants knew for sure, and they weren't talking.

But one thing was certain. The infamous whistle sounded at 5:08 a.m., and when it did, the White mob moved forth like a well-trained army, as a single ruthless organism. Its passions were harnessed to a terribly efficient result.

After the last Black defenders had been vanquished, White gangsters moved from house to house and from business to business, ordering people outside or blowing the locks from buildings already abandoned.

They shot Black people who resisted, as well as men in homes where firearms were discovered. At dozens of places, Black people rushed from burning buildings with their hands in the air and screaming, "Don't shoot! Don't shoot!"

Don't shoot! Don't shoot! The White mob then systematically ransacked the residences, ripping telephones from walls and trampling family photos and other belongings that had obvious sentimental value.

White women carrying shopping bags sometimes followed the mob into Black homes, foraging frantically through closets, bureaus, and trunks to snatch clothing, jewelry, silverware, and curtains. They tore into straw-filled mattresses. White men and boys stole Victrolas, furniture, and pianos from Black homes, often loading the possessions onto waiting trucks.

One was heard to complain as he did that "these damn Negroes have better things than lots of White people do."

And in fact many did.

Black-owned automobiles that could not be driven away were stripped of their tires. An office boy at a Tulsan oil company bragged that day about driving off with a luxury sedan owned by a Black doctor.

"You're crazy, man," a coworker told him. "That's stealing."

"Well, if I didn't take it, it would have burned up," the office boy replied.

The arson commenced when the looting was done. The mob piled flammables, such as bedding and wooden furniture, into one room, sprinkled them liberally with kerosene or gasoline, and lit the pile with a torch or a match. White-owned rental properties were virtually the only exceptions, and they were bypassed if the owner was present. The wall of flame moved steadily northward, with Black people, family pets, chickens, cows, horses, mules, and pigs all perishing in the growing inferno.

The efficiency and thoroughness made it seem like the thousands of mob members spread across Greenwood worked from the pages of the same depraved manual—with an efficiency that could be explained, at least in part, by the abundance of White veterans, who employed military tactics they had used at war against their Black fellow citizens at home.

Some historians later suggested that the attack was not at all premeditated but a spontaneous act born of pent-up hatreds that, once released, have their own predictable methodology, one on common display across world history—that White Tulsans on the night of May 31 and morning of June 1 engaged in the lowest of human behavior. A pogrom. Ethnic cleansing. Genocide. A massacre.

Similar behavior has happened since and continues to happen again and again across the globe. From the Parsley massacre of Haitians in the Dominican Republic in 1937, the extermination of the Jewish communities of Germany and Poland two decades later during World War II, Bengali Hindus in Pakistan in 1971, Cambodians in the late 1970s, the Balkan and Rwandan genocides in the 1990s, the Darfuri genocide in Sudan beginning in 2003, and of the Uyghur in China and Rohingya in Myanmar more recently to the steadily rising count of missing and murdered Indigenous women in the United States and Canada.

The Tulsan mob advanced, whether under orders or not—terrorizing, killing, stealing, and burning. In the process, they forged a legacy of atrocity that rivaled the worst of wartime. Many people find it difficult to believe that this degree of savagery took place in the United States.

TERRORIZING, KILLING, STEALING, AND BURNING

And while Tulsa's massacre was perhaps the worst of countless instances of White mob violence, the reality of White mobs terrorizing innocent Black people remained common until the 1960s.

In Tulsa, there were so many horrific stories. All alike in important ways but all so different, too. Most were too terrible, too horrifying, and too reprehensible for the people who perpetrated them to admit, much less for them to own up to or take responsibility for their actions in public. Otherwise reputable citizens ransacked and looted homes, desecrated dead bodies with their bare hands, and attached corpses to their cars and then dragged them through the streets.

As the years passed, both White people and Black pushed the particulars into the hidden corners of reprobate minds and broken hearts. Many of Tulsa's White residents were unable to face what they, their family members, their friends and neighbors, and their civic leaders had done to fellow human beings—with many of whom they had relationships of one sort or another.

What did it say about who they were?

What did it reveal about their souls?

Who was really more civilized?

Greenwood's Black residents didn't talk about the massacre because they felt humiliated, depressed, ashamed, enraged, vulnerable, exposed. Many continued to live and work among murderers, reliant upon them for their livelihood. But truth be told, no place in the United States was safe, even in the big cities up North. Perhaps if the Black survivors didn't bring it up, White Tulsans wouldn't engage in such depravity again.

The memories eventually took on the hazy tint of a dream. Many people tried to convince themselves that none of it had really happened, that nothing so terrible could have taken place right there in Tulsa, that people could not hate that much, that it was all just a particularly awful nightmare.

But then an offhand remark made while rocking on a Greenwood porch swing, sipping lemonade with friends on a hot summer night, would cause a terrible story to come bursting out. Then came another and another because so many people had them. Porch swings rocked faster and faster as the stories came forth, and there could be no more denial of what had happened.

Kinney Booker and George Monroe, old friends, had two of those stories.

Kinney was just eight when it happened. He had huddled with four siblings in the attic of their family's home on Frankfort Street when the mob came and abducted their father at gunpoint.

"Please don't set my home on fire," Kinney's father pleaded.

But the White mob ignored him and did just that. Fortunately, Kinney and his siblings managed to escape, but outside, bullets were zinging everywhere.

"Kinney, is the world on fire?" his younger sister asked.

"I don't think so," Kinney answered. "But we are in deep trouble."

A few blocks away on Easton Avenue, young George Monroe and his family were in deep trouble too. George was only five then, the son of a man who owned a skating rink and a rental house next door to their large family home. From the window, George could touch Mount Zion Baptist Church. He enjoyed watching the people walk by on Sunday mornings in their finest clothes and watching them park their cars on the gravel street on their way to worship.

But during the massacre, four White men carried burning torches toward the house. With George's father away, his mother shooed her children beneath a bed and then hid herself as the White men barged in and set the curtains on fire.

George hadn't pulled his hand completely under the bed, and one mobster stepped on his fingers as he walked by. George would have yelled if his older sister hadn't slapped her hand over his mouth. When the men left, he and his siblings scrambled from beneath the bed and escaped with their mother while their house went up in flames.

Coach Seymour Williams was a gruff fellow, a veteran who insisted on bending the football players at Booker T. Washington High School to his own fierce will with military-style discipline. As a result, his teams always won more games than they lost.

He was just a first-year teacher and coach when the massacre happened. Watching the other houses burn, he resolved that the White mob would not take the home he had made with his wife without a fight.

"Come on out of there," one White man called from outside. "We won't bother you if you come now."

Like hell, the coach thought, his .45-caliber pistol loaded and ready. He knew how to use it too. Those White men out there might get him eventually, but they would pay a dear price in their own blood.

His wife knew him well enough to read his thoughts.

"Don't you dare take that gun out there," she warned him.

"I'll do as I damn well please," Seymour replied.

He started toward the front door, pistol in hand, ignoring his wife and several of her friends, who were also in the house and were hysterical. The women wept, pleaded with him, tugged at his arms. As a last resort, his wife stuck out her leg and tripped her husband. The women snatched away his pistol when he fell to the floor and immediately tossed it out the back window.

"Where's your gun?" a White man asked him when Seymour finally obeyed his wife and walked outside with his hands up.

"Don't have one," he replied, which was the lifesaving truth.

CHAPTER 16

Dr. Jackson

D r. Andrew Jackson could hear the noise and the chaos while he was tending to the wounded inside the hospital.

Many of Dr. Jackson's friends had served as Army surgeons during the war, and he had marveled at their gruesome but exciting tales of their adventures overseas. He often wondered what war must have been like. Now, as he tended to the wounded inside the hospital, he felt he knew—wounded men crying for drinks of water and for their mamas, limbs destroyed, people shot in the head and the gut, the nauseating smell of burning human flesh.

But this rampage had not occurred in some distant, exotic land.

THIS WAS TULSA, OKLAHOMA

This was Tulsa, Oklahoma.

And these dead and wounded weren't strangers; they were Dr. Jackson's friends and neighbors.

In the middle of Greenwood's worst night, as the prominent doctor took a break from his duties, White people were said to be massing for a major attack on Greenwood at dawn. If he wanted to check on his home and get some rest, this might be the only chance he would have.

Dr. Jackson drove by the Elgin Avenue home of his sister Minnie Mae. The windows were dark, and he assumed that his sister, her husband, and their two girls had escaped. Dr. Jackson drove three blocks farther north and decided to park on Elgin, one block east of Detroit, because the White mob had formed a battlefield on Standpipe Hill, just up from the front of his house. *Thank God he'd sent his wife, Julia, away the night before*, Dr. Jackson thought. That was one less worry, at least.

Dr. Jackson grabbed his black leather medical bag from the Ford's backseat and set off on the short hike home. He saw the shadowy silhouettes of White men milling atop Standpipe but was relieved to see that his home was undamaged and a dim light was burning in the window of the basement apartment that he and his wife rented to an older gentleman named Oliver.

The doctor paused and surveyed his block. Dr. Bridgewater's house and most of the others were dark. Dr. Bridgewater had spent part of the night with Dr. Jackson, tending to the wounded. Most of the other families on the block were already refugees. In the other direction, lights burned in the home of Professor Hughes, which reminded Jackson of the house call he had scheduled there for eight o'clock that same morning. Hughes's wife had been running a fever for days, and Jackson had begun to fear the onset of pneumonia. But on a night when so many had died already, her illness seemed almost trivial.

Dr. Jackson knocked lightly on the back door to the basement apartment. His tenant, Mr. Oliver, answered in seconds, as if he had been expecting the doctor, though it was three o'clock in the morning.

"May I stay with you tonight?" Dr. Jackson asked. "It isn't a night to be alone."

"Of course, Dr. Jackson," Mr. Oliver said, flashing a toothless grin. "It is a good night for company, I agree. I've never seen such a thing."

I've never seen such a thing

By candlelight, they spoke about what had been going on but both were exhausted. Oliver blew out the candle and lay down on a pallet on the floor, while Jackson settled into an old rocking chair. Within seconds, both men were sound asleep.

But their slumber was brief.

Gunfire awakened them less than two hours later, so they sat together until the sun came up, listening to what sounded like a persistent thunderstorm though the brightening sky was without a cloud.

Dr. Jackson knew that the latest outbreak of shooting meant more Black men wounded, but he was hesitant to leave Mr. Oliver and his house. When he finally picked up his bag, it was too late. He could see from the window that White gangs had taken over. He and Mr. Oliver were trapped. Soon the smell of smoke grew more intense.

"Mr. Oliver, I think it's time you and I go on," Dr. Jackson said.

"If that's what you say, Dr. Jackson," Mr. Oliver consented.

Dr. Jackson walked out first and started around his house to the right with Mr. Oliver following several steps behind. When he rounded the corner of the house, Dr. Jackson put his hands in the air, leaning into the slight incline that led to the street in front, where several White men with rifles were milling about. He recognized one of them, nodding to the old White judge, John Oliphant, who lived just a few doors over on Easton and whom he had previously treated as a patient.

There were seven or eight White men in all, a couple of them dressed in khaki military uniforms but most wearing civilian clothes. Dr. Jackson quickly glanced around for a uniformed policeman but found none and figured the men standing in front of him would have to do.

"Here I am," Dr. Jackson said to them. "Take me."

Two of the mob members raised their guns.

"Don't shoot him!" Oliphant yelled. "That's Dr. Jackson."

But the boy with the biggest rifle, the one in the white shirt and cap, didn't listen. He fired two shots. When the doctor fell, a second man stood above him and fired another shot into Dr. Jackson's leg. The older Mr. Oliver, who had been walking behind, dove behind a telephone pole when the mobsters turned on him. They fired a couple of errant bullets in his direction before the other White men grabbed away their guns.

The smoke-blackened sky swirled above Jackson's head as White faces peered down at him.

"Is that true?" asked one of the men in khaki. "Are you Dr. Jackson?"

Dr. Jackson nodded.

"Oh, shoot," the man dressed as a soldier said. "Those boys have done it now."

The men wearing military garb hailed a passing car and loaded Dr. Jackson into the backseat, where the world went black.

THOSE BOYS HAVE DONE IT NOW

He woke up to see his older brother, Townsend Jr.; Minnie Mae; and his father, the great captain, looking down on him. All of their faces were shiny with tears. Townsend Jr. cradled his brother in his arms in the shade of a large oak. Shortly thereafter, he passed away.

Dr. Jackson's final journey began a few days later when his family said their tearful goodbyes at the Frisco Station, and his casket was loaded onto a train. Only his father would accompany the body on that trip west to Guthrie, so the rest of the family and scores of the doctor's friends and patients watched the train huff off past the towers of downtown Tulsa and disappear into the distance.

Dr. Jackson's relatives later collected his obituaries that had appeared in newspapers across the nation, stories that quoted both Black and White physicians who paid the slain doctor great tribute.

Once, Captain Jackson had held his son up as a living specimen of Black promise in America, an example of the limitless opportunities for people of his race if they applied themselves with the same fervor and grace exhibited by Andrew.

Now, as the elder Jackson sat alone, shame mixed with his grief.

How blind he had been.

What a fool.

The young Black firebrands in Tulsa and elsewhere across the country had been right all along. Black progress against White mob violence had been an illusion.

BLACK PROGRESS HAD BEEN AN ILLUSION Despite appearances, despite the gains of men like Andrew, White hatred burned with as much intensity in 1921 as it had in the years when Andrew's father was still enslaved by a White man. That was the cruel truth that the short life of Dr. Andrew C. Jackson represented now.

Captain Jackson was sixty-five at the time of the burning.

Finally, after all those years of stubborn optimism came the heartbreak that overwhelmed his resilient hopefulness. As he sat alone in the train, he retraced his journey across the hate-filled nation, from the Civil War battle of Lookout Mountain when he was just a boy to Tulsa's marauding White looters, murderers, and arsonists when he was old.

Why, he wondered on the train, had he taken the trouble to learn Latin on those nights in Memphis?

Why had he and his family fled from Memphis, thinking they could somehow outrun the White lynch mob?

Why had they bothered to leave Guthrie?

The years in Greenwood had been the most illusory, the most falsely seductive, of all.

But now he would finally concede that there was no outrunning hatred of the sort that still lived in the hearts of so many White people.

THERE WAS NO OUTRUNNING HATRED

Back in Greenwood, he would eventually rebuild his home and barbershop on Cincinnati Avenue, which had been among the first Black properties White arsonists torched in the madness. But his view of the world would never be the same.

Once, so long ago, he had put his son on a train headed east to medical school. Now he and Andrew traveled together on one final journey, west to Guthrie, where the old man buried his son in the family plot next to his mother, Sophronia.

A lifetime of Townsend Jackson's dreams were buried with him.

CHAPTER 17

June 1, 1921: Troops Arrive

At 9:15 a.m. on June 1, a train carrying 109 members of the Oklahoma National Guard pulled into Frisco Station from Oklahoma City.

The soldiers were groggy after the trip and sweating through their mohair uniforms in the morning heat. Many were World War I veterans who had endured similar discomfort before, but they assumed they had left the most apocalyptic visions of war behind them in Europe. Since the National Guard was segregated, all of its members were White. Their mouths hung open as the locomotive inched to a stop in the heart of Tulsa on the railroad tracks that had divided the White lynch mob from Black defenders just a few hours before. The windows of Frisco Station had been shot out and the exterior walls of the building were pocked by bullets in hundreds of places.

But it was the smoke that most reminded the arriving soldiers of the war in Europe—a dense black cloud in the north that transformed a brilliant morning into a premature dusk.

Adjutant General Charles Barrett, another war veteran, commanded the troops. He, too, was dumbfounded by what he saw when the National Guard arrived in Tulsa.

"In all my experience," Barrett said the next day, "I have never witnessed such scenes as prevailed in this city when I arrived at the height of rioting. Twenty-five thousand Whites, armed to the teeth, were ranging in utter and ruthless defiance of every concept of law and righteousness. Motor cars bristling with guns swept through the city, firing at will."

IN UTTER AND RUTHLESS DEFIANCE OF EVERY CONCEPT OF LAW AND RIGHTEOUSNESS

Trainloads of National Guard troops would continue to arrive in the city until about eleven thirty that morning. For most of Black Tulsa, however, their arrival had come far too late. A tremendous amount of destruction had already taken place.

Plus, in spite of the horror General Barrett was witnessing, he was in no hurry to wade into the inferno. Instead, after they piled out of the boxcars, Barrett allowed his men to break ranks and eat breakfast while he consulted with city officials. A civilian who approached one of Barrett's National Guardsmen complained about that outrage and was promptly arrested.

If Barrett and his troops had acted promptly when they arrived, they might have saved the splendid homes of Greenwood's leading doctors, lawyers, and businessmen along Detroit Avenue. Until that point, the dwellings had been spared because the mob mistakenly assumed those substantial residences could only have belonged to wealthy White people. The magnificent homes of Greenwood's Black elite did neighbor homes of some wealthy White Tulsans.

Among the people who owned a home in the neighborhood

near Detroit Avenue was the prominent and retired Judge John Oliphant, Dr. Jackson's neighbor.

Judge Oliphant was seventy-three years old and had been a lawyer in Tulsa since before Oklahoma was a state, when it consisted of Oklahoma Territory and Indian Territory. A major local power broker, he knew every politician and public official worth knowing in the state.

So he, too, was pleased to hear that General Barrett, another of his cronies, would command the arriving troops. He knew General Barrett to be a man of action and integrity, a man who would surely succeed where the Tulsan police and every other responsible authority had failed so miserably that morning.

The approaching troop train's distant whistle was the old lawyer's first real hope that something resembling order might finally be imposed on the insanity that had swept across his city.

Judge Oliphant had built his spacious home near the top of Standpipe Hill sixteen years before. His Easton Street address had a spectacular view of downtown Tulsa in one direction and the foothills of the Ozarks in the other. He had been living there for years by the time Black neighbors began building equally fancy homes on Detroit Avenue just below him.

At first what he viewed as an intrusion rankled Oliphant. But, to his surprise, he soon came to find his new neighbors quite agreeable—more so, in fact, than a lot of the White people he knew. They were educated, polished, and, to judge by the size of their homes, had a good deal of money. They included newspaperman Andrew Smitherman, Dr. R. T. Bridgewater, Dr. Jackson, and the teacher J. W. Hughes.

Educationally and economically, those Black professionals

were a far cry from the low-income Black people that White Tulsans seemed to despise most. With everything happening that morning, Oliphant couldn't help but feel sorry for his Black neighbors. Yet sympathy was not what was on his mind now. Oliphant's house sat virtually next door to Black-owned property, and if the burning wasn't halted somehow, the morning's strong easterly breeze would ensure the flames spreading across Greenwood would dance right up to his doorstep.

What a morning it had been—disgraceful even by the lawless standards of boomtown Tulsa. Oliphant woke up thinking he had landed in one of those war movies with soldiers from local units of the National Guard and veterans in khaki uniforms lined up along the crest of Standpipe Hill, just south of his home. They were firing east toward the Black men holed up in the belfry of Mount Zion Baptist Church, inside Booker T. Washington High School, in the homes along Elgin, or inside the big brick grocery store nearby. The Black defenders fired back, some of their bullets landing almost at Oliphant's doorstep.

Just after dawn, as Judge Oliphant observed the battle, one Black neighbor, the friendly man who ran a grocery store down the way, poked his head out his front door.

WHAT A MORNING IT HAD BEEN

"You better get on out of there and give up so you can get some protection," Judge Oliphant yelled at the man, who waved at him and disappeared inside.

The man and his family emerged from their home with their hands up a few minutes later, heading toward the White soldiers at the top of the hill.

Then Judge Oliphant saw Professor Hughes and his wife, and several other men and their families, come out of their homes on Detroit to surrender to the thugs, leaving their property to the White mob still hungry for Black-owned buildings to destroy. That was not right, Oliphant knew. But of greater interest to him, those homes were the last ones standing between the spreading inferno and his place. So the old man telephoned the police department, reminding whoever answered the phone that John Oliphant was a very important man in these parts and insisting officers be sent to his address.

"Send me ten police officers, and I will protect all this property and save a million dollars' worth of stuff," Judge Oliphant said. "And do it on the double."

"We'll do the best we can" was the answer he received, but the officers never came.

Judge Oliphant called the fire department next but was told the firefighters had orders not to leave the station.

As the sun climbed through the smoke, an angry, frightened old White man stood alone in the street. He confronted four different groups of roaming White mobsters carrying jugs of coal oil, gasoline, torches, and guns.

"If you burn those houses, you'll burn me out, too," Judge Oliphant pleaded with them. "I'm Judge Oliphant, and if you leave those houses alone, I'll make damn sure Negroes never live in that row of houses again."

The judge wasn't sure he could make good on the promise, but it seemed to satisfy the first few bands, which he managed to stave off until he heard the whistle of General Barrett's train.

Only then did the old lawyer allow himself a sigh of relief. He scribbled a note and signed it, sending a neighbor boy to meet the train and deliver his plea to the general.

If Barrett could spare just fifteen troops, he wrote, Judge Oliphant could protect the last homes on Detroit. But they must hurry because clearly the mob's appetite for destruction had not yet been satisfied.

Judge Oliphant heard the locomotive hiss when the train pulled into the station to the south, and he kept glancing over his shoulder in that direction. But precious minutes turned into hours, and no help came.

It was eleven o'clock before Barrett and his soldiers, stomachs now filled with breakfast food, marched over the hill with their bayonets.

By then, the homes on Detroit were gone.

Around the time the National Guard pulled into town, streets that had been full of all-male, White mobs began to fill with White women and children.

After the fiercest fighting was finished, Detroit Avenue began to resemble a street festival. Judge Oliphant witnessed hundreds of jubilant White people pillage the Black-owned homes of pianos, Victrola phonograph record players, clothing of all kinds, and musical instruments.

The White women broke into homes and emerged carrying linens and pillowcases filled with loot. One White man sat down at a piano taken from a Black family's home and tapped out a happy ditty while other White people sang along and danced in the street.

The actual burning was left to the notorious bootlegger named Cowboy Long and his crew. Judge Oliphant had heard versions of the same statement several times from various bands of mobsters that morning: "Cowboy Long will fix this home when he gets here."

When the man finally appeared, Oliphant was stunned to see a shiny badge pinned to the chest of his dirty denim shirt. Two companions were dressed in civilian clothes and also wore badges.

The fourth man with them was a uniformed police officer.

None were in the mood for Judge Oliphant's protestations or his promise to keep the Black people out of the neighborhood.

"We're going to make the destruction complete," one of the men bragged.

WE'RE GOING TO MAKE THE DESTRUCTION COMPLETE

They went after Dr. Jackson's house first, barging inside with their torches and canisters of gasoline.

Of course, Dr. Jackson was long gone from his home by then, shot down by those boys two hours before. Oliphant was standing twenty feet away when that had happened, and of all the miserable things he had witnessed that morning, to him, the treatment of the kindly physician was easily the worst. But now, as he watched Jackson's house burn, and the others with it, he wondered if Jackson wasn't better off dead after all.

CHAPTER 18

Sickening Aftermath

Margaret Dickinson's mother was often too ill to care for her youngest child, so from the time Margaret was old enough to walk, the little girl accompanied her father to job sites, to meetings with Tulsan power brokers, or to any of the other myriad engagements befitting the owner of the young city's most prominent construction firm.

Wilfred Dickinson's company had built the Tulsa Hotel, the movie theaters, the Drew Building, and the homes of Tulsa's millionaire oilmen and its most prominent doctors. He had achieved success beyond the wildest imaginings of a man who came to the United States from Britain around the turn of the century.

Margaret loved observing the way that Tulsa's most important men treated her father with deference. And she loved the way his workers revered him, the dozens of men—mostly Black carpenters and bricklayers—who tipped their hats to Margaret's father as a sign of respect. In turn, the White company owner called each of his workers by name and never failed to inquire about their families, humane behavior very uncharacteristic of a White boss.

In fact, one of the Black employees, a man named Charlie Mason, was both Wilfred Dickinson's foreman and his best friend.

Margaret's father might have been well acquainted with the mayor, the city commissioners, the police commissioner, and Tulsa's business leaders, but when faced with a particularly perplexing concern, it was with Charlie that he consulted.

A common memory of Margaret's childhood was seeing her father and Charlie Mason sequestered to the side of a construction site, carrying on a long and obviously important conversation.

None of that struck her as odd whatsoever. Befriending Black people seemed as natural to her father as breathing was, and it was something quite typical of his expansive spirit.

Over the years, Margaret came to think frequently about her father's relationship with Charlie Mason and of his fondness for his Black employees. She remembered his great satisfaction in knowing that he made life better for those men and their families. As time passed, Margaret eventually came to understand that those feelings were largely responsible for her father's anguish on June 1, 1921, and in the days that followed. His violet eyes were ablaze beneath the brim of his bowler that day as he and Margaret first surveyed the stricken city, his skin blazing red from his forehead to the collar of his crisp white shirt. Even his mustache seemed to glow.

"Are you mad, Daddy?" Margaret asked him that day as they drove.

THIS IS THE PLACE HATRED CAN LEAD

"No, I'm just sick from what I see," he said. "Margaret, this is the place hatred can lead."

About midnight the night before, Wilfred Dickinson had awakened his wife and children, hurrying them into the basement and insisting everyone be silent. They didn't need to ask why because, from the cold cement basement floor where they huddled together in blankets, they listened to gunshots and sirens that wailed continuously outside.

At midday, Margaret's father learned that the National Guard had finally arrived to patrol the streets and that the governor had declared the city to be under martial law. She'd followed when her father left the house a few minutes later and climbed into the passenger seat of the Dodge.

As they drove off, Margaret was mesmerized by a black cloud of smoke so close it made her eyes water. All that smoke, yet so many White people were milling around on Main Street—hundreds of them, maybe thousands—out on a Wednesday afternoon when everyone should have been working or at school.

And she had never seen so many guns. All the men seemed to have one, particularly those piled into the touring cars that raced up and down the street.

Then another strange sight. Margaret wondered, *Why, in the midst of all the ruckus, would a Black man be sleeping on the Frisco railroad tracks?* He was dressed in overalls and a gray shirt with one sleeve ripped away to reveal a thick, brown arm.

Margaret realized then that the man was dead.

The men in the two cars just in front of them saw the man too. They shot up his corpse then roared away, laughing gleefully.

"Don't look," her father said. "That is not a good sight to see."

But Margaret could not look away. She looked directly at the dead man. A terrible thought came to her as she studied him.

"Daddy, is that one of our [men]?" she asked.

"No," her dad answered, his face burning red.

They crossed the railroad tracks, passing the edge of the devastated Black district. She saw a few old Black couples on the front steps of places that had burned or in chairs near the street, staring blankly at Margaret and her father as they drove slowly past.

Two White farmers saw dark shapes appear on the horizon about daybreak, moving slowly toward them out of the huge cloud of smoke to the south.

"What in hell is that?" one said to the other. "A herd of buffalo?"

"I'll be damned," the other said.

There were hundreds of Black people of every age and description fleeing from the violence. Many were carrying children or pulling mules or horses haltered to ropes.

The people seemed to be in a collective trance until they saw the White farmers standing at the fence along the road. They snuck fearful, sideways glances at the men, half expecting them to produce guns and resume the shooting. Not knowing whether or not these White men were safe, the people picked up their pace until they had passed them.

Similarly, every time a car approached from the direction of

Tulsa, dozens of displaced Black people would flee into the nearby woods until the vehicle had gone by. Then they would return to the road and continue their trek to nowhere.

A similar sight played out all day on every road and every set of railroad tracks leaving Tulsa. Masses of Black people trudged away from the inferno like characters from some biblical passage in the book of Exodus. Most of the way, they walked in silence, but sometimes they commented on the day's growing heat or asked for the whereabouts of loved ones.

Or they asked this question: "How far had they burned when you left?"

They walked, and carried their children, and herded their animals from Greenwood all the way to the edge of towns like Sapulpa, Owasso, Broken Arrow, and Sperry, places twenty and thirty miles away. White people in those towns heard that Black people had tried to take over Tulsa, and they met the escaped families on the outskirts with rifles, even though they rarely crossed the city limits and never caused the slightest disturbance. Instead, the Black survivors congregated in the hills and wooded hollows and in places like Flat Rock, where five hundred refugees built a crude camp along the Delaware Creek.

With every step, they wondered when the White mob would come back with their guns and torches and airplanes to finish what they had begun in Tulsa. One little girl, spooked by the sound of nearby gunfire, sprinted from the band of refugees, so fearful that she attempted to ford a fast-flowing creek near Sperry and drowned.

THEY WALKED, AND CARRIED THEIR CHILDREN

Sometimes the fleeing Black families encountered caring White allies.

Every day for a week after the burning, Merrill Phelps and his wife, Ruth, hid twenty or more Black refugees in the basement of their new home in the country, a day's walk north of Tulsa.

The White couple were teachers before they'd been lured to northeast Oklahoma by the higher pay of the oil refineries. Both believed the Golden Rule applied equally, no matter a person's race. So Ruth put on extra pots of beans and pork belly, feeding the families who hid in their basement during the day before they escaped toward the Osage Hills under the cover of darkness.

Each morning, another group would appear at their door, pleading for food and sanctuary, then huddling quietly in the basement to rest. They would eat Ruth's beans and cry and stare blankly into the shadows before setting off to God knows where when the sun went down.

The people didn't talk much about what had happened to them in Tulsa, and the Phelpses didn't think it polite to pry. The couple had heard about a Black uprising, of course, but could not imagine what might have inspired such terror and despair in those people, at least not until Merrill Phelps and his wife drove into Tulsa to tour the ruins of Greenwood several days later.

The horror was self-evident then, and the couple was doubly glad to have offered the smallest comfort to the victims of those depredations.

Additional help showed up on the afternoon of June 1.

Red Cross volunteers had been dispatched into the country-side surrounding Tulsa to try to end the exodus, pleading with the Black families they encountered to return to the city, promising that they would be safe there now.

One Black pastor finally convinced seventy-five members of his congregation to hike back into town. Once they arrived, they were promptly marched to the detention camp at the Tulsa County Fairgrounds and treated like criminals or prisoners of war. Women, children, and old people were placed under the guard of soldiers who often added to their humiliation by taunting them.

Other Black Tulsans trickled back in small groups over the next several days. Or they never returned at all; thousands moved to Chicago, New York, San Francisco, Los Angeles, or smaller towns in Oklahoma and Arkansas, where they tried to put the great burning behind them. But most found that impossible because Tulsa's disgrace had traumatized them.

It is likely that many of Greenwood's Black residents suffered mental and even physical health issues for their lifetime. Symptoms such as edginess, fear, fatigue, flashbacks, nightmares, difficulty concentrating, shame, hopelessness, and a sense of helplessness are those that we now know can be associated with mental

They tried to put the great burning behind them

illnesses such as depression, anxiety, post-traumatic stress disorder, and others, which are often triggered by traumatic events.

White Tulsan grocer Hugh Gary was determined to make sure his children knew the price of sin. He may have been fond of the "good" Black people who worked for him and helped to raise his children, but for Black people to stand up against White supremacy was immoral to him, so naturally they must pay the price.

That afternoon of June 1, Gary loaded his oldest sons, Hubert and Richard, into his Dodge, and they set off driving north into the heart of the devastation. Once they crossed over into Greenville, the boys' jaws dropped open and their eyes were like saucers. But Gary could hardly blame them, for the destruction surpassed anything in his own wildest imaginings.

Some walls of the larger brick buildings still stood in places, but the roofs were gone and the interiors were completely gutted. Skinny chimneys rose toward the sky, but the buildings to which they had been attached were disintegrated. Wooden homes were intact here and there, as were almost all of the outhouses because the mob had not wanted to waste their coal oil and gasoline on those. But most of the homes were piles of smoldering gray ash, with metal bedsteads or stoves or pipes occasionally protruding from the mess. Mules, horses, and cows remained nervously tethered to naked trees, whose leaves had been burned away.

Then they drove west toward Standpipe Hill to obtain a panoramic view. After that, they drove to Convention Hall, where

White men marching around with guns were detaining Black people. Flatbed trucks rumbled back and forth with Black people sitting gloomily in back. A new group of Black prisoners was marched in every few minutes.

Gary sped the boys south out to Cedar Bluff Dairy, then off of the paved road and onto a rough dirt road that curved through the hills outside of town. After a few bumpy miles, they spotted a flatbed truck, laboring to get close to the edge of a deep gully. Hugh parked his car nearby, and he and the boys got out and watched. It took only a few seconds for the boys to realize what was on the truck: the bodies of about twenty-five dead Black people.

Two men unloaded the corpses into a gully, one at a time. After every third or fourth body, they would stop and shovel dirt on top of them. The men were burying Black Greenwood residents in a mass grave.

"It'll take a week to get them buried at this rate," Gary said, chuckling at how hard it was to dislodge the rocky soil. But humor aside, he was not about to let the boys miss the lesson.

"This is what happens when you sin," he told them as they watched the bodies being swung off the truck. "They did something mighty wrong, so they deserve what they got."

They returned to the car after a few minutes and drove back to town. Hubert and Richard were particularly obedient for a long time after that.

The Stanley-McCune Funeral Home provided S. M. Jackson with a place to sleep because the White funeral parlor was swamped with both Black and White corpses, but particularly Black bodies. The White funeral directors had somehow located Jackson that afternoon among the mass of Black prisoners at Convention Hall and requested his help with the bodies. They thought it best that the Black dead be embalmed by one of their own, so they offered Jackson twelve dollars and fifty cents a body to accomplish the task. That was half of what White undertakers were paid, but Jackson figured he was lucky to have the work with the way things were in Tulsa at that moment.

The White mob had torched Jackson's own funeral parlor at 600 Archer Street, also incinerating the four bodies he had been preparing for burial before the burning broke out. That galled Jackson as much as anything, but now he had no other place to lay his head. Maybe it was easier for Jackson than most to stomach the horror because he was used to seeing dead people.

They first sent him on a truck with a bunch of White men to pick up the dead all over Greenwood. They returned to the funeral home toward evening, and Jackson got to work, embalming twenty-six Black bodies over the next few days, though he knew that was just a fraction of the number who had been killed.

HE KNEW THAT WAS JUST A FRACTION OF THE NUMBER WHO HAD BEEN KILLED

Indeed, the rumor mill was rife with stories of how many Black folks had been slaughtered.

Some people talked about seeing sixty bodies laid out on a sandbar in the Arkansas River. Others said they saw many others just dumped into the river itself, or they ended up in common graves out in the country, where they couldn't be found.

The only bodies that really needed embalming were those with an upstanding family seeing to them. For every one of those, Jackson figured there were five others that just disappeared.

He was grateful that he knew only two of the people he worked on that week. One was a neighbor named Mr. Howard. The other was Dr. Andrew C. Jackson, the kindly physician.

Later that afternoon of June 1, Margaret and Wilfred Dickinson set out again, this time to survey the situation downtown. The two walked hand in hand up the street, eavesdropping on conversations among desperate restaurant owners, shopkeepers, and hoteliers. Suddenly, they had no Black employees to cook for them, or wash their dishes, or stock their shelves, or fix up their beds in the hotels.

Tulsa was now experiencing the greatest labor problem in its history. All the Black folks who kept the city running were dead, wounded, burned, locked up in detention camps, or wandering around in the countryside like lost sheep. Rumor had it that many White women in town had to cook their first meals in years and suffered the great indignity of having to hang their own laundry.

Near the courthouse, Margaret and her father met a skinny, nervous-looking man with round glasses and a pointy nose, Mayor Thaddeus Evans. The two men gravely shook hands.

"We've got all these Negroes rounded up in McNulty Park, but we can't keep them there," the mayor said. "Some of them are sick, and some of them are hurt, and I don't know what in the world we will do when it rains. So we've got to get them out of there."

"That's true," Wilfred said.

"I've seen a lot of your men in there," the mayor said. "I'll call you when I'm ready, and I'll release them all to you if you'll vouch for them. We're not letting any of those Coloreds out unless a White will give the okay."

"You let me know," Margaret's father said.

They shook hands again, and Mayor Evans rushed off down the street. Sure enough, the mayor's call came shortly after Margaret and her father returned home. Wilfred left by himself a few minutes later, saying he was heading for McNulty Park. His Dodge lumbered back up the street a few hours after that, weighted down with his workers and their families.

Charlie Mason drove one of the two Dickinson Company trucks that followed Wilfred's car, each loaded with homeless Black families. At the rear was the horse and wagon her father's workers usually used to haul bricks. But now the wagon was full of people. When the trucks and the wagon pulled up, the men hopped down from the beds, assisting their wives, children, and the elderly to the ground.

Neighbors glared from their front doors or windows at the dozens of Black people in front of the Dickinson place, so Wilfred quickly herded them inside.

Some of the men recognized Margaret, tipping their hats to her and smiling sadly. Margaret's mother held the door as the families made their way inside, jostling for places to sit on the floor of the basement, in the garage, or in an apartment behind the house.

Small children scrambled about the knees of women who moaned and wept. Some of the men cried too. Some looked angry. Others looked ashamed. But all looked so weary.

For much of the next week, Margaret's mother and the Dickinson family's Black maid cooked around the clock. Margaret, her older siblings, and her father carried tubs of food to the families from morning until night—fried chicken, mashed potatoes, soups, stews, meat sandwiches, oranges and apples, lemonade, cookies for the children, and cakes.

When the people were fed, Margaret watched her father move from family to family, quietly commiserating with them. At other times, Margaret saw her father sitting alone behind the desk in his study, staring out the window with puffy sacks beneath his eyes.

The children became Margaret's playmates, so she was sad when her father began loading families into the Dodge. He said that the Red Cross was erecting tents in Greenwood where the homes had been. That was where the families would have to live for the time being. Margaret's father drove them to their new homes, promising to do what he could to get them back on their feet. Understandably, many were reluctant to leave.

Margaret always remembered one of the men in particular.

"Don't send us back, Mr. Dickinson, sir," the man said to her father, tears streaming down his face. "My wife, she's afraid to go on back to Greenwood. At least we're safe here."

Wilfred looked ready to cry himself.

"I'm sorry," Margaret's father told him. "There aren't any beds. There's no room. There's hardly anything for you here."

"Yes, sir, Mr. Dickinson," the man said. "Whatever you say. We thank you kindly for what you and your family have done."

Then the man led his family toward the Dodge. He sat in the front passenger seat and took a young son onto his lap. As they drove off down the street, Margaret saw the little boy poke his hand out the window and wave.

CHAPTER 19

June 1, 1921:
The Assignment
of a Lifetime

N ewspaper reporter Faith Hieronymus scarcely believed her good fortune when she reported for work at the *Tulsa World* on the morning of June 1, 1921.

In her late twenties and ambitious, Faith had come to Tulsa from a small paper in Enid, Oklahoma, the year before, desperate for the challenges the larger city could provide. In the media of the 1920s, tragedy translated into opportunity, and for young reporters like her, the greater the heartbreak, the greater the opportunity to achieve journalistic glory.

The *World*'s coverage of the previous night's chaos had been reserved for the male reporters. But now that the fighting was over and Greenwood was completely burned out, the paper needed a front-page feature to tug at people's heartstrings. One that would support the outrage of the *Tulsa World*'s publisher, Eugene Lorton, whose June 2 editorial would compare Tulsa's marauding White mob with German soldiers who burned, looted, and executed scores of citizens in Belgium during the Great War.

"Members of the superior race," Lorton wrote of the massacre, "boastful of the fact, permitted themselves to degenerate into murderers and vandals; permitted themselves to deal their home community the foulest blow it has ever received in history."

So the editors looked around the newsroom and picked Faith Hieronymus. If anyone could

Murderers and vandals

capture the tragedy of the moment, it was Faith. She was a woman, after all, and fitting the stereotypes of the era, she was certain to be more inclined to feel compassion toward the thousands of homeless Black folks.

The city editor called Faith into his office for a brief pep talk. He said something about seizing the moment, her story being part of history, and the necessity of capturing the small details that would make her writing come alive. Faith's heart pounded with anxiety and excitement as she rushed out of the newsroom.

She jumped off the streetcar a block from the ballpark, and her resolve disappeared the minute McNulty Park came into focus. Her youthful ambition melted away as she took in an otherworldly sea of human misery.

The sight of McNulty Park on that hot afternoon stunned her. The young newspaper reporter gawked for several minutes before remembering to take out her pencil and notepad and start writing down some notes.

The shouts of the National Guard soldiers were what finally jolted her back to her senses.

"Get back!" the soldiers shouted to the White curiosity-seekers crowded along the baseball park's outer fence. "Please get back!"

Someone counted more than four thousand Black people imprisoned at McNulty Park that afternoon, three times more than had been interned at Convention Hall.

Some of the men wore white shirts, bow ties, and expensive hats, with suit coats thrown over their shoulders. Others wore baggy overalls over denim shirts, or they stood without shirts or shoes, their skin glistening with sweat as the sun boosted the afternoon temperature into the humid mid-nineties. Others lay in the soft grass of the outfield.

Women filled the shaded grandstand, fanning themselves with straw hats, weeping, staring off into space, and trying to placate howling infants and confused toddlers. Young children clutched tattered dolls as they wandered through the throng, wailing and calling loudly for mamas and papas they had not seen since the White onslaught began at daybreak.

White soldiers and Red Cross volunteers worked frantically. They hauled tub after tub of ice, water, lemonade, and coffee from trucks parked outside the gates as well as vats of soup, boxes of cheese, crackers, and sandwiches that were rushed to the front of the food line that stretched from the backstop behind home plate to the foul pole in the right-field corner.

Faith wandered through the mass of humanity, trying to get her bearings and jotting down observations here and there.

But eventually she felt embarrassed by her pencil and notepad. She wanted to reach out to the people herself, to help as the Red Cross volunteers were helping. At the same time, she felt constrained by the conventions of journalism, which dictated that she remain detached, as the words of her city editor rang in her head. How could any person, ambitious young reporter or not, remain the least bit indifferent in such a place?

She witnessed one old woman seated on the steps of the dugout, a gray handkerchief tied around her weathered face, staring blankly at the sky as she held a ration of hot vegetable soup that the Red Cross was doling out.

Faith couldn't help herself. She sat down on the step next to the woman.

"Sister, why don't you eat your soup?" she asked softly.

The old woman looked at Faith. The single tears that slid down her face traced a crooked path through the dust on her skin.

"Oh Lordy," she moaned, rocking back and forth. "Me an old woman who's worked so hard all her life, now everything gone. My house burned, my chairs burned, my chickens burned, my carrots and onions burned. Nothing I have but the clothes on my back. Oh Lordy. That I should live to see such trouble come to me."

A young woman stood nearby. When she heard that lament, she added one of her own. She and her husband had saved for years to buy their

THAT I SHOULD LIVE TO SEE SUCH TROUBLE COME TO ME

place, and now it was gone. So was everything else they owned but the rags they wore.

Just then, her husband approached through the crowd, carrying half a loaf of bread.

"Here's some bread, honey," he said. "Can't you eat it?"

The young woman angrily turned her back on him, as if he were the cause of her troubles.

"Eat?" she asked. "And us paupers? I can't eat!"

Faith rose, fighting the urge to drop her notepad and run, ashamed of having intruded on such despair.

A few yards down the grandstand, a Black woman in a clean white maid's uniform sat reading a Bible to a group of young children. The woman was one of the lucky ones. She lived in servants' quarters with a White family on the south side of town. She had come to McNulty Park to tend to the children of her burned-out friends and relatives.

Next to her, a woman cuddled a beautiful baby to her chest. The baby cooed and gurgled and happily kicked its little bare feet. The mother looked up at Faith and smiled.

"He don't know what this is all about," the woman said. "My husband and I left before daylight, and we don't know whether our home is standing yet or not. It doesn't seem possible that this thing is happening in Tulsa, does it, sister?"

"No," Faith said. "It doesn't."

Faith walked on for a few yards, then stopped to lean on the fence at the end of the grandstand.

With every passing minute, more White people drove up in limousines and long sedans—the men wearing business suits and the women wearing fine dresses and sunbonnets. They rushed from their cars into the park and began calling desperately at the top of their lungs.

"Annie, are you here? Annie?"

Or—

"Luella? Where are you, Luella?"

Or—

"Aunt Lizzie? It's me, Mrs. Thomas."

Every so often, people answered their calls, and the White

folks rushed to embrace them, and, after the happy reunion, walked the bewildered-looking Black people to a table near the entrance where some soldiers sat.

There the White people signed papers promising to look after the refugees and to keep them out of trouble. Then they dragged them away from the stadium as if worried the authorities would change their mind and insist they stay behind at McNulty Park with the others.

Back at Convention Hall, sometime in mid-afternoon, a soldier pointed at Bill Williams and said, "Young fella, you follow me." Bill first thought he would be taken outside and shot as punishment for helping his father defend Greenwood. But the friendly demeanor of the soldier, a young man with bright red hair and freckles, put him at ease.

"Looks like you could use some fresh air," the soldier said to Bill.

They passed through the front door and into the commotion outside, then walked toward a truck loaded with Black men and boys; a few White men stood among them, holding shotguns. "Hop on, young fella," the soldier said, smiling cheerfully. "You're gonna get to play some ball."

So Bill climbed onto the back of the truck next to the rest of the men, and in a few minutes, the truck rumbled off through the sea of White faces that still lined the road.

A man slumped next to Bill on the truck looked vaguely familiar, probably from nights at the confectionery. He seemed to recognize Bill too.

"Guess there wasn't no lynching after all," the man said.

"I wouldn't know," Bill said.

"Nope," he said. "No lynching at all. Some deputies snuck that Rowland boy out of jail and drove him outta town about eight this morning. That's what I heard, so all this for nothing. That's a shame, isn't it?"

"I guess it is," Bill said.

That's a shame, isn't it?

The truck pulled up to the front gate of a baseball stadium, and the White men ordered the Black men off and marched them inside the fence. If anything, Bill saw more Black folks here than he had at the hall. He wandered over to the outfield and sat down by himself, leaning on the fence, closing his eyes against the glare of the hot sun, wondering where his mother and father and Posey had gone or if they were still alive at all.

A giant sob welled up in his chest, and he swallowed hard several times to force it back. Once evening arrived, he saw a familiar White face come heading toward him across the field.

"Come on, Mr. Bill," said Henry Sowders, the Dreamland projectionist. "Let's get you out of here."

Bill followed Henry through the crowd to a table by the front gate, where Henry signed papers handed him by some soldiers. The soldiers gave Bill a piece of green paper and told him to keep it with him at all times, because if he didn't, he would end up right back here with the others. Then Bill followed Henry out through the front gate.

"Those boys stole my car outside the Dreamland last night, Mr. Bill," Henry said. "You up to walking a spell?"

They walked to Henry's house. On the way, the projectionist said there had been no word about Bill's parents. That night, Bill put on clean clothes belonging to Henry, and Henry's wife fed him dinner.

After breakfast the next morning, Bill thanked the couple and walked back downtown. He didn't have any money, so he took a job washing dishes during the lunch rush for two dollars. Afterward, he left the restaurant without knowing what to do next, so he decided he would try to walk to Greenwood, hoping he might find his parents there.

As he turned the corner on Main Street, he almost bumped into his mother. She was on her way to the office of her White lawyer, hoping the attorney could help her find Bill. Loula swept her son into her arms, and he buried his head on her shoulder and cried loudly. White people averted their eyes from the mother and son as they stepped around them on the sidewalk.

Loula wept, too, patting her son's head, telling him that both his father and Posey were safe and staying with relatives in a house that hadn't burned. The theater and the confectionery were gone, but they were all alive.

And wasn't that the important thing, after all?

O. W. Gurley knew the Black folks were watching him.

The richest man in Greenwood—for years he had cultivated that image. But the rain falls on the rich and poor alike, doesn't it? What good did Gurley's riches do him now? That's what the people thought as they watched Gurley wander aimlessly across the ballpark, keeping his eyes to the ground. As rich as he was, he had fallen that day. Just like everyone else.

Then, in front of the grandstand, he heard a glorious noise.

"My Lord, it's Gurley!"

It was his wife's voice.

Gurley squinted against the shadows of the grandstand, and in a second he made out Emma, hurrying down the bleachers in his direction. She was alive after all and, right this moment, rushing through a gate onto the field and into her husband's arms.

She hadn't been shot that morning on Archer Street; she had fainted! That's all. There wasn't a mark on her, thank the Lord.

For a long while, Faith Hieronymus was lost in the ocean of faces. Then the intense energy of a slender Black woman in a white dress caught her attention. The woman stood near the gate leading into the grandstand, desperately scanning the imprisoned throng.

"Excuse me," Faith said. "Did you lose something?"

She regretted the question the second the words left her mouth, knowing how ridiculous it sounded under the circumstances.

"Lose something?" the woman asked, turning to look at Faith fiercely. "You ask me if I lost something? I done lost my home. I done lost my clothes excepting these here on my back. And my shoes are burned."

The woman held up one charred shoe as proof.

"And I ain't seen my husband since we left this morning with our house a-burning." The woman's anger gave way to weeping then to a loud wail. "It seems to me that nothing would matter no more if I could just see my husband."

Faith approached and touched her shoulder.

"Is there anything I can do?" she asked.

The woman suddenly stopped weeping and looked at Faith.

"There is if you can find my husband," she said. "Figure you can do that, young miss? Of course, there's nothing you can do. Get away from me, if you please."

GET AWAY FROM ME, IF YOU PLEASE

Faith backed away as the woman buried her head in her hands and again began to sob. Feeling ill then dizzy, her stomach tumbling, Faith staggered toward the gate hoping she might escape the misery.

A tiny old Black lady sat on a cot just before the exit. She smiled as Faith neared her.

"Darlin', you look pale as a clean sheet," the old woman said. "Come sit here a spell."

She slid over, making room for Faith. Faith was baffled by the act of kindness, but in her condition, she had no choice but to sit.

"Take some of this," the old woman said, offering a tin cup half full of cold water.

Faith took a small sip and handed the cup back.

"Thank you," she said. "That's better."

"Surely, darlin'," the old woman said. "That sun getting to you?"

"No, ma'am," Faith said. "Not the sun."

"What, then?"

"All this, I guess," Faith said, looking out at the ballpark. "All these poor people."

"It is a vision, ain't it, child?" the old woman agreed.

"I don't know how this could happen," Faith said.

"How could it *not* happen?" the old woman asked.

They sat silently for a few minutes, watching the people, passing the cup of water back and forth for small sips. The woman

HOW COULD IT NOT HAPPEN?

asked Faith her name, and what was she doing out among all these Black folks? Faith told her how she had moved to Tulsa the year before to work for the newspaper, which explained her notepad. The old woman said that was nice.

Her name was Easter Smith because that was the day she was born a long, long time ago, though everyone called her "Auntie."

Would Faith believe that Auntie would be ninety-seven years old in a few weeks? But she was still as fit as a young filly. In fact, she had hiked that morning from the home in Greenwood where she lived with her son and daughter, led along with a band of captured Black folks to Convention Hall. Then she was trucked to McNulty Park because Convention Hall was full.

She hadn't seen her son and daughter since the burning began, but she had faith in the Lord they would turn up eventually so they could go home and start putting things back together. She was impatient for that to happen.

"At home, I packed water and did washing, even though my son and daughter both fussed at me," she told Faith. "They say, 'Auntie, you're too old to be working this hard.' But I can't sit and fold my hands after all these years being so busy and a good cook. I began cooking in my eleventh year. I cooked all the days I was a slave. In a hotel, I cooked some of the time, then after the War. I don't cook in hotels no more."

The old woman paused and drifted off into a memory.

"I was born in Georgia," she said after a minute. "Did I tell you that?"

"No, ma'am," Faith said.

"I was born in Georgia, but my master, he lived in Arkansas," she said. "He was a nasty old man. Sold my mama and two of my brothers to this other fella in Tennessee. But I did his cooking and his washing 'cause I was told to. I was a young woman when they fought that war to set us free. That was something, let me tell you, child. The master comes and says, 'You don't belong to me no more. Go on before I shoot you.' But I stayed there in Arkansas until my son come down here to Tulsa 'cause he heard about all these Colored folks getting rich. So I came, too."

The woman paused again, took another sip of water, and offered the cup to Faith.

"I've seen lots of trouble," Auntie said. "But in all my born days, I never seen a day like this."

"Me either," Faith said.

Auntie looked over at Faith. The old woman began to quiver with laughter, her tiny frame shaking.

I NEVER SEEN A DAY LIKE THIS

"No, darlin'," Auntie said finally. "I don't suppose you have."

Faith rose from the cot, took Auntie's cup, stood in line to have it refilled, then returned it to her.

Both Auntie's kindness and her laughter convicted Faith that afternoon and burdened her with a shame that lingered inside her for the rest of her life.

Faith's story, which appeared on the front page of the *Tulsa World* on June 2, 1921, would be remembered as one of the most skillfully written, most heartrending articles ever published by the paper. But it was years before Faith could read it again.

That same day, the *World*'s rival, the *Tulsa Tribune*, published a front-page article that was every bit as masterful but whose tone could not have been more different. The *Tribune* story reflected the sense of triumph shared by many White people in the city. And though the article ran without a byline, it was most surely written by *Tribune* editor and publisher Richard Lloyd Jones.

It didn't matter to him that most authorities blamed the *Tribune*'s reckless and inflammatory coverage of Dick Rowland's arrest for inciting the courthouse confrontation and the much larger tragedy that came of it. In a *Tulsa World* story published a few days after the burning, James Patton, Tulsa's chief of detectives, said officers investigating Sarah Page's accusations were doubtful about the case against Rowland.

"If the facts in the story as told to the police had only been printed, I do not think there would have been a riot whatsoever," Detective Patton said.

The *Tribune* defiantly denied any role in the catastrophe.

If anything, Jones's racism became even more publicly virulent.

Events in Tulsa in the following weeks and months—a time when the Black families of Greenwood struggled to rebuild their devastated community with almost no assistance from White people—demonstrated the degree to which White folks shared Jones's sentiments.

Jones survived and eventually prospered in the newspaper business in large part because he was not afraid to give voice to the hateful racism clouding so many American souls. Some people would contend that if it hadn't been for Dick Rowland and the *Tribune*'s incendiary coverage of the case, something else would have come along to ignite Tulsa, just as White mobs had engaged in atrocities in cities and towns across the nation.

Mayor Thaddeus Evans, speaking at a city commission meeting a few days after the burning, said the catastrophe was probably inevitable. Mayor Evans said the belligerent Black folks were to blame.

Indeed, hate-mongering resonated not only in the hearts of Tulsa's oilfield roughnecks, bootleggers, and assorted White ruffians but also among its political leaders, lawyers, doctors, ministers, and businessmen.

In the months after the burning, thousands of Tulsans joined the Ku Klux Klan. Five days later, the coverage of the burning had ended. The dominant photograph on the *Tribune*'s front page featured the winner of the newspaper-sponsored beauty contest.

CHAPTER 20

Thursday, June 2, 1921: A Conspiracy of Silence

No matter what they personally thought about the massacre, Tulsa's leaders knew that the city faced a public relations nightmare of staggering proportions.

By Thursday morning, June 2, Greenwood's decimation dominated the front page of every major newspaper in the nation.

"One of the most disastrous race wars ever visited upon an American city," wrote the *New York Times*, which condemned the Tulsan White mob's behavior as "indefensible violence."

Tulsa was similarly skewered on editorial pages across the nation.

A *Houston Post* editorial was typical of the condemnations. "Americans have been loud in the denunciation of pogroms in Poland, of the massacres in Armenia and Russia and Mexico, and they were ready to go to war to avenge the victims of barbarous German warlords," said the *Post*. "But unless we can create a public sentiment in this country strong enough to restrain such intolerant outbreaks as Tulsa has witnessed, we shall be unable in the future to protest with any moral weight against anything that may happen in less favored parts of the world."

Mind you, a White mob in Houston had massacred Black citizens as recently as 1917.

"The bloody scenes in Tulsa, Oklahoma," wrote the *Philadelphia Bulletin*, "are hardly conceivable as happening in American civilization of the present day."

Philadelphia had three similar but less disastrous incidents of racist mob violence during the summer of 1919.

Racial violence, including lynching, was so commonplace in the United States that the NAACP had launched a movement to raise awareness among White people to end it. The Tulsa calamity seemed to shock the conscience of the nation to an extent greater than any of the previous violent outbreaks, reminding many of the mammoth atrocities that Americans attributed to people they claimed lived in less sophisticated and less righteous parts of the world.

The burning was indeed of a magnitude almost unimaginable in peacetime, with destruction rivaling the worst that any of the visiting press correspondents had seen during the recent war in Europe.

THE TULSA CALAMITY SEEMED TO SHOCK THE CONSCIENCE OF THE NATION

Panoramic photographs of the decimation bore a haunting resemblance to those after the atomic bombings of Nagasaki and Hiroshima a quarter-century later: Thirty-five square blocks of the Black community lay almost completely in ruin, save for hundreds of outhouses and a few isolated residences.

As noted earlier, White people burned more than eleven hundred Black people's homes to the ground along with all of Black Wall Street, the pride of so many industrious Black business people, Greenwood residents, Black America, and the nation.

Most of the Black families' personal belongings were torched or looted as well, along with savings that Greenwood families typically kept tucked away under mattresses or hidden in cupboards because no Black banks existed on the north side of the tracks. White curiosity-seekers poking around in Greenwood's rubble regularly plucked coins from the ashes. Later, dozens of Black survivors attempted to redeem charred currency at White Tulsan banks, usually without much success.

The toll of dead and wounded was even more staggering, but for a variety of reasons, the true extent of the casualties may never be known. Determining the exact number of injured was impossible in part because so many Black victims fled to be treated for burns and gunshot wounds by doctors as far away as St. Louis or Kansas City.

THE TOLL OF DEAD AND WOUNDED WAS EVEN MORE STAGGERING

Many White mobsters were reluctant to seek local medical treatment for injuries they sustained while engaged in looting, arson, or murder. Other White people presented themselves to Tulsan hospitals insisting they had been hurt as innocent bystanders.

In any event, every Tulsan hospital was swamped with the injured. Surgical teams operated around the clock for days afterward on both White and Black casualties. Basements of White churches, the National Guard Armory, and a private residence were commandeered for the purpose of treating the wounded.

The Red Cross also converted the classrooms of the Booker T. Washington High School into a hospital, where the largest number of injured Black people were treated. Red Cross records reflect that the agency treated 531 men, women, and children in the week after the riot, only forty-eight of them White. Twenty doctors working for the Red Cross, half of them Black, performed 163 operations.

In the burning's immediate aftermath, a Tulsan fire official estimated the dead at 185, saying that many of the victims had been incinerated in their homes. But Tulsa's official estimate was quickly revised downward to seventy-seven dead—nine White and sixty-eight Black. In the coming days they adjusted the number even further to ten White people and twenty-six Black people.

Anyone in Tulsa on the day of the burning knew that death estimate to be ludicrous.

Hundreds of Tulsans' most vivid memories were the unbelievable scenes of trucks hauling piles of Black bodies through the city, apparently to be buried at unknown destinations out in the country. Dozens of other bodies were seen stacked like firewood onto railroad flatcars.

In reality, the Tulsa Race Massacre was the deadliest domestic outbreak of violence in America since the Civil War.

In the early 1970s, a White Tulsan named Ed Wheeler—a writer and amateur historian who rose to the rank of brigadier general in the Oklahoma National Guard—spent seven months researching the destruction of Greenwood for an article he published in *Oklahoma Impact*, a Black publication.

For his article, which had first been rejected by the White publications in town, Wheeler interviewed about ninety elderly survivors and witnesses, both Black and White. Five people independently recalled watching National Guard soldiers lay out about sixty bodies on a sandbar in the Arkansas River, apparently using the hidden spot as an open-air morgue until arrangements could be made to permanently dispose of the corpses.

Most had spoken to Wheeler only with his promise that they would remain anonymous. During their interviews, they pulled out dozens of old photographs showing charred corpses lying in the street and in stacks on the back of trucks and railcars.

Wheeler concluded that the number of dead probably approached three hundred. White Tulsans ridiculed Wheeler, but shortly after the piece printed, a man named Bill Wilbanks called to say that he had come across some old documents that Wheeler might find pertinent.

Wilbanks, then the retiring commander of the Tulsa Police Academy, had been cleaning out old files when, at the bottom of an old police department cabinet, he discovered five yellowed pages stuck together with a rusty paper clip. The papers lacked headings or descriptions but were filled with two columns of entries, fifty on each page, reading:

```
Black female, mid-20s, shot
White female, mid-30s, shot
Black male, teenager, shot
Black female, hanged from a lamppost.
Black male, mid-forties, burned.
White male, mid-20s, shot.
Black infant, dead of unknown causes.
```

The roughly 250 victims were listed by race but not by name. Black victims outnumbered White by two to one.

"Any prudent person would probably think this was an informal body count," Wheeler said. "Somebody was keeping count of what they found but didn't want to make an official report."

In an emergency meeting of the Tulsa Chamber of Commerce on June 2, 1921, a gathering widely attended by journalists from around the nation, civic leaders competed to offer the most hyperbolic statements of regret.

While blaming the riot on "some lawless [Black] leaders," Alva Niles, president of the Tulsa Chamber, said the city "feels intensely humiliated and standing in the shadow of this great tragedy pledges every effort to wiping out this stain at the earliest possible moment."

A previous Tulsan mayor, Loyal J. Martin, was even more emphatic, stating that Tulsa could only redeem itself by completely restoring Greenwood at its own expense. The former mayor was then named to head a committee of influential Tulsans to lead the Greenwood recovery effort.

All of the members of the committee were White.

In their efforts at damage control, Tulsa leaders pointed out to journalists that scores of White families were housing hundreds of Black victims in their homes and servants' quarters. They emphasized that thousands of White people had donated food and clothing for the suffering Black families. They claimed that White teachers had taken their Black colleagues into their homes by the dozens.

While some of those facts may have been true, it was also true that, by June 2, four thousand Greenwood residents had been moved from McNulty Park and Convention Hall into pig and cow barns at the Tulsa County Fairgrounds, where they were held in custody.

Away from the headlines, Tulsa's White leaders treated the Greenwood community as a hostile and vanquished force, subtly at first, then overtly.

Until July 7, 1921, any Black person who had secured their release was forced to wear or carry a green card stamped "Police Protection" on one side, with their name, address, and employer recorded on the other. Any Black person found on the street without this green card was subject to arrest.

Black men were ordered to dig latrines and repair roads around the camps where White men were detaining them. White employers securing the release of Black people were forced to promise that they would be kept "indoors or at the scene of their labor."

BY JUNE 4, THE BURNING WAS NO LONGER FRONT-PAGE NEWS IN AMERICA

Several days after the massacre, Tulsa police decreed that White Tulsans could no longer provide shelter for Black people who were not their employees, most likely because White neighborhoods had become overrun with Black people made homeless by the great conflagration.

Tulsa benefited enormously from the national media's short attention span. By June 4, the burning was no longer front-page news in America.

Once the national spotlight had extinguished, White Tulsa's commitment to make amends or help rebuild evaporated. By June 5, Tulsan leaders decided they would not accept outside donations to help with the rebuilding, though offers were pouring in from across the country.

Instead, Tulsa's leaders washed their hands of any responsibility toward the stricken community by turning every facet of the recovery work over to the Red Cross. Civic leaders instead seemed more concerned with capitalizing on what was increasingly viewed not as a tragedy but an opportunity.

Negro Section Abolished by City Order read a headline in the June 7 edition of the *Tulsa Tribune*. The story that followed began: "Thirty-five blocks south of Standpipe Hill now in ruins following the fire Wednesday morning will never again be a Negro quarter but will become a wholesale and industrial center."

Less than a week after the massacre, the city proposed to transform the devastated area into the site of a new railroad station, White-owned manufacturing plants, and warehouses.

Indeed, White businessmen had attempted to purchase burned-out property from stricken Black owners, generally for a few cents on the dollar, before the last fire had died out. Most refused.

But on June 7, the city commission gave Black property-owners further incentive to sell out and relocate. Fire Ordinance No. 2156 mandated that rebuilt buildings must be constructed of concrete, brick, or steel and be at least two stories high. Those requirements were clearly prohibitive to most of the survivors, who were now impoverished and many of whom no longer had jobs. Under the new ordinance, wooden houses were permitted only on Greenwood's northern edge. Many ignored the ordinance and began to put up shacks on their property anyway.

The city's land grab also fueled suspicions that have survived in the Black community for decades. White Tulsa, especially the downtown area, was hemmed in on its south side by the Arkansas River and didn't have room to grow. One rumor had it that city leaders had actually planned and orchestrated Greenwood's destruction to gain access to the land north of the Frisco tracks.

THE WHITE LEADERS OF TULSA WERE TREATING THEIR PROPERTY LIKE IT WAS THE SPOILS OF WAR

From the perspective of Greenwood's Black community, the White leaders of Tulsa were treating their property like it was the spoils of war.

On the morning of Thursday, June 9, 1921, dozens of Black survivors filled the halls of the county courthouse, jockeying to be the first to testify before a special grand jury that Oklahoma Governor J. B. A. Robertson had ordered. The governor had made clear that he wanted a thorough and unbiased probe of what happened. Each of the twelve men selected to participate on the panel was White; however, the Black survivors at the courthouse had apparently taken Robertson at his word—that he wanted to know what had taken place. Finally, they had the chance to tell their side of the awful story. Not surprisingly, White people were much more reluctant to testify. In fact, there were so few White witnesses that authorities put out a plea in the local papers, begging for people who had knowledge to come forward.

After several days of testimony, the all-White grand jury returned eighty-eight indictments, including a charge of attempted rape against Dick Rowland, who was still being held at an unknown location. Dozens of White people were charged with rioting, arson, theft, and assault, including Cowboy Long, the notorious hoodlum who led the crew of arsonists along Detroit Avenue. Tulsa Police Chief John Gustafson was indicted for failing to take action to control the disturbance and on unrelated charges that he had conspired with a local car-theft ring.

But most of the criminal charges were against Black people, even though the overwhelming majority of the marauders, arsonists, and murderers were White. Fifty-seven Black people were charged in all, including Peg Leg Taylor, the one-legged veteran of the Spanish War who supposedly killed a dozen White people while firing down from a Greenwood hilltop, and O. B. Mann, who disappeared from Tulsa after the final battles against the White mobs on June 1.

Those Black men, the indictments said, "assembled together armed with rifles, shotguns, pistols, razors, and other deadly weapons," and attacked downtown Tulsa in cars, trucks, and on foot, killing several peaceable White people and wounding many others.

Tulsan authorities singled out two men as the Black ringleaders: *Tulsa Star* editor Andrew J. Smitherman and his friend

John Stradford. White Tulsans had long felt that Smitherman and Stradford were the most uppity, contentious Black men in Greenwood. Both had slipped out of Tulsa when Greenwood was overrun. Stradford fled to his brother's home in Independence, Kansas.

Lawmen had caught up with Stradford on June 3, but by the time the Kansan governor ordered his return to Tulsa, he had vanished. This time, he headed to his son's home in Chicago. Tulsa's attempt to find and prosecute him ended there. Smitherman escaped to points unknown but eventually turned up in Buffalo, New York, where he edited another Black newspaper. Neither man ever returned to Tulsa.

In most other cases, the grand jury indictments were empty gestures. One Black man was sent to jail but for only thirty days on a charge of carrying a concealed weapon.

A CITY DETERMINED TO ERASE FROM ITS COLLECTIVE MEMORY WHAT HAD HAPPENED IN GREENWOOD

After a raucous trial in July, Chief Gustafson was convicted, fined, and fired.

But the rest of the indictments against White and Black folks alike were either dismissed or ignored in a city determined to erase from its collective memory what had happened in Greenwood.

And in spite of the fact that hundreds of Black people were killed and thirty-five square blocks of Greenwood were burned down, including all of Black Wall Street, not one White person was sent to jail.

In fact, the grand jury report issued at the end of its deliberations briefly criticized inflammatory local newspaper accounts for helping precipitate the tragedy. But jurors reserved most of the blame for the Black community.

The report read: "We have not been able to find any evidence, either from White or Colored citizens, that any organized attempt was made or planned to take from the sheriff's custody any prisoner; the crowd assembled about the courthouse being purely spectators and curiosity-seekers resulting from rumors circulated about the city. There was no mob spirit among the Whites, no talk of lynching and no arms. The assembly was quiet until the arrival of the armed Negroes, which precipitated and was the direct cause of the entire affair."

The report also charged that Black Americans had changed, becoming agitated by propaganda promoting ideas of social equality.

"This agitation resulted in the accumulation of firearms among the people and the storage of quantities of ammunition," the report concluded, "all of which was accumulative in the minds of the Negro, which led them as people to believe in equal rights, social equality, and their ability to demand the same."

Black people, in other words, should remain in their place, their necks under the heel of White supremacy. The report ignored the fact that Black Greenwood residents armed themselves in an attempt to protect themselves from White-on-Black violence.

Though Black people would rebuild Greenwood and Black Wall Street with shocking speed, no public debates about race or reparations would take place in Greenwood for decades.

BLACK PEOPLE WOULD REBUILD GREENWOOD AND BLACK WALL STREET WITH SHOCKING SPEED

That summer and fall, as Black Tulsans subsisted in tents and cooked their meals outdoors, White Tulsans returned to business as usual. Adding insult to injury, they joined the Ku Klux Klan by the thousands. Indeed, almost immediately after the burning, the KKK had become a major facet of life in Tulsa. Hundreds attended nighttime initiation ceremonies held around burning crosses on hilltops. Some of the order's largest downtown marches took place within weeks of the Greenwood tragedy.

For the Black people of Greenwood, this new reality must have been horrifying.

That August, thousands of White Tulsa's men, women, and children crammed Convention Hall, the same facility that just two months earlier had been filled with homeless, terrorized Black citizens. But the atmosphere that night was more mindful of a pep rally or tent revival. The crowd had gathered to hear the speech of a visitor from Atlanta, a man named Caleb Ridley, who would tell of the past and present glories of the Ku Klux Klan, its sacred principles, and the requirements for membership.

Ridley was enthusiastically introduced that night by the prominent Tulsan attorney Washington Hudson, whose clients included Dick Rowland.

Indeed, mayors, city commissioners, sheriffs, district attorneys, and many other city and county officeholders who were either Klansmen or Klan supporters were elected and reelected with regularity throughout the 1920s.

In 1922 the Klan built Beno Hall, a stucco palace at Main Street and Easton Avenue downtown. Supposedly, Beno was short for the word "benevolent," but others claimed the name was short for "Be No Negro, Be No Catholic, Be No Jew." Its auditorium could seat more than a thousand members, and monthly meetings were generally packed.

The chapter had a women's auxiliary, called the "Kamelia," and a junior Klan for boys ages twelve to eighteen. There were Klan funerals and Klan fundraisers. White robes and hoods were the most popular Halloween costumes for children for years.

Apparently, national Klan officials had been correct when they had instructed their brethren in Tulsa. The best way to boost Klan membership was to have a good riot.

CHAPTER 21

Rebuilding

That September, only a few days after he had introduced the speaker at the Klan rally at Convention Hall, attorney Washington Hudson drove across the Frisco tracks to deliver news to Damie Rowland, who was now living in a tent on Archer Street.

Mr. Hudson rolled up in his expensive Ford, wearing a beautiful brown suit with a vest and bow tie and a nice straw hat, which he tipped politely to Damie before bending to step into her tent.

Then he delivered his wondrous news: Sarah Page had decided to drop her charges.

Dick Rowland was a free man, at that very moment probably strolling the streets of Kansas City, where Sheriff McCullough had hidden him since the burning.

Damie nearly fainted. She made Hudson repeat himself to make sure she wasn't dreaming.

It was over.

Dick was free.

THERE WOULD BE NO HANGING, NO MORE DEATH

There would be no hanging, no more death.

But the whole community was in ruins. Because of that, there were plenty in Greenwood who felt that the mob should have had its way with Dick Rowland that night at the courthouse, even if the boy was guilty of nothing worse than stupidity.

He came in the night and only one time. At first, Damie didn't recognize him, thinking he was just another young Black man desperate for some food. Damie heard a man whisper her name outside her tent, and when she poked her head out, he stood to the side, outlined in the shadows.

"Isn't this an awful mess that I caused?" he whispered.

Damie nearly fainted. She rushed the few yards toward Dick and hugged him. He smelled like several days of riding in boxcars.

What was done was done, Damie said. She looked closely at her boy in

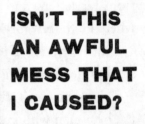

ISN'T THIS AN AWFUL MESS THAT I CAUSED?

the thin light of her gas lamp. Dick's diamond ring was gone from his finger. A dirty piece of string was tied around that finger instead, as if to remind him of his flamboyant life and where that life had led him. Eyes that once twinkled were now dull and old, even though Dick had just turned twenty.

He asked Damie about the folks around Greenwood, wondering who died in the burning and who survived. He asked what she would do with her boardinghouse and with all her money gone. Damie said she would find a way to get back on her feet and that Dick shouldn't worry.

Well before dawn, Dick hugged her one last time and disappeared into the night.

He wrote to her every month from Kansas City. Damie was surprised when he told her that Sarah Page had moved back to Kansas City, too, the place where she had grown up and divorced her husband before moving to Tulsa.

From what he wrote in his letters, it sounded like Dick and Sarah saw a great deal of each other. Dick said that Sarah felt terrible that the police had arrested him for something he didn't do. But she never talked at all about the burning and killing set in motion by her lies.

Then again, as harmful as the lie was, it should never have resulted in genocide.

If Dick loved Sarah, he didn't say. Then her name disappeared from his letters, and not long after that, he moved to Oregon, where he found work in shipyards along the coast.

For forty years, Dick wrote to Damie about his work and the sea, but he never mentioned a wife or a family or even a friend.

Then, one day in the 1960s, a letter came from Oregon written by a man who said he had been Dick's roommate there. He was sorry to inform Damie that Dick had been killed in an accident on a wharf.

Damie was the only person that Dick ever really loved, the man said.

Bill Williams first heard the sound about a week after the burning. A blues melody someone was tapping out on a piano drifted toward them from a tent across Greenwood Avenue. Not long after that, Bill heard a sax wailing along Greenwood Avenue,

212

and within a few weeks, regular crowds gathered along the street to eat ribs and greens cooked over open fires and to listen to the music. The jazz and blues expressed feelings that the Black folks of Greenwood couldn't otherwise put into words.

Somehow life in Greenwood continued.

To be enslaved before the Civil War, or to be a Black person in America afterward, was to learn how to demonstrate endurance and resilience, to assume the moral high ground in the face of depravity, to possess the ability  to advance toward a vision that didn't yet exist, to create something out of nothing with every faithful step, and to express love in the face of hate. It meant figuring out how to move onward through terrible things that White folks did and to deal with the troubles that Black folks had come to expect life to bring.

Things that would make members of a weaker people turn to dust.

So, though shell-shocked, brutalized and horrified, Greenwood's Black citizens mounted a heroic and courageous comeback. Expecting and receiving next to no assistance from White Tulsans, Greenwood's residents leaned into each other as they engaged in self-help and assisted their neighbors in getting back on their feet.

Within one week, people had built vegetable stands among the tents. They milked cows and collected eggs from nervous hens. Then thousands of Black workers resumed their daily treks back across the railroad tracks to shine shoes, to hang a White family's laundry and do its cooking, to trim hedges and cut lawns, to drive limousines, to run elevators, or to wash dishes in White restaurants. Then they came home to their tents across the tracks and made do, the rich Black folks and the poor Black folks alike, because after the burning, there wasn't much to distinguish the two.

"We had to save our own, use what small means we had, and cooperate together," wrote Mabel Little, who ran a beauty parlor alongside her husband Pressley's shoeshine stand. "Our top wages then were five to ten dollars a week [That's about sixty to one hundred thirty dollars weekly in today's dollars.], and we couldn't even borrow money. We had to cooperate together; for there was no other choice. Little by little, we built our businesses back up—beauty shops, our own drugstores, grocery stores, and our own barbershops, tailor shops, you name it."

Before the burning, the fellow named C. L. Netherland lived in a ten-room home with a basement, and cut hair in a Greenwood Avenue shop with five enamel chairs, four baths, a set of electric clippers, an electric fan, two lavatories and shampoo stands, a double shine stand of marble, and an income of five hundred dollars a month, or almost seven thousand dollars today. After the burning, he lived in his coal barn and cut hair in a folding chair set on the sidewalk because life went on, no matter how terrible it could be.

Townsend Jackson cut hair in his tent on Cincinnati, grieving for his son, the doctor.

Young Robert Fairchild, Dick Rowland's old buddy, shined shoes downtown.

Professor Hughes taught his classes at Booker T. Washington High School.

H. A. Guess hung his law shingle in his family's tent, assuring his wife and two daughters all along, "Don't worry, girls. I'm gonna build you a nice new house, better than the last one."

Within a few months, he did.

Right away, members of Mount Zion gathered to pray and assess the damage. The church had insurance, but as the insured owners of many Greenwood businesses would find, the policy excluded damage caused by a riot, as the massacre was labeled for decades. Though fifty thousand dollars in debt, the congregation made a vow to take on what they believed was a moral imperative to repay the debt. They struggled to pay off their debt and rebuild the church. At the same time, they were counting their coins and scraping together every penny to rebuild their homes and businesses.

It took the flock until November 1942—twenty-one years— to pay off the original structure. The new building was completed in 1952 at the steep cost of three hundred thousand dollars.

Vernon Chapel had been destroyed as well. It took that assembly until 1945 to clear its debt. In 1995—almost seventy-five years after the original structure had been torched—the church opened the doors to its new building. Today, the basement of Vernon A.M.E. Church is the only original structure to have survived the 1921 massacre.

First Baptist Church—where Captain Townsend D. Jackson had spoken that night—bordered a White neighborhood. Believing it was a White church, the members of the mob let it stand. But though it survived unscathed, its Black members did not.

John and Loula Williams plowed forward, as they had since the first day they were married.

They started rebuilding with the savings they had placed in a White bank downtown, and by September, the family was able to move from their tent along Greenwood Avenue to the second floor of the new Williams Building, which was almost exactly like the one before.

Crowds stood in line to get into Williams' Confectionery the day it opened, desperate for Greenwood life as it used to be. People congregated around the soda fountain, and young men resumed their marriage proposals there. The Dreamland also came back to life that autumn, but half of the seats sat empty for many months, except on the nights when Loula decided to show movies for free.

John rebuilt his engine shop, too, and within a few weeks, the rich White men brought their cars back north across the tracks so he could work on them.

A few of the White people told John they were sorry, but most said nothing at all about the tragedy. They just looked a little sheepish when they walked into the garage with this or that complaint about their car, wondering if old John could have a look under the hood.

John fixed their cars anyway because life went on.

By winter, most of John and Loula's neighbors along Greenwood Avenue were back in their buildings too. Deep Greenwood, in fact, looked almost exactly as it did before the burning, except newer.

BY THE END OF THE YEAR, BLACK TULSANS HAD BUILT MORE THAN SIX HUNDRED HOMES

Indeed, by the end of the year, Black Tulsans had built more than six hundred homes in Greenwood. "The rapidity with which businesses, buildings and residences are being rebuilt, in most instances, better than before, is proof in wood and brick and in stone, of the Black man's ability to make progress against the most cunningly planned and powerfully organized opposition," Tulsa's East End Relief Committee wrote to the Red Cross.

Central to the effort to reconstruct the neighborhood were three Black lawyers who formed the law firm of Spears, Franklin & Chappelle, which they ran from their tent. Over the coming months, these three men counseled thousands of Black Tulsans, kept Black organizations nationally apprised of the extent of the devastation, and issued a nationwide appeal for financial assistance.

That August, they filed a successful lawsuit against the City of Tulsa to stop it from seizing property from Black people and making the cost of rebuilding prohibitive. All totaled, they filed more than four million dollars in claims against the City of Tulsa and various insurance companies for property damage as a result of the riot.

By November, they had moved into a permanent office.

In December, Red Cross workers cut a huge spruce tree in the country and hauled it outside the new Black hospital on Hartford Avenue, where twenty-seven victims of the burning were still on the mend. A wealthy White businessman named Charles Page, from nearby Sand Springs, purchased lights and other decorations for the Christmas tree, including the huge white cross that was placed on top. Only two years earlier, Page had sold the *Tulsa Tribune* to Richard Lloyd Jones, who had written the incendiary lynch mob headline. Page also offered to supply bricks to rebuild Mount Zion, but he passed away before he could make good on his offer.

On a night shortly before Christmas, Black families gathered around the Christmas tree in the evening chill. Red Cross workers distributed twenty-seven hundred half-pound packages of fruits and nuts to the children, as well as spools of thread, pillows, children's underwear, and quilts to the adults. The singing began after the last gifts were given.

Two thousand voices raised to the heavens as Greenwood sang traditional Christmas carols, interspersed with spirituals like "Swing Low, Sweet Chariot." The throng clapped for "Down by the River Side." Men and boys removed their hats for "Standing in the Need of Prayer."

Then, when the singing was over, a Black preacher climbed onto the back of a truck and began to speak. He wished the crowd a Merry Christmas and reminded the people that they had much to be grateful for.

"Let us always remember the old Negro tradition," the preacher concluded. "There is no room in our hearts for hatred."

"Amen," some of the men and women replied.

Then the crowd began to drift away, dispersing back across Greenwood to new homes in some cases, to tents in others.

Standing at the edge of the crowd that had gathered around the Christmas tree was maybe the only person in the throng who didn't sing. O. B. Mann had been walking across Greenwood on one of his nightly strolls when he heard the strange noises in the dusk. So he turned to investigate and saw all those Black families at the Christmas tree, singing and taking handouts from White people. On the evening before his birthday, his blood boiled once again.

O.B. had snuck back into Tulsa only the week before, ending a six-month exile that began the day after the burning, when he'd run into his brother McKinley staying with a bunch of other Black survivors in an abandoned barn in the country.

On June 2, McKinley had cleaned out the safe at the grocery store before fleeing. He handed his brother a stack of bills, telling O.B. to head north because word was getting around about how many White men the youngest Mann brother had killed during the burning.

"Canada might be a good place for you about now," McKinley said. "I hear Toronto's got a fair number of Negroes."

"I ain't running from nothing or nobody," O.B. stated.

"Well, suit yourself," McKinley said. "But if you stay in Tulsa, I'm telling you, you're as good as hung."

I AIN'T RUNNING FROM NOTHING OR NOBODY

Thinking better of his bravado, O.B. hopped a train to Kansas City. From there, he bought a rail ticket to Chicago, then to Detroit, then to Toronto. The Canadian city had plenty of other Black people and poor White people from Europe who couldn't speak English— men who worked next to O.B. building bridges.

O.B. took a bed in a boardinghouse with the bridge builders and at night wrote to his family in Tulsa. The letters that came back said the grocery store had burned along with almost everything else in Greenwood, but because of all the money he'd deposited at the White bank downtown, there had been plenty of money to rebuild the store.

In July, McKinley wrote to say that an indictment at the courthouse had O.B.'s name on it, and that five White deputies had come looking for him at the store. But about four months later, McKinley wrote another letter telling O.B. to come on home if he wanted to. The White folks no longer seemed interested in anything about the burning, including messing with Black folks, whether they had been indicted or not.

So O.B. rode the train from Toronto to Detroit to Kansas City and finally to Okmulgee, where a friend he knew from the Army drove him into Tulsa in the middle of the night, dropping him off in front of the new Mann Brothers Grocery Store on Lansing Street.

For weeks after that, O.B. put on his apron and worked behind the counter, stocked shelves, or slaughtered chickens. He ventured outside only at night, leery that some deputy might still want to make a name for himself by capturing the Black man with so much White blood on his hands.

On his evening strolls, O.B. nervously checked over his shoulder as he saw the new homes taking the place of the ones the White mob had burned down, the new brick buildings that Black people rebuilt in Deep Greenwood, and the piles of bricks where Mount Zion Baptist used to be. He heard the Christmas carols on one of those strolls and stood at the edge of the crowd, fuming. Sleep in heavenly peace. How could anyone sleep in peace again?

He almost couldn't restrain himself at the end, when that fellow stood up on the truck and yelled, "There is no room in our hearts for hatred."

Where White people were concerned, there was no room in O.B.'s heart for anything but hatred. The sight of blue eyes nearly drove him crazy. But the people of Greenwood, these sorry folks singing their carols, they had been beaten down. They were still enslaved. They would keep their mouths shut, except to sing carols, and keep their heads down to take whatever the White folks wanted to give.

The crowd at the Christmas tree began to disperse, hauling away their Red Cross packages, and O.B. went mumbling off into the night, wrestling with his rage.

A few days later, on January 1, 1922, the last of the Red Cross workers, who had come from around the nation, packed up and left town for good.

By the spring of 1922, the last of the tents were gone, and the only reminders of the massacre were the occasional piles of rubble, the empty shotgun and rifle shells that kept turning up in the dirt like the arrowheads of the area's original Native American residents, the residents' thousand-yard stares, or the nightmares that afflicted almost every Greenwood house.

Still, Greenwood residents rebuilt doctors' offices, law offices, funeral homes, night spots, hotels, cafés, grocery stores, florists, bowling alleys, dress shops, jewelry stores, newspaper offices, drugstores, cleaners, barbershops, taverns, variety stores, realtors, popcorn stands, and more.

"There were mostly good people, but there were some 'underworld' characters, too, mainly bootleggers and numbers runners.

There were cultivated, sophisticated Black people, there were working class, salt-of-the-earth people, and there were a few eccentrics," wrote survivor Juanita Alexander Lewis.

"A little over a decade" later "everything was more prosperous than before. Most of these businesses even survived the Depression," wrote Tulsan historian Henry Whitlow, a former principal of Booker T. Washington High School.

As fabulous as Greenwood had been before the massacre, it wasn't until the 1940s that it reached its heyday. By 1945, 242 Black-owned and operated establishments were in business— the most there had ever been.

Fortunately, O. B. Mann lived to see it. By then, he and McKinley had grown rich with their grocery store. Nephews remembered their Uncle O.B. coming to visit them in Southern California in a chauffeur-driven limousine.

In 1952, Don Ross relocated to Tulsa from the small farming town of Venita, sixty miles away.

CHAPTER 22

The Veil Lifted

In 1946, a White Chicago native named Nancy Feldman accepted a job teaching sociology at the University of Tulsa. Not long afterward, she met a Black man named Robert Fairchild while she was moonlighting at the Tulsa Health Department. One of just a handful of Black municipal employees, Fairchild organized recreation programs for Tulsa's youth.

The two quickly became friends, and Feldman was highly curious about Fairchild's life as a Black man who had grown up in Tulsa. It wasn't long before he began recounting his days of shining shoes with the notorious Dick Rowland, of Rowland's ultimate misfortune, and of the cataclysm that happened because of it.

Feldman was stunned.

The way Fairchild described what had happened, the burning of Greenwood surely ranked among one of the nation's worst racial atrocities, yet the young scholar could not recall a single mention of the catastrophe in any of her history texts.

Not that Feldman doubted Fairchild. Something in his manner convinced her it had happened just the way he described it. She was so sure of it, in fact, that she decided to introduce his horrifying recollections to her classroom. What better topic for Tulsa sociology students than the historic example of hatred's handiwork so close to home?

Feldman was eager to get her White students' perspective. But the day she repeated Fairchild's story in class, she was dumbfounded by the response. The students seemed surprised, defensive, or greeted her with uncomprehending stares. None admitted to knowing about the burning, and a few argued it was impossible that such a terrible thing could have happened in such a prosperous and tranquil city.

> **NONE ADMITTED TO KNOWING ABOUT THE BURNING**

To prove it, Feldman invited Fairchild to tell his story in person. They remained stubbornly disbelieving. Many mentioned the classroom debate to their parents, who insisted it was nothing but a lie. Not long afterward, Feldman's dean encouraged her to drop the subject. She ignored him, inviting Fairchild back the next semester. Those students were just as oblivious.

The oblivion about the slaughter was a Tulsa-wide contagion.

In the immediate months and years afterward, White racists bought and sold postcards depicting burning Black homes and businesses and charred Black corpses on Tulsa's downtown streets. White participants openly boasted about notches on their guns, earned during Greenwood's obliteration, which initially was a widespread source of civic pride.

But before long, the events of 1921 became an embarrassment, something better forgotten.

Tulsa much preferred to promote itself as a thriving city

with an impressive skyline and a sophistication that belied the lawlessness of its early days. The burning was like an ugly birthmark that would forever disfigure the place unless it was covered up and forgotten. White people consoled themselves with the notion that the massacre had been the fault of the Black community—the White people had merely acted to put down an uprising of uppity and lawless Black people.

Thus Tulsa's remarkable conspiracy of silence was born.

TULSA'S REMARKABLE CONSPIRACY OF SILENCE

Communities across the nation had struggled mightily to sweep their racial atrocities under the carpet, but in no other city were the horrors as great and the cultural amnesia so complete as in Tulsa. What was at first called a race riot would later be compared to the pogroms of Europe or to ethnic cleansing. One scholar termed it the American Kristallnacht, referring to that infamous night in 1938 when the Nazis torched and vandalized Jewish neighborhoods, terrorizing and killing approximately one hundred Jewish people. But the American Kristallnacht was not mentioned in an Oklahoma history book until 1941, and that first mention came in a single paragraph. Texts in the years to come generally described the catastrophe in passing, a footnote to what were described as greater historical events of the day.

Though it had generated front-page headlines around the world at first, the tragedy quickly disappeared from Oklahoma newspapers, particularly those in Tulsa. On June 1, 1936, in its regular feature called "Fifteen Years Ago Today," the *Tulsa Tribune* of Richard Lloyd Jones recalled that, on the day of the burning, "Miss Carolyn Skelly was a charming young hostess of the past week, having entertained at a luncheon and theater party for Miss Kathleen Sinclair, and her guest, Miss Julia Morley of Saginaw, Mich." The massacre was not mentioned, nor did it come up in the paper on the event's twenty-fifth anniversary on June 1, 1946.

The *Tulsa World* didn't observe the date, either.

In the spring of 1971, the writer Ed Wheeler submitted his account of the burning to Russell Gideon, editor of the *Tulsa World*'s Sunday magazine.

"This is a hell of a good article," the editor told Wheeler. "But there is an unwritten rule at this paper that we don't touch this subject with an eleven-foot pole."

Wheeler was not surprised.

Earlier that spring, while walking in downtown Tulsa, he'd felt a tap at his shoulder and turned to see a White stranger.

"Don't print that article," the man said before turning and walking casually down the street. The phone calls to Wheeler's home warning him off writing the story began at about the same time. In early May, he found a message scrawled in soap across the windshield of his car:

"Best look under your hood from now on," the words said.

Wheeler had been a military intelligence officer in Vietnam and had subsequently attained the rank of brigadier general in the Oklahoma National Guard. He didn't scare easily, though he couldn't dismiss the threat to his family. He moved his wife and son across town into the home of his wife's mother, while he completed what became Tulsa's first detailed account of the racial bloodbath in fifty years.

The assignment had begun innocently enough in a casual conversation between Wheeler and Larry Silvey, editor of Tulsa's Chamber of Commerce magazine. Silvey asked Wheeler if he'd be interested in writing about the burning. The fiftieth anniversary of what was then known as the Tulsa Race Riot was rapidly approaching. In Silvey's estimation, a story about the event would be a positive thing, demonstrating the city's progress in race relations. Who could object to something like that, especially a half-century later?

Wheeler agreed to write the story. But within weeks, he realized the horror of what had happened in 1921 extended far beyond anything that had been discussed publicly in Tulsa for decades.

The Black survivors' fear remained palpable, even five decades later. None would allow Wheeler to use their names in his story. Most insisted on meeting only at night in the sanctuary of their churches and with their pastor present. Grandchildren accompanied some of the survivors, and Wheeler knew by the shocked look on their faces that the young people were hearing the story of the massacre for the first time.

Word also quickly spread to the White side of town about his interviews with White Tulsans and about the hours he spent in the public library poring over old newspapers. Wheeler's White sources insisted on anonymity as well. Among them were two remorseful Klansmen, who said they had merely tried to teach the Black people in Greenwood a lesson, a lesson that had gotten out of hand.

A third Klansman said his only regret was that more Black people weren't killed, that more Black-owned buildings had not been destroyed.

"This is the story of a race riot," read the first sentence of Wheeler's story. "It is not a pretty story, and it is not told for its shock value or to reopen old wounds. It is presented because it happened fifty years ago to another generation whose story is pertinent to a contemporary generation.

"The blame for the riot was heaped upon ' . . . Negroes of the lower class—gamblers and bootleggers . . . and . . . a group of Negroes who . . . had been worked upon by a lawless element of White agitators, reds and bolshevists.' But this was hogwash," Wheeler wrote. "Prejudice, suspicion, ignorance and hate caused the riot. Intolerance, anger, rumor-mongering and fear fanned its flames. Such elements were prevalent in abundance on both sides of the racial fence."

PREJUDICE, SUSPICION, IGNORANCE AND HATE

They were courageous words for a White writer in 1971 Tulsa, though the piece that followed was restrained and understated.

After estimating the death toll at three hundred and describing how thousands of homeless Black people had been imprisoned, Wheeler retold the tragedy hour by hour.

Silvey immediately made plans to publish the piece in the Chamber of Commerce magazine, but the Chamber's general manager, Clyde Cole, was unenthusiastic.

"This article will start a race riot," Cole told Wheeler and rejected the story.

The *Tulsa World* wouldn't run the story, either.

Wheeler began to realize that his only hope of salvaging the months of work that had brought such fear and pain to his own family was a publication in the Black community.

So Wheeler reached out to a Black magazine publisher named Don Ross.

Ross was not the same Greenwood pool shark he'd been before his life had been transformed in the 1950s by Bill Williams's grim history lesson. No, since then, Don Ross had joined the air force, participated in the civil rights movement, and studied journalism in college. He had also begun publishing a Black periodical called *Oklahoma Impact*. He'd hoped the *Impact* would someday tell the real story of the Tulsa massacre and who was to blame. He could scarcely believe his good fortune when Wheeler walked into his office. He would publish Wheeler's story.

In 1971, the cover of the June/July edition of *Oklahoma Impact* read: PROFILE OF A RACE RIOT. Wheeler's piece took up most of the pages inside and was wrapped around grisly photographs of the burning that were published for the first time. The magazine printed five thousand copies, twice its normal press run. They were swept up by Black Tulsans the moment they hit the newsstands. Within hours, Black readers flooded Ross and Wheeler with calls of congratulations. The secret of the massacre was finally out.

Copies also made their way across the tracks to White Tulsa, where they were passed from hand to hand and read surreptitiously. Some of those who called to compliment Wheeler were White. Other White Tulsans grumbled, chastising Wheeler particularly for what they believed was his inflated estimate of the dead. But for the most part, in White Tulsa, the article was

> THE SECRET OF THE MASSACRE WAS FINALLY OUT

publicly ignored. Wheeler had not named names, which was a relief, and the threatening calls to his home ended.

Remarkably, the White press, both in Tulsa and around the nation, ignored Wheeler's article and the historic nightmare it described. In the years to come, only occasionally would White or Black writers attempt to continue the process Wheeler and Ross had begun.

Ruth Sigler Avery—the little girl who had watched Klan members torture a Black man in the hilltop cross-burning ceremony and who would never forget the truck piled with bodies that rumbled past her window on the morning of the burning—was one of them. Avery spent much of the 1970s interviewing Black survivors and White witnesses. Her book was never published, but her interviews would become a crucial resource for journalists, authors, and historians to come.

By the mid-1970s, a White college student named Scott Ellsworth had also begun his own long investigation. Born and raised in Tulsa's White, middle-class neighborhood, Ellsworth heard about the burning as a teenager from his Black coworkers at local restaurants. He wrote about it while astounding his professors at Reed College in Oregon and then at Duke University, where he earned a PhD in history.

In 1982, he published a book, *Death in a Promised Land*, which drew on his interviews with survivors such as Bill and

Seymour Williams, Robert Fairchild, and Wilhelmina Guess Howell; court records; and newspaper accounts. But White Tulsa continued to ignore the reminder of its dark past. As the 1980s drew to a close, the city remained safe with its terrible secret.

CHAPTER 23

Reparations

They were just children back then. The seven elderly men and women who gathered in the Old Capitol Building of Tallahassee, Florida, stood nervously while surrounded by family and friends, the daunting glare of television lights, and the gaggle of journalists.

These African Americans had survived a massacre at a place called Rosewood.

After decades of hauling their memories of gunshots, deaths, and the fire during the first week in January of 1923 in private, on this day they dressed in red and white: white for Rosewood's innocence and red for the blood of innocent people whom a rampaging White mob had killed.

It is such a public spectacle that, after all these years, there will finally be a measure of justice. The amends may be paltry when you consider what had happened to their little village so long ago, but they are amends just the same.

Seated before them on May 4, 1994, is Florida Governor Lawton Chiles. Television cameras prepare to capture this historic moment, the first time any state has compensated the survivors of racial violence.

Shadow of shame

Chiles tells the television cameras that the bill before him will help disperse the "shadow of shame" that had lingered like a fog over his state for more than seven decades.

It had begun on New Year's Day of 1923 with a White married woman named Fannie Taylor claiming that an unknown Black man knocked at her door that morning and beat and robbed her when she answered. Little matter that Taylor's Black laundress saw the woman's White boyfriend come and go from the house around the time of the supposed attack. Back then, White people didn't need much of an excuse to ruthlessly vent their racial hatred.

Just three years earlier, a White mob had snatched four Black men in Macclenny, Florida, lynching them for the alleged rape of a White woman. Five more Black Floridians were killed and a Black community at Ocoee was destroyed in a dispute over voting rights. Another Black Floridian man was lynched in Wauchula for yet another purported attack on a White woman. Still another Black man in Florida burned at the stake in Perry for allegedly killing a White schoolteacher.

On New Year's Eve 1922, the Ku Klux Klan celebrated the holiday with a huge march in Gainesville. The next day, forty miles away in Sumner, a crying Fannie Taylor claimed a Black man was responsible for the bruises on her face.

Angry White mobs gathered in that rural part of Central Florida, cleaning out the local hardware store of its ammunition and setting off into the woods with their guns and dogs in search of a Black felon who supposedly escaped from a nearby chain gang. The mob encountered one Black man. They shot him to death and hung him from a tree.

The mob kept moving toward Rosewood, home to a few dozen Black families, a general store, a sugar mill, a one-room school, three churches, and a nifty baseball team called the Rosewood Stars. Many of the Rosewood residents worked in the White sawmill nearby or as domestics for White families in Sumner, then came home to their tranquil place hidden in the pine woods—at least until the mob came looking for Fannie Taylor's assailant and tried to force its way into the home of a Black woman named Sarah Carrier. Sarah's son was a proud man named Sylvester, who greeted the intruders with a cloud of buckshot. Sarah, Sylvester, and two White people died in the exchange, which newspapers around the state trumpeted as a full-fledged race war, inaccurately making the Black people seem like the aggressors.

So White people converged on little Rosewood, seething, many of them drunk. As the local sheriff and Florida's governor looked the other way, the mob torched the town. Six Black people were dead by the end of that week, yet a state grand jury could not find enough evidence to return a single indictment. The people of Rosewood scattered forever, keeping their secret until 1982, when a newspaper reporter from St. Petersburg caught wind of the atrocity and wrote about it. The secret was finally out.

The survivors' descendants began insisting the state of Florida make good. Some of them were surprised when the government decided to do just that.

"The long silence has finally been broken and the shadow has been lifted," Governor Chiles said on that day in May 1994, as seven old people stood around him. "This legislation assures that the tragedy of Rosewood will never be forgotten by generations to come."

Chiles signed a bill that paid Rosewood survivors up to two million dollars and provided college scholarships for Rosewood descendants and other minority students.

By that spring day in 1994, Don Ross—the same man his history teacher once called Fat Mouth, the onetime crusading magazine editor—was now among the senior members of the Oklahoma House of Representatives. He represented the place still called Greenwood on the north side of Tulsa. He kept a close eye on the situation in Florida and spoke on several occasions with lawmakers who led the Rosewood reparations fight.

He knew that someday the same battle awaited him.

The more he learned, the more Ross was amazed by how much the story of Rosewood resembled the horrible tales he had been hearing from Greenwood folks since he was a teenager. But there was at least one crucial distinction. The whole community of Rosewood would have fit into one small corner of the thirty-five square blocks of Greenwood's sprawling, thriving community.

If Florida was making amends, Oklahoma would have to do so as well.

The moment Ross had been waiting for since that day in the high school yearbook meeting was growing near.

Approximately one year later, on the morning of April 19,

1995, a White man named Timothy McVeigh set off a truck bomb that reduced the Alfred P. Murrah Federal Building in downtown Oklahoma City to a pile of rubble and a skeleton of twisted steel. The blast killed 168 people, many of them children.

Television crews captured the images of dazed survivors and grim rescue workers. Journalists searched for superlatives to describe what some called "the worst episode of civil violence in America since the Civil War."

But what if television crews had been present a hundred miles east as the sun came up on June 1, 1921?

What if the cameras had recorded Black families racing from burning homes in their nightclothes, or Black Americans screaming as they were burned alive, or Black people shot dead by the White mob because they didn't empty their pockets fast enough, or truck after truck piled high with Black corpses, or the vibrant Black community reduced to nothing but rubble and ash, or the sea of despair in the detention camps where thousands of Black citizens were forced to congregate after White arsonists made them homeless?

What then?

That was what Don Ross and so many others in his community wanted to know. Yes, what had happened at the Murrah Building had been an unthinkable tragedy, but the media was mistaken.

TELEVISION CAMERAS WEREN'T AROUND ON THAT MORNING OF 1921

The explosion was not the worst thing that had happened in this country since the Civil War.

That dubious honor belonged to Tulsa. The

television cameras weren't around on that morning of 1921 when the White mob came pouring over the tracks. And most of the victims were Black, so instead of days of national mourning and the race to build a fitting monument, the world got out a big broom and swept Greenwood's obliteration under a huge carpet.

In 1997, Don Ross introduced a bill demanding five million dollars in reparations for Greenwood's destruction.

"Reparations for what?" Oklahoma legislators asked, because at the time, only a handful of them had any notion at all that the catastrophe had ever happened.

So the Oklahoma legislative leaders proposed a compromise to Ross: the promise of a state-funded commission to undertake a thorough study of what had happened in Tulsa and suggest an appropriate remedy.

Just what Ross wanted.

It became known as the Tulsa Race Riot Commission, and it was comprised of eleven people—Black and White, scholars, businesspeople, and state legislators—appointed by the governor.

And that's how the word got out.

In newsrooms around the world, reporters and editors read wire stories about a new state commission created to study the incident in Tulsa, Oklahoma, where up to three hundred people had been killed and mobs of White racists had wiped out what had been called the Black Wall Street of America, a uniquely prosperous community of ten thousand Black people.

What?

Television stations, newspapers, magazines, and film crews descended upon the city. Their stories detailed the commission's search for mass graves and the heated debate over reparations.

"Why should we pay for something that happened eighty years ago?" went the arguments on one side.

> **WHY SHOULD WE PAY FOR SOMETHING THAT HAPPENED EIGHTY YEARS AGO?**

"How can we not?" said those on the other.

Most of the stories from around the world also reflected people's shock that something so horrible could have remained a secret for so long.

Finally, the Greenwood survivors no longer felt afraid. No longer was it necessary to speak about the burning and bloodbath only at night in their churches with their pastors seated nearby as witnesses and protectors. In fact, many survivors became minor celebrities, particularly those with the most horrifying memories. Dozens were also videotaped while telling their stories to Riot Commission investigators.

And for the first time ever, White Tulsans spoke out in numbers. A commission investigator logged hundreds of telephone calls, some made anonymously but most of them not, from White people who were children at the time of the burning or who had heard stories passed down from parents or grandparents. One elderly man told a story of going to a young friend's house just after the massacre and seeing a photograph of fifty Black bodies piled on a truck, an image that had stayed with him all these years. Dozens of others had similar memories or told stories of Black bodies dumped into trenches out in the country, into the Arkansas River, or into abandoned mines. A White nurse called to describe caring for an elderly White man who bragged of shooting Black people during the slaughter, insisting that he would do it again if he had the chance.

Another man called to say that some Black victims were still alive when his father trucked them to a mass grave near Dawson Road. The trucker always cried when he drove by the place in years to come and began to drink heavily, and years later, he confessed to what he had done to his Black coworkers.

Caller number thirty-five was a man named Clyde Eddy, an elderly Tulsan who said he knew precisely where some of the Black bodies were buried. Eddy had been a boy of ten when the burning happened. A few days later, he and a cousin were walking by Oaklawn Cemetery when they noticed several men digging a large pit. A group of big wooden crates sat nearby. The boys peeked under the lid of the first crate and saw that it contained the bodies of three Black men. They saw four more Black bodies in the second crate before the gravediggers shooed them away.

Among the last to call was an old man named Lee Cisco, who had lived in Southern California for most of his life. He, too, was a child when the burning happened, living next door to Tulsa's Convention Hall. He watched White people drag Black corpses down the streets behind their cars and stack them in ugly piles just a few feet from the boy's front porch. When the burning was over, Cisco's father drove his family through what was left of Greenwood.

"This is what happens when people start hating each other and it gets out of hand," the father said. A few weeks later, Cisco's father loaded his wife and children into the car and headed to California because he didn't want his family to live in a place that hated like that.

HE DIDN'T WANT HIS FAMILY TO LIVE IN A PLACE THAT HATED LIKE THAT

Eldoris Ector McCondichie lived to be ninety-nine years old, and until the Riot Commission was impaneled, when she was in her eighties, she hesitated to discuss the burning, and her own mother's frightening words on that rosy morning so long ago. "Eldoris, wake up! We have to go! The White people are killing the Colored folks!"

By February 28, 2001, those recollections had been folded into the Riot Commission's final report. On that cold, rainy day in late winter, the report, which called for reparations similar to those received by the survivors and descendants of Rosewood, was formally presented to Oklahoma Governor Frank Keating, Tulsa Mayor Susan Savage, and state legislative leaders. Among the recommendations, the commission suggested cash payments to survivors and their descendants who had lost property during the massacre, a scholarship fund for the heirs, financial support to redevelop Greenwood's business district, and a national museum to commemorate the massacre.

"We accept this report with an open heart," Keating said that day in an ornate room of the Oklahoma Capitol. Three massacre survivors sat before him in the audience, wearing buttons that said REPARATIONS NOW! "I do not know what the legislature will do, but I assure you that something will be done."

Representative Don Ross, his work almost done, stood in the wings while the governor spoke. Whether reparations were paid or not, there was now no escaping the truth. In the spring of 1921, Greenwood had been destroyed by an act of evil worthy of Nazi Germany.

"We told these people to lift themselves up by their bootstraps," Ross told reporters afterward, nodding to the three aging survivors. "And they did, by forming the most successful Black community in America.

"And once they had lifted themselves up by their bootstraps," Ross went on, "we destroyed them for it."

John and Loula Williams would know their building today, three sturdy stories of red brick at the corner of Greenwood and Archer, the same place they rebuilt within months of the massacre. But now the confectionery is gone, replaced by small businesses and the offices of the Greenwood Chamber of Commerce. The Dreamland Theatre is long gone too. State offices have settled into the other old buildings on the same block. There's a place that rents medical equipment and there are a few restaurants, but otherwise the area is quiet during the day and deserted at night.

A short distance away, the once-fine neighborhoods of

Detroit and Elgin Avenues are just empty, grassy hills in the shadow of Tulsa's skyline. The Black neighborhoods now lie farther north, stretching away for miles into the rolling hills where Greenwood's refugees once hid.

From the 1950s through the 1970s, the city drove a dagger through Greenwood's heart, condemning properties, discouraging investment, reclaiming lands, and constructing highways right through the heart of Black Wall Street. One historic block of Deep Greenwood is all that remains of the way things used to be, those familiar buildings now tucked into the shadows of a freeway overpass. For most visitors, it requires a great act of imagination to envision what the place must have been like all those years ago, when you had to push through the happy throngs, especially on a Thursday, the maids' day off. Today, the neighborhood is being gentrified, primarily by White people, many of whom know little about the land upon which they walk or about the community they live within.

But some still remember. Though only a handful of the massacre's survivors remain, the legacy of the burning and massacre live on. The railroad tracks that once separated the White side of town from the Black side of town still symbolize the racial divide.

THE LEGACY OF THE BURNING AND MASSACRE LIVE ON

The massacre cost Black Tulsans an incalculable inheritance. Financially, Black Tulsans lost an estimated five hundred thousand to one million dollars in wealth back then. That's the equivalent of fifty million to one hundred million dollars today, an irreplaceable loss of money that likely would have grown and been passed down to the victims' descendants, many of whom now struggle economically.

Still, the spirit and legacy of Black Wall Street cannot be extinguished. John Hope Franklin, the son of B. C. Franklin, one of the three lawyers who operated out of a tent in the days after the burning, went on to become one of the nation's greatest scholars of African American and American history, as well as the author of *From Slavery to Freedom: A History of African Americans*. Duke University operates an academic center in his name, and the John Hope Franklin Reconciliation Park sits on North Elgin Avenue in Greenwood.

The light of the many descendants shines brightly. Among them, John W. Rogers Jr., the great-grandson of J. B. Stradford, founded and chairs Ariel Investments, a firm in Chicago that manages a more than $4.5 billion financial portfolio. "Greenwood shows that when we are left to our own devices and don't have a knee to our neck, we can achieve extraordinary things," Rogers said to Forbes.com. "On the other hand, it shows you that unfortunately so many times in our history, when Black folks get a few steps ahead, we get pulled back down . . . It's why the wealth gap in this country is so dramatically worse than it was twenty-five or forty years ago." One of Andrew J. Smitherman's descendants, Raven Majia Williams, a Los Angeles digital marketing entrepreneur and businesswoman, has established a foundation in her great-grandfather's name, and is working on both a book and documentary about him. There are thousands more descendants.

The Vernon A.M.E. Church, previously known as Vernon Chapel, is the only Black-owned structure that remained standing in Greenwood after the massacre. Every Wednesday since September 2018, its pastor, Dr. Robert Richard Allen Turner, has stood in front of Tulsa City Hall, protesting for repentance and reparations. During the COVID-19 pandemic, White supremacist anti-mask protesters physically and verbally attacked him.

"It is a sad day in Tulsa, but I will not be deterred in this fight. By God as my helper, I will endure this fiery furnace, and we as a people will make it to the promised land. Our people will know justice," Dr. Turner said. "The racism that destroyed Black Wall Street in 1921 is alive and well in 2020. I have

THE RACISM THAT DESTROYED BLACK WALL STREET IN 1921 IS ALIVE AND WELL IN 2020

never, in person, seen mobs so filled with hate as I did today. I hope our city leaders will stand up and repudiate the racist attacks we endured today on the steps of city hall."

Organizations such as the young Black entrepreneurs and innovators of Dream Tulsa are among the many groups working to rebuild Black Wall Street, to encourage people to support Black businesses and entrepreneurship, and to create Black economic freedom. "The spirit of Black Wall Street is very much alive and there is a growing momentum around reclaiming a legacy that was so brutally interrupted," Dream Tulsa coordinator Onikah Asamoa-Caesar told Black Enterprise. Today, *Forbes* lists Tulsa as a hot spot for young entrepreneurs. The Greenwood Cultural Center anchors much of the effort to keep the flame of Black Wall Street alive for the world to see.

EQUAL JUSTICE OR NAH?

Terence Crutcher's great-grandmother owned a barbecue restaurant on Black Wall Street. Like so many others, she fled from the massacre. Terence, his twin sister, Tiffany, and their other siblings grew up in North Tulsa. On September 16, 2016, Terence was driving home from his first day of class at Tulsa Community College, where he was planning to study music, when his car stalled out in the middle of East Thirty-Sixth Street North in North Tulsa. While on her way to another call, Officer Betty Shelby and her partner happened across Terence and began to investigate why both he and his Navigator were in the road, the SUV straddling the yellow line.

People disagree about what happened next, but multiple police videos show Shelby and a group of three officers—some with weapons or tasers drawn—following him closely as he walked away from them and toward his SUV with his hands above his head. After Terence reached the driver's door, Officer Shelby shot him. Terence crumpled to the ground, his face toward the heavens and hands remaining above his head. Rather than helping him right away as they're supposed to, officers allowed several minutes to pass before they offered first aid. They found no weapons on his body or in the car. Days later he died. Subsequently, Shelby claimed Crutcher wasn't behaving normally or responding to her commands. In court, she would claim that she perceived Terence to be a threat and that he was reaching into his car to retrieve a weapon. Though lawyers represented him, we will never know his side of the story. We do know that the police never found a weapon.

By killing Terence, Officer Shelby joined a long list of police officers, the vast majority of whom are White, who have claimed to be justified in shooting a Black person whom they also asserted was threatening them but who turned out to be unarmed. In 2013, three Black women organizers—Alicia Garza, Patrisse Cullors, and Opal Tometi—co-founded the Black Lives Matter social and political movement in response to the ceaseless killings of unarmed Black people and a lack of justice for victims and their families, with law enforcement repeatedly not held accountable even when shootings are caught on camera. The trio kicked off the movement immediately after a jury acquitted George Zimmerman of murdering seventeen-year-old Trayvon Martin.

According to a report by the international organization Human Rights Watch, in Tulsa, Black people experience what it labels a "case study" in "abusive, overly aggressive" policing. This includes being stopped by the police more frequently and for longer periods of time than their White neighbors. In fact, the Tulsa Police Department is more than two times as likely to arrest Black Tulsans as White Tulsans. They arrest larger percentages of North Tulsans and are more likely to pull over Black Tulsan residents in low-income neighborhoods than high-income neighborhoods.

In fact, out of all of the people police officers arrest in the United States, two North Tulsa zip codes fall on the list of the ten with the nation's highest incarceration rates. There are forty-two thousand zip codes in the United States. The Fourteenth Amendment guarantees equal justice no matter a person's race. So it's essential that we ask ourselves why two of the top ten zip codes come from the nation's forty-seventh largest city and an area containing only about fifteen thousand people? What's wrong with this picture?

The same report also states that poverty rates are almost three times higher among Black Tulsans than White Tulsans. Poor people are more likely to be arrested, but it's not necessarily for the reasons you might imagine. For example, in Tulsa, almost forty percent of arrests occur because people can't afford to pay the fines or court fees they are assessed after they're given a ticket or arrested for minor infractions like running a stop sign or speeding. When people receive these kinds of citations they often miss hours of work or even lose their job—a devastating consequence for something so minor. Beyond that, people may need to spend money for cash bail to get out of jail. They may lose their driver's license, get evicted from their house or apartment, lose custody of their children, and more. Even if they never get charged with a crime, spending even a little bit of time in jail can lead to financial ruin, which keeps folks from being able to pay any fines or court fees. Far too many low-income and working-class people get caught in one huge loop, and disproportionate numbers are Black.

We already know that the original residents of Greenwood had either been enslaved or were the descendants of enslaved people who had worked for generations without being paid—and that White people and American society benefited from their labor. Imagine how hard those first residents worked and what they overcame to establish their community. And all while Jim Crow laws kept them from getting the best jobs or getting good pay or participating in mainstream society. Allow yourself to imagine what they lost when their homes and businesses were burned to the ground. Not only did the conflagration consume all their belongings, the residents received no insurance money or compensation for losing their homes and businesses, as people normally would following such a disaster. They then had to rebuild their homes and businesses from the ground up, from nothing, aware that White Tulsans had not only set fire to their homes and businesses, they had also stolen their money and possessions during the burning. Knowing this, and aware that similar White-on-Black mob violence took place throughout Oklahoma and the United States—it's easy to see how some of Greenwood's descendants would struggle more financially than their White neighbors.

The types of racial disparities that Black Tulsans face are similar to those faced by Black Americans nationwide and contribute to a dramatic difference in wealth between Black and White communities. Though the media often shows us Black athletes, entertainers, celebrities, and other Black people who have been very successful financially, the average White family in the United States has ten times the wealth of the average Black family. Experts trace these inequities back to chattel slavery, Black Codes, Jim Crow laws, and discrimination—the tools of White supremacy.

On May 16, 2017, after nine hours of tense deliberations, a jury that included three Black people acquitted Officer Shelby of first-degree manslaughter. Several jurors cried as the judge read the verdict. In a letter the jurors filed with the court, they stated that they did not find her "blameless." Two years later, a federal judge ruled that Officer Shelby would not be charged for violating Terence's civil rights. As occurs in many cases in which a police officer kills a civilian, the definitions of what constitutes a crime when a police officer is involved and the ways in which laws protect most officers make it almost impossible to hold even the most irresponsible officer accountable, especially when the victim is Black.

Crutcher's father, Minister Joey Crutcher, and his twin sister, Dr. Tiffany Crutcher, spoke to reporters in the Tulsa County Courthouse.

"Let it be known that I believe in my heart that Betty Shelby got away with murder. I don't know what was in the mind of that jury, how they could come to that conclusion. There was precise evidence that said she was guilty," Pastor Crutcher said before addressing the jury directly. "You did your job, but I'm wondering what you were thinking about."

THE SAME RIGHTS BLACK AMERICANS HAVE SOUGHT FOR CENTURIES

Dr. Crutcher said, "Betty Shelby murdered my brother, and after she murdered my brother all of the officers involved with the Tulsa Police Department covered for her. What I got out of this case was that a cover-up was exposed."

To this day, Black Americans around the nation are still fighting for "due process" and "equal protection under the law," the same rights Black Americans have sought for centuries.

WHERE ARE WE NOW?

In 2016, Tulsans elected G. T. Bynum as mayor, a native with deep roots in the city. Bynum's great-great-grandfather ran the city between 1899 and 1900; his grandfather led it between 1970 and 1978; his uncle served as mayor from 2002 to 2006; and his father headed the Tulsa Historical Society. Yet Bynum said he had never heard of the Massacre until 2001, when a cousin ran for mayor and a resident referred to it in a forum.

"I thought that was insane. No way something like that could have happened in Tulsa," he told the *Washington Post*. "And I started looking into it and found it had been true. It was a big shock. You don't think you could live in a place, and no one would talk about it at all. They never brought it up in our history course in high school. It never came up in meetings at the historical society."

But then he began to ask his grandparents if they knew anything about it. Turns out, they did. His maternal grandmother told him that her family had just moved to Tulsa and hid in an attic, afraid that, as Catholics, the Ku Klux Klan might harm them as well. He also acknowledges having lots of ancestors whose actions he isn't certain of.

After a 2018 story about the massacre ran in the *Washington Post*, Mayor Bynum announced he wanted to be on the right side of history and would reopen the investigation. This stunned Black Tulsans.

"He is the first mayor in almost one hundred years who did something," said Don Ross's son J. Kavin Ross.

But the decision to pursue justice hasn't come without a cost. Mayor Bynum has experienced backlash from some racist White Tulsans. And it may have cost him some points politically.

"I don't view it from a partisan standpoint at all. I view it as basic decency," he said.

Under Mayor Bynum's leadership, researchers began to scour the area looking for abnormalities that were consistent with mass graves.

In 2019, the Unites States Senate, led by three Black Senators—Kamala Harris, Cory Booker, and Tim Scott—unanimously passed legislation that would make lynching a federal crime. In February of 2020, the Emmett Till Antilynching Act—named for a fourteen-year-old Black teen who was lynched in Mississippi in 1955 after Carolyn Bryant, a White woman, lied and claimed he'd whistled at, touched, and said crude things to her—

passed the United States House of Representatives. Till's mother, Mamie, had held his funeral with an open casket so that the entire nation could witness how the lynchers had brutalized her son, hoping to rally the public support that would bring the barbaric practice to an end. Finally, the grotesque public murder of Black people seemed on the verge of becoming among the highest level of crimes.

Around the same time, the United States began to experience the coronavirus pandemic, a worldwide epidemic that claimed a disproportionate number of lives of Black, Latinx, and Native American people as compared to their White neighbors. As tens of millions of Americans sheltered in place at home in an effort to protect themselves and each other from the deadly disease, they witnessed tremendous numbers of their Black and Brown neighbors both lose their jobs and serve the community—grocery store clerks, transit workers, health care providers, and so on. Suddenly, many White people could see the integral role so many Black people play as essential workers who keep society running, similar to how Greenwood residents kept Tulsa functioning a century ago. Many White Americans could no longer deny the gap between their quality of life and that of so many of the nation's Black and Brown citizens.

Then, while quarantined in their homes, in late April 2020, Americans witnessed on viral video a group of armed White men stalk a twenty-five-year-old Black man, Ahmaud Arbery, in their cars and murder him as he jogged through a coastal South Georgia housing development for exercise. The nation also began to learn of a twenty-six-year-old Black emergency room technician, Breonna Taylor, killed back in March by Louisville police officers carrying out a "no-knock" search warrant at almost one o'clock in the morning. Believing they were experiencing a break-in as they watched a movie, Breonna's boyfriend fired his gun, at which point one officer fired blindly into the apartment, killing Taylor, who lay in bed, unarmed.

Then, on May 25, 2020, the public watched Minneapolis Police Officer Darren Chapin kneel on the neck of George Floyd for eight minutes and forty-six seconds, snuffing the life out of him as he called for his mother—another murder of an unarmed Black human being caught on tape for the entire world to see. In the Twin Cities, the community rose up to protest. So did people in cities nationwide. But then an interesting thing happened: The protests kept growing and growing and growing. Increasingly, White people who previously had not believed that racism exists, had not supported Black Lives Matter, and had never protested police killing a Black person before now joined Black and Brown people and anti-racist White activists in the streets, protesting the injustice that Black and Brown people face in general and at the hands of law enforcement.

Many White protesters were met with similar types of repressive violence that some members of law enforcement had previously reserved for Black and Brown people. These uprisings became what may be the largest social movement that has ever taken place in United States history. Massive numbers of White Americans began to take small steps forward to stand up against the forces that make Black life so difficult and unjust, and to consider becoming more anti-racist.

In the midst of the outcry, Kentucky Senator Rand Paul blocked the anti-lynching law named for Emmet Till, stymying, once again, an effort to criminalize the unconscionable act that members of Congress first began fighting against back in 1900.

THE LONG ARC OF JUSTICE

On September 2, 2020, the organization Justice for Greenwood Advocates—a group of civil and human rights lawyers led by a Black Tulsan attorney, Damario Solomon-Simmons, who also represented the Crutcher family—filed a lawsuit demanding reparations. The lawsuit's lead plaintiff was a woman, Lessie Benningfield "Mother" Randle, who was 105 years old and one of only two massacre survivors still alive—and who still experienced flashbacks of Black bodies stacked up on the street as her community burned. The lawsuit identified five defendants—the City of Tulsa, Tulsa County, the then-sheriff of Tulsa, the Oklahoma National Guard, and the Tulsa Chamber of Commerce—as directly involved in the massacre. The grandchildren of massacre victims and survivors—Dr. Andrew Jackson, J. B. Stradford, Clarence Rowland (Dick Rowland's uncle), and Andrew J. Smitherman—were among the plaintiffs.

In October 2020, consistent with eyewitness, funeral home, and newspaper reports following the massacre, a research team uncovered ten badly decayed coffins in a trench located in Oaklawn Cemetery. Though the remains were in poor condition, they may well be the bodies of Black Greenwood residents who were slaughtered during the burning. Newspaper and funeral home reports from the era suggested that eighteen victims were buried in the cemetery.

"We have a lot of work to do to determine the nature of [this] mass grave and who is buried in it, but what we can say is that we have a mass grave in Oaklawn Cemetery where we have no record of anyone being buried," said Mayor Bynum at a news conference.

We have a lot of work to do

The wait for justice continues, but in the words of Dr. Martin Luther King, "the arc of the moral universe is long, but it bends toward justice."

As for Don Ross, the man who once hated to go to school, he has not only become a scholar—he has an undergraduate degree in journalism, a master's degree in labor relations, and has also studied some law—but he is also one of the state of Oklahoma's greatest heroes. Ross served in the air force, was a leader in Tulsa's local civil rights movement, and became an award-winning journalist. As a member of the state's House of Representatives, he initiated laws that made Oklahoma's system of college education fairer, allowing greater numbers of Black and Brown people, as well as White women, to obtain their degrees. He successfully led the fight for the state to remove the Confederate flag, which had hung above the statehouse for generations, sending a traitorous, offensive, and intimidating message to many of the state's residents. He was named "legislator of the year" thirteen times by various organizations, including Americans for Civil Liberties. As a lawmaker, he has brought more than seventy-nine million dollars in funding to North Tulsa and has helped stimulate the community's redevelopment. If you ever go to Greenwood, look for the Black Wall Street Memorial, which he helped establish.

But more than any other American, Don Ross is responsible for bringing to light the truth about the Tulsa Race Massacre and the fight for justice for the survivors and their descendants—not just in Tulsa or even Oklahoma but around the nation and even the world.

Not a bad legacy for a young man whose dreams for himself once centered around running the table at the community pool hall.

Author's Note

For many years, I worked as a reporter at a newspaper in Fort Worth, Texas, but I had not heard about the Tulsa Race Massacre until a day in the winter of 2000 when my boss stopped by my desk. She handed me a copy of a wire service story that described a deadly outbreak in 1921 that left as many as three hundred people dead, most of them African Americans. A thriving community of Black people called Greenwood—thirty-five square blocks and thousands of homes, businesses, churches, and schools—had been destroyed by a White mob in Tulsa that numbered in the thousands.

I was stunned when I read the story that day at my desk. How could we not have known about such a thing? If the Tulsa Race Massacre of 1921 was as horrible as the story seemed to suggest, it deserved a place among the most important moments in American racial history. But the Tulsa massacre had never been mentioned in any history book I had ever read.

That year, my boss assigned me to write my own story about what happened in Tulsa in 1921. I interviewed a handful of elderly African Americans, people who remembered the terrible hours of June 1, 1921, when the White mob swarmed over the railroad tracks separating White Tulsa from the side of town where Black people lived. On that first trip I also met Oklahoma State Representative Don Ross, a longtime African American legislator who had grown up in Greenwood and had devoted much of his life to restoring the Tulsa massacre to its proper place in history. My own article ran in the *Fort Worth StarTelegram* on January 30, 2000, beneath the headline TULSA'S TERRIBLE SECRET.

In important respects, I was an unlikely candidate for such a newspaper assignment. I was born and raised in a small farming community in the north of Minnesota, where the only people of color were the Hispanic migrants who came up from Texas each summer to work in the sugar-beet fields. By and large, through the first twenty years of my life, television was the only place I saw a Black face. Racial issues were not important to me when I was young, and that continued to be true even after I moved to Texas, where I lived and worked for the first time with people from other cultural backgrounds. In retrospect, my lack of curiosity about those people and their experience in America was stunning. I will never forget my first night in Tulsa, having dinner with Don Ross in a quiet Chinese restaurant, and the look on his face as I asked questions such as, "What was it like for Black people after the Civil War?"

Ross was stunned at first, then angry. "How can you not know these things?" he demanded. Then, his voice rising to the point that others in the restaurant looked uncomfortably over at our table, he said, "And you're one of the educated Whites. If we can't count on you to understand, who can we count on?"

My own education about the history of race in America began with my newspaper story and continued with the research and writing of this book. I'm not nearly as ignorant as before. I will never be able to look at a Black person the same way again. I think I'm beginning to understand.

Not long into my research, I realized that what happened in Tulsa in 1921 was not an isolated event. It might have been the worst incident of its kind in our history, but almost every month, American newspapers of that time carried stories of racial bloodshed in another town or city, new horrors inflicted on African Americans by White mobs.

Most of my research focused on a particular moment in that wretched history, and my debt to those who helped me understand what happened in Tulsa cannot be overstated. In every instance, I found the Black survivors and White witnesses to be gracious and very helpful. I'm so thankful to Black survivors George Monroe, Otis Clark, Eldoris Ector McCondichie, Veneice Sims, and Wilhelmina Guess Howell, and to White witnesses Lee Cisco, Clyde Eddy, Philip Rhees, Richard Gary, and Margaret Anderson.

From our first telephone conversation, historian Scott Ellsworth was extremely generous with his time and knowledge. Ellsworth is among the handful of individuals whose courage and determination have helped coax the burning of Greenwood from the shadows of history.

Ellsworth's book *Death in a Promised Land: The Tulsa Race Riot of 1921* was the first scholarly examination of the massacre ever published, and it was an essential guide to my own attempts to understand what happened. Equally valuable were taped recordings of Ellsworth's interviews, conducted as far back as the 1970s with massacre survivors who were teenagers or young adults at the time of the massacre. Those people have been deceased for many years.

My research included dozens of conversations with descendants of Greenwood residents, most notably Jack Adams and his brother Don, Obera Mann Smith, and J. D. Mann, who shared family stories that had been passed down for generations, stories so crucial to my understanding of some of this book's most prominent characters. My reporting also included reading dozens of Tulsa newspaper stories from that time, as well as stories from the *New York Times* and other major national newspapers and magazines that covered the massacre in the days and weeks after it happened.

Finally, I'm deeply grateful to Hilary Beard. I'm honored that such an accomplished writer and researcher would devote herself in the last year to adapting my book for a new generation of young readers.

For me, work on this book has been a life-changing experience. Early in the process, I began to suspect that a crucial piece remained missing from America's long attempts at healing our problems with racism. Too many in this country remained as ignorant as I was. Too many were just as unaware of some of the most terrible moments in our history, of which Tulsa is a tragic example. How can we heal when we don't know what we're healing from? I hope this book contributes in some small way toward that broader understanding. Such is the spirit in which it is written.

—Tim Madigan

December 2020,
Fort Worth, Texas

Acknowledgments

I awaken daily in awe of God's wonders. I'm grateful to the Lenape people upon whose land I live in present-day Philadelphia. Thank you to my Beard and Lanton ancestors, who suffered and strived sensing the promise of free descendants. Big love to my heavenly parents Charles and Peggy Beard; Alison, Jonathan, Jennifer, Kailey, Jadon, Alex, Ralph, and Hughy; and my Beard, Stanley, Lanton, and Carson champions.

Tim Madigan, I have mad respect for you. What a blessing to reshape your astonishing work. I pray that I've honored the spirits murdered during the Massacre, Greenwood descendants, and Tulsa. I'm heartbroken I couldn't write there, but COVID.

Appreciation to Jennifer Lyons, Kate Farrell and the Henry Holt team, my Cleveland friends, Black Princeton, my Philly and Enon families, Black women, and #BLM.

—Hilary Beard

CHAPTER NOTES

For Original Research by Tim Madigan

PROLOGUE

I first heard the story of Eldoris McCondichie from Eddie Faye Gates, a member of the Tulsa Race Riot Commission, and it was Gates who arranged my interview with Mrs. McCondichie on a cloudy morning in the spring of 2000. The elderly burning survivor had lost a son to cancer only a few weeks before, but was patient, poised, and gracious during our talk in the living room of her home. And her statement about the burning, made while grabbing tissues from a box on her bookcase, testified to the fact that old horrors and heartbreak also remained vivid.

CHAPTER 1

Oklahoma Stale Representative Don Ross was nothing but helpful from the moment of our first telephone conversation. Becoming his friend has been one of the great pleasures of this work. Of course, Ross is also one of the key characters in the story of the burning and how it came to be restored to its proper place in history. Over several long conversations, Ross told me about the day in the yearbook meeting with Bill Williams and the impact it had on his life.

CHAPTERS 2, 3, AND 4

My account of Townsend Jackson's address at the First Baptist

Church in Greenwood is drawn from the *Tulsa Star* of May 30, 1913. Front-page coverage of the meeting of the United Brothers of Friendship, a leading Black fraternal organization of that time, was no doubt written by editor Andrew J. Smitherman himself. In addition to describing the attire of the men and women in attendance, Smitherman's paper also provided a complete text of Jackson's speech, which "went deep into the hearts of those who heard it," the *Star* reported. That fawning coverage was typical of Townsend Jackson's early years in Tulsa, when he was something of a media darling, at least in the *Star*. Two months after his speech at First Baptist, another story in the *Star* announced that the Oklahoma governor had appointed Jackson a representative to the National Negro Education Conference in Kansas City. Other stories regularly promulgated Jackson's political views, articles that ran beside the increasingly familiar portrait of the handsome, middle-aged Black man in a starched white shirt.

In 1914, the *Star* published short profiles of Black Tulsa's leading citizens, including John Stradford, John and Loula Williams, O. W. Gurley, and Barney Cleaver, articles that were invaluable sources of information on those prominent individuals and their community.

CHAPTER 3

My depiction of early Tulsa history was based on several sources, including *Tulsa: Biography of an American City*, by Danney Goble (Council Oaks Books, 1997); Angie Debo's *Tulsa: From Creek Town to Oil Capital* (University of Oklahoma Press, 1943); *Death in a Promised Land* (LSU Press, 1982), by Scott Ellsworth; and the report of the Tulsa Race Riot Commission.

Ellsworth's work was also crucial to my attempts to place

the burning in the ugly context of the times. Other sources that described the rampant paranoia, nativism, the Red Scare, and the rise of vigilantism were *The Fiery Cross: The Ku Klux Klan in America*, by Wyn Craig Wade (Simon and Schuster, 1987); John Hope Franklin's *From Slavery to Freedom* (McGraw Hill, 1994); and Frederick Lewis Allen's *Only Yesterday: An Informal History of the 1920s* (Harper and Row, 1931).

The description of O. W. Gurley's journey to Tulsa was drawn largely from the aforementioned profile in the *Tulsa Star*, as were passages describing the achievements of John and Loula Williams. My description of early Greenwood was synthesized from many sources, including *Black Wall Street: From Riot to Renaissance in Tulsa's Historic Greenwood District* (Eakin Press, 1998), by Hannibal Johnson. The story of the Williams family was also regularly told by Bill Williams in his later years. A recording of the retired teacher's interview with historian Scott Ellsworth is included in the race riot materials at the McFarlin Library at the University of Tulsa. Bill Williams also discussed the lives of his parents, his own childhood, and the origins of Greenwood in an interview with *Oklahoma Impact* magazine in the early 1970s, and with Ruth Sigler Avery on November 29, 1970.

CHAPTER 4

Townsend Jackson's odyssey from slavery to the battle of Lookout Mountain, to Memphis and Guthrie, and finally to Greenwood, was described in one of those newspaper profiles.

My descriptions of life in Memphis and Guthrie and the insights I gained into that time came from several sources, including Joseph H. Cartwright's *Triumph of Jim Crow: Tennessee Race Relations in the 1880s* (University of Tennessee Press,

1976); *Crusade for Justice: The Autobiography of Ida B. Wells*, edited by Alfreda M. Duster (The University of Chicago Press, 1970); Shields McIlwaine's *Memphis: Down in Dixie* (E. P. Dutton and Company, 1948); and *Guthrie: History of a Capital City 1889–1910*, by Lloyd C. Lentz III (Logan County Historical Society). The classic work of historian John Hope Franklin, *From Slavery to Freedom* (McGraw Hill, 1994), is essential reading for anyone trying to understand the experience of Black Americans in the century after the Civil War and to learn how men such as Booker T. Washington and W. E. B. Du Bois led efforts to transcend decades of horror and injustice.

CHAPTER 5

Damie Rowland was eighty-seven years old when Ruth Sigler Avery interviewed her on June 22, 1972. "She was a tiny, wrinkled Black woman wearing a white, dotted-swiss cap over her gray hair," Avery later wrote. "In her apartment she proudly showed me the ring her husband had given her the day they were married. Then she began to tell me the story of the little boy, Jimmie Jones, whom she had raised."

My account of Dick Rowland's life is drawn largely from the transcript of Avery's interview with the shoeshine boy's caregiver—beginning with his appearance at Damie's door in Vinita, continuing through the tragedy in Tulsa, to Dick Rowland's eventual death on the West Coast.

Ruth Avery mentioned her childhood memories of the hilltop cross burning and torture of the Black man in one of our first conversations. She also wrote about the event in her unpublished account of the Tulsa burning.

My description of the kidnapping and torture of the Tulsa

members of the I.W.W. was based largely on Scott Ellsworth's *Death in a Promised Land*, and on accounts in both the *Tulsa Tribune* and *Tulsa World*.

CHAPTER 7

On October 8, 1939, the *Tulsa Tribune* commemorated the twentieth anniversary of the paper's purchase by Richard Lloyd Jones with several long articles, prominent among them a long essay written by Jones himself. The publisher's piece traced the arc of his remarkable life—from his early love of writing to his frustrations as an aimless young adult, his success at *Collier's* and the purchase of the Lincoln birthplace, followed by his entry into newspapers and his eventual purchase of the *Tribune*.

A description of the events inside the *Tulsa Tribune* on the afternoon of May 31, 1921, came to me secondhand, but from two excellent sources. In the 1960s, a senior writer with the *Tribune* told the story of what went on at the paper that day to a highly respected Tulsa historian. That historian passed the account on to me on the grounds that I would not divulge his name.

The infamous missing editorial of May 31, 1921, the piece so widely blamed for precipitating the burning, may be gone forever. But *Tribune* stories and editorials that survive offer a clear window into the editor's opinions about race, including the front-page piece of February 4, 1921, that announced the KKK's intention to expand into Oklahoma, and the *Tribune* editorial on June 4, 1921, that declared, "A bad [n-word] is about the lowest thing that walks on two feet."

In an August 19, 2000, telephone interview with Jones's son, Jenkins Lloyd Jones was surprisingly candid about his father's shortcomings, conceding that father and son did not have a close relationship. "He was very opinionated and argumentative. We often clashed," Jenkins Lloyd Jones said. "Or he would run *over* people. It's hard to describe that as a clash. He had a strong temper. You can never out-argue people with a strong temper."

My description of Sheriff William McCullough and McCullough's reluctant role in the hanging of a young Black man in 1911 comes from a 1954 profile in the *Tribune*. McCullough was in his eighties when reporter Toby LaForge wrote about the ex-lawman. McCullough's involvement in the burning of 1921 was never mentioned in that story, which focused on McCullough's lingering regret about the 1911 hanging, the only execution over which he presided.

Descriptions of the Tulsa County Courthouse and the fourth-floor jail were taken from interviews that Ruth Avery conducted with former members of the Tulsa County Sheriff's Department.

CHAPTER 8

My description of the escalating tensions on both sides of the tracks that afternoon was drawn from several sources, including Scott Ellsworth's *Death in a Promised Land*, the report of the Tulsa Race Riot Commission, and newspaper accounts in the *Tulsa Tribune* and *Tulsa World*. In interviews with Scott Ellsworth conducted in the 1970s, Greenwood residents Robert Fairchild and Bill Williams described the scene along Greenwood Avenue late that fateful afternoon and early evening. Fairchild also recounted his friendship with Dick Rowland, and the statements of the Greenwood pool sharks who vowed retaliation should White people attempt to lynch a Black Tulsan.

It was my great good fortune to make the acquaintance of Obera Mann Smith, the daughter of O. B. Mann. Mrs. Smith's recollections of her father were sketchy, but she provided me with an outstanding photographic portrait that itself gave me an insight into the towering veteran of World War I. Obera also pointed me toward John D. Mann, O. B. Mann's nephew, who now lives in Michigan and is well versed in his remarkable family history. It was John Mann who told me about the birth of O. B. Mann's mother to the White slaver from Texas, about O.B.'s notorious temper, and his role in attempting to fend off the White attack on Greenwood.

My descriptions of the experiences of Black soldiers in World War I and German propaganda directed toward them were taken from *The Unknown Soldiers: Black American Troops in World War I* (Temple University Press, 1974), by Arthur E. Barbeau and Florette Henri.

My description of the deteriorating racial climate and racial violence in the years after World War I was based on several sources, including but not limited to John Hope Franklin's *From Slavery to Freedom*; *The Unknown Soldiers: Black American Troops in World War I*, by Arthur E. Barbeau and Florette Henri (Temple University Press, 1974); Wyn Craig Wade's excellent book *The Fiery Cross: The Ku Klux Klan in America* (Simon and Schuster, 1987); Scott Ellsworth's groundbreaking *Death in a Promised Land: The Tulsa Race Riot of 1921* (LSU Press, 1982); the Tulsa Race Riot Commission Report written by Scott Ellsworth and John Hope Franklin, and by numerous newspaper articles from that time.

CHAPTER 9

Mann's loud appearance in the Dreamland Theatre on the night of May 31, 1921, was based on several sources, including the testimony of Dreamland projectionist Henry Sowders and interviews with Bill Williams, who was in the theater that night. A few days after the burning, Mann's role in what was happening in Greenwood was also described by O. W. Gurley in the *Tulsa Tribune*.

"The real leader of the gang was a tall, brown-skinned Negro named Mann," Gurley said. "This boy had come back from France with exaggerated ideas about equality and thinking he can whip the world."

In 1924, William Redfearn, the White owner of the Dixie Theater on Greenwood Avenue, went to trial against an Oklahoma insurance company, seeking payment for losses incurred on June 1, 1921. The insurance company had refused to pay, arguing that the policy had been voided because the fire that destroyed Redfearn's theater occurred in the course of a race riot. Redfearn, who lost the case at trial, appealed all the way to the Oklahoma Supreme Court, losing there eventually too. But the defeated property owner left a grand legacy for future researchers and writers. Transcripts of testimony in his case are among the richest veins of information I found anywhere.

O. W. Gurley was among those who testified in the Redfearn case. My depiction of Gurley's actions on the afternoon and evening of May 31, 1921, are taken largely from transcripts of that testimony. The tense scene as described in the *Tulsa Star* that evening is also based in part on Gurley's later interview with the *Tulsa Tribune*, one that did little to endear him with his brethren on the north side of the tracks. "I entered the *Star* office about nine o'clock and found activities far advanced," Gurley was quoted by the *Tribune* as saying. "Men were coming singly and in little groups in answer to the call to arms. And guns and ammunition were being collected from every available source, and many of the men were making open threats and talking in the most turbulent manner." Jonathan Z. Larsen's excellent article in the February/March 1997 issue of *Civilization* magazine also describes the volatile meeting that night in the *Star*, quoting from the unpublished memoirs of John Stradford in which Stradford vowed to go to the courthouse alone if the need arose.

In describing the escalating tensions at the courthouse and the Black men's first trip to the courthouse, I consulted Tulsa newspaper stories of the time, Scott Ellsworth's *Death in a Promised Land*, Gurley's court testimony, the *Tulsa Tribune* story in which he is extensively quoted, and later interviews with Bill Williams.

CHAPTER 10

The White men's rush for weapons at the National Guard Armory was recounted in Major James A. Bell's duty report for that night.

My account of the fateful attempt by the old White man to disarm O. B. Mann comes from several sources, including newspaper accounts, Scott Ellsworth's interview with Bill Williams, and my own interviews with Mann's descendants. Gurley's interview with the *Tribune* was helpful once again. "This fellow Mann fired the first shot," Gurley was quoted as saying. "That brought calamity."

It is here that I will state my debt to a late World War II veteran named Loren Gill, who returned from Europe to attend the University of Tulsa and picked the burning as his topic for his master's thesis.

Any investigative journalist would have been proud of Gill's work. He interviewed dozens of witnesses, most of them White, studied newspaper accounts of the time, Red Cross records, and government documents to produce a history of the burning invaluable to me and essential to anyone attempting to understand what happened.

CHAPTER 11

It was my good fortune that Henry Sowders was among the witnesses in the Redfearn case. His remarkable story about events in Greenwood on May 31 is contained in transcripts of that case.

My description of events immediately after the first shots were fired at the courthouse were again drawn from the writings of Scott Ellsworth, from newspaper accounts, and on the fairly voluminous after-action reports written by the Tulsa members of the National Guard.

CHAPTER 12

The story of the old Black couple murdered while kneeling in prayer was first told by Walter White, an assistant secretary of the NAACP who was investigating lynchings, and who arrived in Tulsa hours after the burning was over. White was a light-skinned Black man who moved freely among the Tulsan Whites. He said he based his accounts of the atrocities on statements made to him by top law-enforcement officers in Tulsa.

The story of Black officer H. C. Pack is also contained in the transcripts of the Redfearn case.

CHAPTER 13

Young Bill Williams was one of those who heard the whistle at 5:08 a.m. on the morning of June 1, and decades later continued to speculate as to its origin, though no one had any doubt as to its intent.

The dreadful story of what young Walter Ferrell witnessed came from Ferrell's interview with Ruth Avery on March 3, 1971. "I've never forgotten that horrible sight, and knowing what was happening to my friends," Ferrell, a maintenance worker for the Tulsa school district, told Avery that day. "That's all I can tell you of my personal experience. It is just too terrible to talk about even decades later."

Choc Phillips's compelling story of those hours comes from the Riot Commission Report. I also gleaned a few details of Phillips's story in an interview with Tulsa resident Ron Trekell, a friend of the late Phillips, who described for me how the teenager and his barbershop quartet were practicing on the steps of Central High School as the Black platoon came marching downtown.

The story of John Williams and his son, Bill, and what happened to the Williams family on the morning of June 1, is taken from the previously mentioned series of interviews that Bill Williams conducted in the 1970s. My description of the plight of O. W. Gurley and his wife, Emma, derives from Gurley's testimony in the Redfearn case and his appearance as a witness in the July 1921 criminal trial of Police Chief John Gustafson.

My description of the White mob's modus operandi derives from several sources, including Scott Ellsworth's book, newspaper and magazine articles, and interviews with witnesses.

CHAPTER 14

Reverend C. Calvin McCutchen preached his first sermon at the Mount Zion Baptist Church on October 20, 1957. In our telephone interview, he described much of Mount Zion's history, told me about Pastor R. A. Whitaker's oratorical gifts, and traced the congregation's long odyssey to rebuild, efforts that were not completed until the 1950s.

My description of the battle for Mount Zion was drawn from several sources, including Choc Phillips's account published in the Riot Commission Report, Tulsa newspapers of the time, and an article in *The Crusader*, a publication of The African Blood Brotherhood. The article, which was written by a Black Tulsan and published in July 1921, described the casualties taken by White people who attempted to charge the church held by a "handful of ex-soldiers, fifty to be exact. Five times they came against it in mass formation, and five times were they repelled with deadly loss. However, what they had not valor enough to accomplish by force, they treacherously achieved. Under cover of a white flag of truce, several of them sneaked forward and set fire to the sacred building. As the fate of the church was recognized, the Negro heroes, who had given such a good account of themselves and had held it so valiantly, determined not to die like rats in a hole, and taking up their few wounded comrades, intrepidly charged through the mocking foe, suffering severely, but nevertheless breaking through the enemy line to safety. Ten heroes were left behind, however, stricken to death. Upon these the White barbarians vented their wrath by further riddling their bodies and kicking the lifeless clay after they felt sure that no spark of those heroic lives remained."

O. B. Mann's part in the battle of Greenwood Avenue and his dash to Mount Zion were part of my discussions with John D. Mann, the Black defender's nephew.

Ruth Sigler Avery's account of that morning is taken from her own writing, and from our interviews.

Events at Central High School were variously described by White people interviewed by Avery decades later. References to the weary man's hand-off of gun and ammunition to the boys came to me via the research of Scott Ellsworth.

CHAPTER 15

No one can testify more dramatically to Tulsa's conspiracy of silence than Ed Wheeler, whose life was threatened while he researched the burning for a Tulsa magazine article published in the spring of 1971. Wheeler is the magazine writer to whom the three Klansmen spoke, two of them with regret, one without the slightest remorse.

The official position of Tulsa authorities was taken from newspaper accounts of that time, from books and other articles written about the burning, and through numerous interviews with Tulsans, including some who continued to try to minimize what happened.

The testimony of Fire Chief R. C. Adler was contained in the Redfearn documents, as were the stories of several other Tulsa firefighters who said that their superiors prevented them from combating the Greenwood conflagration. I found the account of Van Hurley among newspaper accounts collected by the Tuskegee Institute. The statements of Thomas Higgins and V. B. Bostic were contained in the report of the Tulsa Race Riot Commission, as was the story of the White policeman who changed out of his uniform, then hurried to Greenwood to join the looting. The story of the Tulsa detective's daughter passing out chewing gum came from my interview with Philip Rhees, a White Tulsan who lived near the girl. Laurel Buck's story came from his testimony at the criminal trial of Police Chief Gustafson.

Stories of the Black survivors came from several sources. I first read of Kinney Booker's experience in Brent Staples's *New York Times Magazine* article of December 19, 1999, titled *Unearthing a Riot*. I heard George Monroe's recollections firsthand during one of several interviews with Monroe at his Tulsa home in the spring and summer of 2000.

Seymour Williams's story was based on an interview the old coach did with Scott Ellsworth in the late 1970s. A recording of the conversation resides at the University of Tulsa's McFarlin Library.

CHAPTER 16

Dr. Andrew C. Jackson has long been described as one of the burning's most tragic figures, a man whose death symbolized both the larger atrocity and the state of race in America at that time. Thus I was fortunate to discover the recording of the speech Wilhelmina Guess Howell made in 1989, Eddie Faye Gates's profile of Wilhelmina in the book *They Came Searching*, and to track down Jack and Don Adams, Wilhelmina's nephews and keepers of the family stories. It is through those sources that my portrait of Andrew Jackson emerges.

CHAPTER 17

Because of the court testimony of John Oliphant, I had access to a contemporary and highly detailed account of the Black physician's death. Transcripts of Oliphant's testimony at the criminal trial of Police Chief Gustafson rank among the most chilling descriptions anywhere of the burning.

CHAPTER 18

As part of my research, I contacted many of the people who had called Riot Commission investigator Dick Warner with their memories of the burning or to share stories of the event that had been passed down through the years. Only a small percentage of these conversations produced relevant information for me, so my expectations were low on the afternoon I called Margaret Anderson at her Tulsa home. Nearly *two* hours later, I possessed an account of the burning and its aftermath that still causes my stomach to stir. Her name had been Margaret Dickinson then, the young daughter of Tulsa's most successful builder. I was astounded not only by the story she told me, but by the small details she was able to remember. Clearly, her experiences during the burning have been much on her mind over the years.

My description of the Black exodus derives from several sources. It was Red Phelps, son of Merrill and Ruth Phelps, who told me of how his parents ran what amounted to a stop on an underground railroad in the days after the burning. Red Phelps still lives in the house where his parents gave shelter to the fleeing survivors.

Details of Hugh Gary's trip with his boys to survey the destruction of Greenwood, and the subsequent observation of the truckload of bodies in the country, were obtained in a long interview with Hugh Gary's son Richard.

S. M. Jackson discussed with Ruth Avery in the early 1970s his work embalming Black victims.

CHAPTER 19

It's worth noting that Faith Hieronymus was the only reporter of the *Tulsa World* to receive a byline in the paper's coverage of the burning. Hers was an excellent and haunting piece that brought the misery of McNulty Park into multisensory focus. It was abundantly clear from her writing that she had been deeply affected by what she saw. The pathos of her words provided a dramatic and telling contrast to the stories that appeared after the burning in the *World*'s rival, the *Tulsa Tribune*. The *World*'s coverage, with the Hieronymus story as the most dramatic example, was full of remorse. *Tribune* stories reflected a mood that was almost celebratory.

CHAPTER 20

Most sources here are self-evident—the *New York Times* and other papers around the nation, and the coverage of the burning's aftermath in the local papers. Within hours, Red Cross volunteers were on the scene, and the precise records kept by that agency also provided much insight into the scope of what happened.

We will never know exactly how many were killed during those terrible days in Tulsa, but Ed Wheeler's assessment is bound to be closer to the truth than the ridiculously low figure promulgated by official Tulsa.

A list of indictments and the grand jury's report are part of the public record. O. W. Gurley's name appears prominently on the list of witnesses, but not among those who were indicted. Based on his interview with the *Tulsa Tribune* and his other public statements subsequent to the burning, there is no doubt that Gurley was among the most damning witnesses where the Black defenders were concerned, and no doubt he was considered a traitor to his people.

My description of the Klan in Tulsa is based on several

sources, including my interviews with Philip Rhees and Richard Gary, two White Tulsan men who were boys at the time of the riot and who remember watching the Klan parades with their fathers; transcripts of Ruth Avery's interview with Klansman Andre Wilkes; and Avery's interviews with other White people knowledgeable about the KKK's influence in the city at the time.

CHAPTER 21

The account of Dick Rowland's exoneration, his last visit to Tulsa, and his life and death on the West Coast were part of Damie Rowland's interview with Ruth Avery in the 1970s.

Descriptions of the rebuilding of Greenwood are based on several sources, including interviews with Bill Williams, the work of Scott Ellsworth, Hannibal Johnson's *Black Wall Street*, and Mary E. Jones Parrish's *Race Riot 1921*.

It was John Mann who told me the story of O. B. Mann's flight to Canada and his return to Tulsa after six months, just in time for the Red Cross Christmas party in Greenwood. An account of that hopelessly bittersweet moment was written by Maurice Willows, who led the Red Cross efforts to assist the survivors, and whose name still evokes reverence among Black Tulsans today.

CHAPTER 22

Nancy Feldman's experience at the University of Tulsa is taken from the Riot Commission Report.

Scott Ellsworth coined the term, "the American Kristallnacht."

I learned of Ed Wheeler's chilling adventures during a long interview in Wheeler's home and in several follow-up conversations on the telephone.

It was no accident that Don Ross was the editor of *Oklahoma Impact*, the Black magazine that published Ed Wheeler's account of the burning, or that Ross should be the legislator whose work led to the creation of the Tulsa Race Riot Commission. The horror of 1921 Tulsa has seemed to follow Ross around all of his adult life.

CHAPTER 23

My description of the ceremony where Florida Governor Lawton Chiles signed the Rosewood reparations law was taken from the May 5, 1994, edition of the *Miami Herald*. Details of the 1923 attack on the Rosewood Community were drawn from *The Rosewood Report*, a 1993 study led by Professor Maxine D. Jones of Florida State University. The linkage of the Rosewood reparations, the bombing of the Murrah Building, and Ross's legislative efforts to exhume the Greenwood tragedy were explained to me by Ross in several conversations.

The accounts of Clyde Eddy and Lee Cisco are based on my interviews with both of those men, who were children at the time of the burning.

My description of the presentation of the Riot Commission Report to Governor Frank Keating, Tulsa Mayor Susan Savage, and legislative leaders is based on the reporting of Randy Krehbeil in the *Tulsa World* and on a *New York Times* article of March 1, 2001.

For several weeks in the summer of 2000, I drove the north

side of Tulsa, searching for relics of the burning—buildings or places that might look the same as they did in 1921. With the exception of that one block of Deep Greenwood, few remain. But many people remember. *Fort Worth Star-Telegram* photographer Jill Johnson and I were charmed during our visit with survivor Otis Clark. Wilhelmina Guess Howell, though her memory failed her for the most part, was radiant when I visited her in the waiting room of her nursing home. And I will always treasure the burnt penny George Monroe placed in my palm during my last visit to his home.

SOURCE NOTES

For Additions to the Adaptation by Hilary Beard

CHAPTER 2

17. "I would set no limits": John Hope Franklin, *From Slavery to Freedom* (New York: McGraw-Hill, 1980), p. 276–277.

CHAPTER 21

214. "We had to save our own": Hannibal B. Johnson, *Black Wall Street* (Fort Worth, Texas: Eakin Press, 1998), p. 80.

217. "The rapidity with which": Johnson, *Black Wall Street*, p. 99.

222. "A little over a decade": Scott Ellsworth, *Death in a Promised Land: The Tulsa Race Riot of 1921* (Baton Rouge: Louisiana State University Press, 1982), p. 108

CHAPTER 23

243. "Greenwood shows that when we are left": Antoine Gara, "The Bezos of Black Wall Street," *Forbes*, Accessed January 14, 2021, https://www.forbes.com/sites/antoinegara/2020/06/18/the-bezos-of-black-wall-street-tulsa-race-riots-1921/?sh=1af22e23f321.

244. "The spirit of Black Wall Street": Brandon Andrews, "Here's How Oklahoma's Black Entrepreneurs Are Rebuilding 'Black Wall Street,'" *Black Enterprise*, March 22, 2018, https://www.blackenterprise.com/dream-tulsa-black-entrepreneurs-rebuild-black-wall-street/.

248. "Let it be known that I believe": Paighten Harkins, "Crutcher Family Stunned After Not Guilty Verdict in Betty Shelby

Case," *Tulsa World*, May 17, 2017, Updated February 18, 2019, https://tulsaworld.com/news/local/crutcher-family
-stunned-after-not-guilty-verdict-in-betty-shelby-case
/article_08bfb5c5-ea61-5371-80a9-5f58b5c2a2ad.html.

250. "I don't view it from a partisan": DeNeen L. Brown, "A White Republican Mayor Seeks the Truth About Tulsa's Race Massacre a Century Ago," *The Washington Post*, March 13, 2020, https://www.washingtonpost.com/history/2020/03/13
/tulsa-mayor-bynum-mass-graves/.

253. "We have a lot of work to do": Randy Krehbiel, "Mass Grave Found in Search for 1921 Tulsa Race Massacre Victims; 10 Coffins Found in Trench at Oaklawn Cemetery," *Tulsa World*, October 22, 2020, Updated November 28, 2020, https://tulsaworld.com/news/local/racemassacre/mass
-grave-found-in-search-for-1921-tulsa-race-massacre
-victims-10-coffins-found-in/article_78e3008a-13dc-11eb
-a10a-e7bbbfbf616f.html.

RESOURCES

BLACK WALL STREET

Bloomberg. "Black Wall Street's Tragedy Didn't End in 1921." https://www.youtube.com/watch?v=mRIGiHiPWCw.

CBS *60 Minutes*. "Uncovering the Greenwood Massacre, nearly a century later." https://www.youtube.com/watch?v=yA8t 8PW-OkA.

CBS *60 Minutes*. "Tulsa Burning (1999)." https://www.youtube.com /watch?v=EgUrsmzFAd4.

CNN. "The history of Tulsa's 'Black Wall Street' massacre." https:// www.youtube.com/watch?v=EO3Fxe4mDP4.

Greenwood Cultural Center. greenwoodculturalcenter.com.

History.com. "Tulsa's 'Black Wall Street' Flourished as a Self-Contained Hub in Early 1900s." https://www.history.com/news/black-wall -street-tulsa-race-massacre.

LYNCHING AND RACIAL VIOLENCE

BlackPast.org. "Ida B. Wells, 'Lynching, Our National Crime' (1909)." blackpast.org/african-american-history/1909-ida-b-wells-awful -slaughter.

Equal Justice Initiative Videos. eji.org/videos. *See topics Racial Justice and Lynching in America.*

Equal Justice Initiative. "Report: Lynching in America: Confronting the Legacy of Racial Terror." eji.org/reports/lynching-in -america.

Facing History and Ourselves. "The Origins of Lynching Culture in

the United States." youtube.com/watch?v=hPdh46k7b38&feature
=emb_logo.

Human Rights Watch. "Policing in Tulsa." hrw.org/video-photos
/interactive/2019/09/11/policing-poverty-and-racial-inequality
-tulsa-oklahoma.

Lynching Sites Project Memphis. lynchingsitesmem.org.

National Geographic. "'It Was a Modern-Day Lynching': Violent
Deaths Reflect a Brutal American Legacy." nationalgeographic
.com/history/2020/06/history-of-lynching-violent-deaths-reflect
-brutal-american-legacy.

New York Times. "Lynch Mobs Killed Latinos Across the West. The
Fight to Remember These Atrocities Is Just Starting." nytimes
.com/2019/03/02/us/porvenir-massacre-texas-mexicans.html.

New York Times. "Overlooked: Ida B. Wells." https://www.nytimes
.com/interactive/2018/obituaries/overlooked-ida-b-wells
.html.

PBS. *American Experience.* "The Murder of Emmett Till: The Legacy
of the Lynching of Emmett Till." pbs.org/wgbh/american
experience/features/legacy-lynching-emmett-till.

Smithsonian Institute. "American Indian Removal: What Does It
Mean to Remove a People?" americanindian.si.edu/nk360
/removal/index.cshtml#titlePage.

The Marshall Project. "Ahmaud Arbery and the Local Legacy of
Lynching." themarshallproject.org/2020/05/21/ahmaud-arbery
-and-the-local-legacy-of-lynching.

RECONSTRUCTION

Equal Justice Initiative. "Reconstruction in America: Racial Violence
After the Civil War." eji.org/reports/reconstruction-in-america
-overview.

Facing History and Ourselves. The Reconstruction Era Video Series. Parts Four and Five. facinghistory.org/reconstruction-era /video-series

Teaching Tolerance. "Race Riots." tolerance.org/classroom-resources /texts/race-riots.

Teaching Tolerance. *Teaching Hard History*. Podcast. tolerance.org /podcasts/teaching-hard-history.

TULSA RACE MASSACRE

1921 Tulsa Race Massacre Centennial Commission. tulsa2021 .org

Ellsworth, Scott. *Death in a Promised Land: The Tulsa Race Riot of 1921*. Louisiana State University Press, 1982.

History.com. "Tulsa Race Massacre." history.com/topics/roaring -twenties/tulsa-race-massacre.

Johnson, Hannibal B. *Black Wall Street 100: An American City Grapples with Its Historical Racial Trauma*. Eakin Press, 2020.

Johnson, Hannibal B. *Black Wall Street: From Riot to Renaissance in Tulsa's Historic Greenwood District*. Eakin Press, 1998.

Krehbiel, Randy. *Tulsa, 1921: Reporting a Massacre*. University of Oklahoma Press, 2019.

Madigan, Tim. *The Burning: Massacre, Destruction, and the Tulsa Race Riot of 1921*. Thomas Dunne Books, 2001.

Oklahoma Commission to Study the Tulsa Race Riot of 1921. "Tulsa Race Riot." okhistory.org/research/forms/freport.pdf.

Oklahoma Historical Society. "Tulsa Race Massacre." okhistory.org /publications/enc/entry.php?entry=TU013.

Parrish, Mary E. Jones. *Race Riot 1921: Events of the Tulsa Disaster.* Out on a Limb Publishing, 1998.

PBS. *Code Switch.* "Meet the Last Surviving Witness to the Tulsa Race Riot of 1921." npr.org/sections/codeswitch/2018/05/31 /615546965/meet-the-last-surviving-witness-to-the-tulsa -race-riot-of-1921.

Smithsonian Magazine. "A Long-Lost Manuscript Contains a Searing Eyewitness Account of the Tulsa Race Massacre of 1921." smithsonianmag.com/smithsonian-institution/long-lost -manuscript-contains-searing-eyewitness-account-tulsa-race -massacre-1921-180959251.

Tulsa City County Library. "Tulsa Race Riot of 1921." tulsalibrary .org/tulsa-race-riot-1921.

Tulsa Historical Society. "1921 Tulsa Race Massacre." tulsahistory .org/exhibit/1921-tulsa-race-massacre.

White, Walter Francis. "The Eruption of Tulsa," *Nation* 112 (29 June 1921): 909.

OTHER BOOKS OF INTEREST

Alexander, Michelle. *The New Jim Crow.* The New Press, 2010.

Bolden, Tonya. *Inventing Victoria: Her Past Isn't Her Future.* Bloomsbury Children's Books, 2020.

Bolden, Tonya. *Up Close: W. E. B. Du Bois.* Viking, 2008.

Douglass, Frederick. *Narrative of the Life of Frederick Douglass.* Anti-Slavery Office, 1845; Signet Classics, 2005.

Dunbar-Ortiz, Roxanne. Adapted by Jean Mendoza and Debbie Reese. *An Indigenous Peoples' History of the United States for Young People.* Beacon, 2019.

Giddings, Paula. *When and Where I Enter: The Impact of Black Women on Race and Sex in America*. Bantam Books, 1984.

Hine, Darlene Clark and Kathleen Thompson. *A Shining Thread of Hope: The History of Black Women in America*. Random House, 1998.

Kendi, Ibram X. and Keisha N. Blain. *Four Hundred Souls: A Community History of African America, 1619–2019*. One World, 2021.

Lewis, John, Andrew Ayden, and Nate Powell. *March, Books One, Two and Three*. Top Shelf, 2013, 2015 and 2016.

Loewen, James W. *Sundown Towns: A Hidden Dimension of American Racism*. Touchstone, 2005.

Reynolds, Jason and Ibram X. Kendi *Stamped: Racism, Antiracism, and You*. Hachette Book Group, 2020.

Truth, Sojourner. *Narrative of Sojourner Truth*. Penguin Classics, 1998.

Wells, Ida B. Edited by Alfreda M. Duster. *Crusade for Justice, the Autobiography of Ida B. Wells,* University of Chicago Press, 1970 and 2020.

Wilkerson, Isabel. *The Warmth of Other Suns: The Epic Story of America's Great Migration*. Vintage, 2011.

Zinn, Howard. *A Young People's History of the United States: Columbus to the War on Terror*. Triangle Square, 2009.

INDEX